COOKING
Without Fat

A Healthy Eating Guide with More than 100
Delicious, Easy, High-Energy Recipes

George Mateljan

Villard • New York

 Printed on Recycled Paper

Also by George Mateljan:
Baking Without Fat

This is an updated edition of *Cooking Without Fat,* originally
published in 1994 by Health Valley Foods.

ISBN: 0-679-77071-2
LC: 95-062001

Manufactured in the United States of America
98765432
First Villard Books Edition

Praise for "Cooking Without Fat"

Please accept my sincere congratulations for the wonderful service that you are providing humanity by making it so much easier for people to follow a low-fat vegetarian diet.

Dean Ornish, M.D.
Author of "Dr. Dean Ornish's
Program for Reversing Heart Disease"

"Cooking Without Fat" is a welcome addition to the heart-healthy bookshelf. I believe the public has been lulled into a false sense of complacency when it comes to the fat content of the diet. While the 30-percent-of-calories-as-fat approach is a step in the right direction, a lower fat diet is definitely better. The book offers delicious suggestions for a complete menu, from appetizers to desserts. Many of the recipes call for Health Valley Foods products which I heartily endorse. Choosing dishes prepared from the book will provide the leeway for enjoying a splash of olive oil here or a dash of salt there without guilt."

Robert E. Kowalski
Author of
"The 8-Week Cholesterol Cure"

Your battle to save this battered and abused planet is far more important than the wars I write about. Keep fighting.

Colonel David H. Hackworth
Author of "About Face:
The Odyssey of an American Warrior"

American families are increasingly concerned about how to limit the amount of fat in their daily meals. Mr. George Mateljan of Health Valley has already helped millions of people to accomplish that worthwhile goal with the fat-free products his company makes. Now, his book offers sensible recipes and clear guidelines that families can use to follow this healthy practice in home cooking as well.

Deralee Scanlon, RD
The Media Dietitian

acknowledgments

The collaborative efforts of many dedicated and knowledgeable individuals made this book possible.

Barbara Luboff, a Registered Dietitian, worked with me to ensure that all the recipes taste good and are also nutritious.

Jim Burns contributed his extensive publishing experience to this project.

Renee LaBriola, also a Registered Dietitian, assisted with recipes.

Terry Taketa assisted me with the editorial content.

Harry Urist assisted in many ways, and took on the tremendous responsibility of checking and proofing the text and recipes.

Sarah Lewkowicz, John Convey and Cristina Aldana tested the recipes and helped insure that all the directions are accurate.

Michael Clayton, Lessa Woods and Donna Mitnick did a wonderful job of designing and executing the graphic elements of this book, making it attractive and easy to read.

Gary Moats was the photographer who made the photos of our recipes so appetizing, with the assistance of food stylist Robin Tucker.

I especially want to thank Nikki Goldbeck who was a most important consultant in the development of the recipes.

I also want to thank Eli Khoury, Charles Brockett, Rod Crossley, John Fulkerson and Ray L'Heureux for their various contributions.

All these people worked tirelessly and patiently, and without them this book could not have been completed.

Answers to the most commonly asked questions from the first printing of this book

Question: *Many of the recipes call for fat-free chicken broth as an ingredient. Where can I find it? Can I substitute for it?*

Answer: Health Valley makes a natural fat-free chicken broth with less salt and no MSG. It is available in many markets and health food stores. If you can't find it, you can substitute regular chicken broth that has been skimmed of fat. If you're a strict vegetarian, you can substitute vegetable broth.

Question: *None of the recipes include salt. Can I add salt to the recipes?*

Answer: We believe that a diet low in sodium is healthier. Feel free to adjust all of the seasonings to your personal tastes.

Question: *I notice that honey is used in many recipes. Can I substitute other sweeteners for it?*

Answer: Honey is specified in these recipes because it does more than just add sweetness. It brings out the flavor of herbs and spices, and it provides thickness and moisture, while substituting for fat. You can decrease the amount you use, or substitute apple juice concentrate in recipes where thickness is not a concern.

Question: *Your cheesecake and some other recipes include an ingredient called "yogurt cheese" that is made by draining the liquid from plain, nonfat yogurt. Which brand of yogurt works best?*

Answer: Any brand that does not have added gelatin or many additives will work. We have had success with Dannon® yogurt. One quart drained for 24 hours will yield two cups of yogurt cheese, and two cups of yellow liquid (which is discarded). See directions, page 138, diagram, page 71.

Question: *I am having difficulty finding low sodium tomato products. Are they essential to the success of the recipes?*

Answer: If you are not on a strict low sodium diet, the recipes can be made with regular tomato products.

Question: *What does it mean when an ingredient is listed as 1 tablespoon + 2 tablespoons?*

Answer: That particular ingredient is used twice in the same recipe. The directions indicate where to use each amount.

Question: *I try to avoid dairy products. Is there a substitute for nonfat yogurt?*

Answer: Many people who are sensitive to milk can tolerate nonfat yogurt. You may, however, wish to try soy yogurt, but be aware that it is higher in fat than nonfat yogurt. We do not recommend making this substitution for the cheesecake recipes.

Cooking without Fat

a message from the author

All my life, I've had a passion for food. Even as a child, I was fascinated by food preparation. By the time I was 5 years old, I already had my own kitchen tasks to perform during the holidays. My mother would measure out the ingredients and give them to me to mix together. When we made bread, I would watch in wonder as simple ingredients such as flour, water and yeast were transformed into something altogether different. It was magical to see the dough rise. And I've always loved the mouth-watering fragrance of baked goods. When the golden loaves of bread finally emerged hot from the oven, I felt a sense of pride and accomplishment that was the greatest reward I could ever imagine.

In 1970, I turned my passion for food into my life's work when I started a small company called Health Valley Foods. The company's original purpose was to prepare only good tasting foods made the healthy way. In the years since then, we have been consistent in maintaining those standards, without regard to profit or effort. It has never been my intention to build a financial empire. I have always received my greatest satisfaction from knowing that our Health Valley foods offer healthy benefits for our customers.

Even in the early years, I realized that it wasn't enough merely to prepare and distribute healthy foods. Health-minded people also need information on how to use our foods as part of a healthier way of eating that contributes to the quality of their health and their lives. That's what motivated me to share my knowledge and experience about nutrition by writing this book.

I have been very gratified by the response this book has received. People who have used it to cut down on fat have been writing to tell us how much better they feel, how they've been able to lose body fat without "dieting," and how well it meets the needs of their busy, active lifestyles.

It has even been used as a guide and textbook.

Sharyl Heavin of Saddleback College in Costa Mesa, Calif., designed a class around it, entitled "Lite Cuisine Strategies" and *Cooking Without Fat* is the textbook used.

The Heart Disease Prevention Center at the University of California, Irvine, used the book as a guide for the "Journey to a Healthier Lifestyle" 12-week program that involved low-fat eating, exercise and stress management to allow participants to successfully lose weight and lower both blood pressure and cholesterol levels.

> *"We learned many new ways to enhance the flavor of healthy foods and to eliminate fats from cooking and baking using natural ingredients.*
> *"More importantly, it was amazing to me that I didn't have to feel hungry or deprived. After years of dieting, Health Valley put back some guilt-free pleasure into eating, which was a major hurdle for me. Thank you, Health Valley—we appreciate your efforts."*
> —Sara Blumberg, Newport Beach, California

The book has also been used by cardiac rehabilitation centers and weight loss centers across the country, including Positive Changes® Here are a few of the many comments from people who have used the book and its meal plan as part of the program at Positive Changes:

> *"By following the plan, weight loss can be done painlessly and without going hungry. I have more energy and more self-esteem, and I feel good that I am doing the right thing."*
> —Dee Mansfield, Deerfield, Illinois

> *"I love to eat, so why not eat lots of great tasting Fat-Free foods. I enjoy eating six times a day…can feel my energy increasing…and will include Health Valley products long term."*
> —Sue Hinkler, Gurnee, Illinois

Cooking without Fat

In addition, many Health Valley customers have enjoyed wonderful results. Here are just a few of the many favorable comments we've received:

> *"Recently, I discovered your book* Cooking Without Fat. *It has changed my life. I have lost in excess of 60 pounds simply by using your recipes, watching my fat intake, and exercising regularly. I am now repulsed by foods dripping with grease. I am pleased to thank you for changing my way of life and probably extending it."*
> — Elizabeth Szoke, Troy, Ohio

> *"I sent for your cookbook* (Cooking Without Fat) *and changed my way of cooking and eating. In the process, I lost 31 pounds during the last six months.*
> *"I have tried many of the recipes in your book and they are really good. I serve them to guests and they enjoy them and have no idea that they are eating healthy food until I tell them. Several of my friends have purchased your book after tasting the food and seeing the results I have had enjoying a no added fat diet (not really a diet, but a new healthy way of eating)."*
> — William L. Stone, Seal Beach, California

This book was originally self-published and sold primarily to Health Valley customers through offers on our packages. So it has been gratifying that over a half million copies were purchased. It was equally gratifying when the good people at Random House approached us and offered to give the book a wider audience by publishing and releasing this printing. Our hope is that the book will allow even more people to experience the personal benefits of healthier eating and living.

One of the most important ways people can begin to eat healthier is by cutting down on the total amount of fat. The event that turned cutting fat into a personal crusade for me was the loss of my brother, John. I am convinced that John's high-fat diet was the major contributing factor to his premature death from cancer. And even though it is too late to do anything for John, it's not too late to help other people.

The goal of this book is not only to help people prevent disease, but also to enhance their health. Because the future belongs to those with the wisdom to take control over their own well-being.

I'm very pleased to be sharing with you the secrets to preparing good tasting, convenient meals without any added fat or high-fat ingredients. I hope it helps you achieve good health and well-being.

Yours in Good Health,

George Mateljan

P.S. This cookbook has a number of good baking recipes, but if you'd like more, be sure to purchase a copy of our follow-up cookbook, *Baking Without Fat.*

Cooking without Fat

table of contents

*Cooking
without
Fat*

introduction

What Makes This Cookbook Different from All Others

This cookbook represents a revolution in cooking methods: it is one of the first books to show you how easy, fast, convenient, good tasting and truly satisfying it can be to cook without any added fat or high-fat ingredients.

Cooking Without Fat is an authoritative, up-to-date guide to the revolutionary new method of cooking that is sweeping the world of healthy eating. This book is based on traditional natural cooking, but it abandons the fat, while using ingredients that are high in nutrition and fiber. The result is lighter, healthier cooking that is more in tune with today's nutritional needs.

Although the recipes in this book are low in calories (up to 50 percent lower than ordinary recipes), this is not a dieter's cookbook. It celebrates natural flavors with new taste combinations and the imaginative use of natural ingredients. With this book, I cover the whole range of healthy dishes, from soups to desserts, while providing the basis for a full understanding of healthy cooking.

I call this revolutionary new way of preparing meals the **"Cooking Without Fat Method."**

(Although this method doesn't use any added fat at all, I don't call it the "Fat-Free Cooking Method" because there are recipes that include ingredients which are **not** "fat-free," such as lean cuts of poultry, and fish.)

By using this new Method, you will learn to highlight the natural flavors of foods without adding fat, plus you will see how to substitute fat-free ingredients to achieve the same flavor satisfaction of recipes with fat.

For the first time, it's convenient and practical to enjoy all the benefits of cutting down on fat, because this cookbook contains **over 100 recipes that supply less than 15 percent of calories from fat.**

What is even more impressive is the fact that of the 108 recipes in this book, 86 recipes contain 6 percent fat or less! Here is a breakdown of the recipes by the percentage of calories from fat they contain:

Number of Recipes	Percentage of Calories from Fat
47	Fat-Free
2	2
6	3
8	4
15	5
8	6
1	7
2	8
4	9
1	10
6	11
3	12
1	13
2	14
2	15

Because these recipes are so low in fat, they allow you to indulge in foods you love that are high in fat, because they balance out the fat. So you can have some avocado, or even the occasional scoop of ice cream, if you use these recipes as your regular way of eating.

By using the Cooking Without Fat Method, you can achieve your ideal weight and maintain it permanently, plus significantly reduce your risk of developing degenerative diseases.

The Only Oil We Used Was to Sharpen Our Knives

There is a lot of talk about the type of fat that is the healthiest to eat: monounsaturated, or polyunsaturated.

The fact is that any fat is still 100 percent fat, regardless of the type! In the 1970's, cutting down on saturated fat and cholesterol was what health-conscious people focused on. Then in the 1980's, the focus was on eliminating tropical oils, such as coconut and palm. But in the 1990's, we now realize that we need to cut down on all the sources of fat and cholesterol to enhance personal health. Since there is some fat present in all natural foods, there's no need to add fat when we chose healthy foods to eat.

However, creating recipes that taste good without any added fat wasn't easy. We had to draw on years of experience at Health Valley, preparing the world's best tasting Fat-Free foods made the healthy way. We started with hundreds of recipes, and eliminated all of them that didn't meet our strict criteria for flavor, nutrition and ease of preparation. We finished with a little over 100 exciting recipes made totally without added fat or high fat ingredients.

You'll also notice that there are no recipes that call for red meat. This was a conscious decision based on the fact that most red meat is high in fat, and one of the main sources of saturated fat in the typical American diet. There is no need to get saturated fat from your diet, and too much of it can lead to elevated blood cholesterol.

You'll also notice that none of our recipes use refined sugar, salt, soy sauce, or any ingredients that contain more than 30 percent of calories from fat. (The one exception is the Tofu section. We have included tofu, even though it is naturally higher in fat, because it is such a nutritionally valuable food, especially for vegetarians.) We recommend using the Light Tofu that is now available.

We also do not use margarine because we consider it as bad, if not worse, than saturated fat. To make margarine, oils that are primarily unsaturated are artificially saturated through a process called "hydrogenation." This process is what turns oils that are liquid at room temperature into fats that are solid at room temperature. Hydrogenated oils have no essential fatty acid activity and may interfere with normal fat metabolism.

What you will find in this cookbook are recipes made without fat, but with plenty of flavor and eating enjoyment. You'll find recipes for virtually everything, even for delicious fat-free cheesecake.

We have spent hundreds of hours in our test kitchens, and made countless revisions to these recipes so that they provide all the taste appeal of recipes made with fat, but without any added fat and with far fewer calories.

By using the Cooking Without Fat Method, you can take a big step in the pursuit of a healthier, happier future.

chapter one

A Personal Journey

My Love Affair with Food

Food has always been a focal point for every society. It not only gives us nourishment, it's also the cornerstone for most social interaction. One of the first ways a mother expresses her love for a newborn is by giving it nourishment. Traditional family life involves gathering around the table for meals together. Virtually all holidays have their own special foods associated with them, as do special events: weddings, birthdays, anniversaries. Even many religious services involve food in their ceremonies.

Yet, in spite of how important food is in our lives, people pay little real attention to it. Food choices are based on convenience and taste, rather than on nutrition. Many still don't see the connection between what they eat and their health.

The reason I'm so aware of the relationship between food and health is because of my personal experiences. As a child, I seemed to have one health problem after another. It wasn't until I was a young adult that I decided to do something positive about it. I read everything I could get my hands on, until I realized that by changing the way I ate and lived, I could also change from being sick to being healthy. I discovered firsthand that the key to controlling my own health and well-being was with diet and nutrition. As a result, I feel better now than I ever have.

Because of the dramatic difference I experienced in my own health, I take food very seriously. In fact, the whole reason I started Health Valley back in 1970 was because I simply couldn't find the kinds of good tasting, convenient, nutritious foods I wanted for myself and my own family. I pledged over 25 years ago to make only the kinds of wholesome, nutritious foods I wanted to eat myself. I'm proud to say I have never wavered from that commitment.

Cooking without Fat

As I've continued to work with food, I've developed a true passion for it. I now feel that I was born to do the work I'm doing. The fact that I can be of service to people gives me great personal satisfaction.

You won't find me to be the typical president of a food company, spending most of my time in conference rooms, talking with the board of directors about how to make more profits. In fact, there are no stockholders to answer to, because Health Valley is a family-owned company.

I like to think of our Health Valley customers as our shareholders, because whenever people purchase our products, they are making a small investment in what we stand for. That's the reason I created the $5 Cash Refund Offer that you'll find on all our packages. It's my way of paying a "dividend" to the people who "invest" in our products. Every year, 200,000 people take advantage of this offer. I invite you to become one of them.

Because I'm the happiest when I'm around food, I spend much of my time in the kitchen, helping to create and improve our products. I believe that the president of a food company has an ethical and a moral obligation to see that his company produces nutritious, safe foods. The only way to succeed in that task is to be personally involved in the creation and preparation of all of our products.

I'm also involved with every one of our products because our foods are a direct reflection of our company philosophy. **(We make business decisions based on what will provide the greatest health benefits to our customers, rather than on what will provide the greatest bottom line profit for the company.)**

The people I've brought to work with me in the company are those who share my commitment. That's why all of us talk about quality, service and making better, more nutritious foods, rather than trying to make the most profit. My greatest personal satisfaction doesn't come from money, but rather from the response of our customers. For example, here is a recent letter we received that meant a great deal to me:

"I could not believe a cookie could taste so good, and they do curb your appetite. I know, because I've now lost 110 pounds (in one year). I don't think I could have made it this far without the help of Health Valley."

—Darlene Stephens, Sumter, South Carolina

Getting such letters as this one from customers who benefit from our products is enormously gratifying to me. I refuse to compromise on quality, because I am committed to creating the best foods in the world for our customers. So it means a great deal to me when you recognize and appreciate all the effort that goes into our products. That's why I invite you to write to let me know your reaction to what we're making. Our address is on all our packages. I even appreciate your critiques, because it makes me aware of how we can improve to better meet your needs. Truly, my greatest joy is hearing how Health Valley foods have contributed to your health and well-being.

How My Love for Food Led to These Recipes

As far back as I can remember, the kitchen was always my favorite spot in the house—always so warm and filled with such irresistible aromas as fresh herbs and pungent spices. I can still almost taste the mouth-watering fragrances of baking breads and cookies! Even as a small child, I was fascinated by food preparation. I credit my mother because she was such a wonderful cook. She spent hours in the kitchen cooking and baking for our family of six.

When I was growing up my family lived on the coast of the Adriatic Sea in the Mediterranean region. So without actually being conscious of it, I became very familiar with what we now call the "Mediterranean Diet."

Today that diet is recognized as being one of the healthiest in the world. It consists of copious amounts of fresh vegetables and fruits, beans and legumes, and whole grains, such as pasta. The Mediterranean diet contains far less saturated fat from meat than the typical American diet, because animal foods such as chicken are used as flavoring elements or condiments rather than as the main part of a meal. In the Mediterranean diet, beef is mostly replaced by fresh fish, and highly-processed ingredients such as hydrogenated fats and refined sugar are virtually unknown. This diet is naturally low in fat, yet one of the most appetizing and enjoyable cuisines in the world. I drew on my great familiarity with the Mediterranean Diet in creating many of the recipes for this book.

One of the reasons the Mediterranean Diet can be so delicious and so healthy is that it is in harmony with nature. For example, it takes full advantage of the special foods of each season.

That was one of the things I remember best about the foods of my youth. In the spring and summer, we had sweet, juicy peaches, nectarines, plums, apricots, cherries, and melons. During the fall, we enjoyed crisp apples, luscious pears, and colorful pumpkins.

This longtime fondness for fruit is reflected in these recipes. Although traditional American cooking tends to use fruit primarily in desserts and breakfast foods, I've used fruits to wonderful advantage in a variety of other dishes, including those featuring poultry, fish and vegetables.

Although the idea may sound unusual to you at first, I think you'll be delightfully surprised. Most of the great cuisines of the world use fruits lavishly to create elegant, delicious dishes. My lifelong love for food is also reflected in some of the ethnic influences in these recipes. Everywhere I've gone in my extensive travels, I've observed the way the local chefs prepared their food.

When it came time for me to create a whole new way of cooking – *The Cooking Without Fat Method* – I had many sources of inspiration to draw upon.

Traveling and Learning About Food

My passion for food has sent me literally to the ends of the earth. Some people go to Paris to see the Louvre; I went there to attend cooking school. While others might enjoy India just for the Taj Mahal, I was busily watching the way native chefs prepared their indigenous curries, and learning the way they combine potato and cucumber with papaya and mango to create an appetizer called *chat.*

I'm not saying that the world's great monuments and treasures of art have no meaning in my life, quite the contrary. It's that I believe food– especially healthy food–is equal to the greatest of life's joys. It was through searching the world and studying the cuisines of over 80 countries that I eventually learned the secrets to highlighting natural flavors without fat.

For example, I learned how other cultures blend fruits with meat, poultry and fish with delicious results. Southeast Asians bake their fish in coconut milk, or use the milk as a base for spicy soups. The French are masters at creating orange and cherry sauces. Middle Easterners prepare their lamb with pomegranate juice.

These cultures realize that by combining sweet flavors with tangy ones, you can greatly highlight the taste of the natural ingredients without adding fat. This food research provided the inspiration for the recipes in this book. I don't think I could have developed a method for cooking without fat that tastes this good or is this convenient unless I had spent as much time as I have studying the cuisines of the world.

Perhaps the most important lesson learned from all these different cuisines is that you don't have to depend on fat to get flavor. There are simple ways to artfully combine and contrast the natural flavors of foods to create recipes with their own distinct and flavorful personalities. That's the basis for the recipes in this book.

Cooking without Fat

My Personal Discovery of "Hidden" Fat

I was shocked and angry when I found out that the majority of fat in the average diet is actually from "hidden" sources where we least suspect it.

Again, I learned about it through personal experience.

For me, it all started with one dish – coleslaw. Yes, coleslaw. I love salads mixed with cabbage, not only for the taste, but because it is one of the cruciferous vegetables that can be such potent cancer-fighters. Coleslaw was always a natural favorite of mine.

What I discovered is that traditional deli coleslaw contains 225 calories and 20.2 grams of fat in a serving. That's 77 percent of calories from fat. Yet in 100 grams of raw cabbage, there's only 0.1 grams of fat. Obviously, it's not the vegetables, but the sour cream, or mayonnaise and oil added to them that turns what appears to be a healthy salad into one loaded with hidden fat.

I eventually developed my own coleslaw made without any added fat. In fact, it's basically the same recipe that I'm sharing with you in this book. To dramatize how much difference it can make when you cook without fat, let's compare a traditional coleslaw recipe with the one in this book made without fat.

Let's look at typical take-out coleslaw.

Dressing for Traditional Deli Coleslaw
⅓ cup olive oil
⅓ cup vinegar
1 cup sour cream (or mayonnaise)
2 tablespoons sugar
1 teaspoon salt
⅛ teaspoon pepper
1 tablespoon caraway seeds (optional)

Compare that with the coleslaw dressing that we originated here in our kitchen. We kept all the flavor, while getting rid of the fat, salt and sugar.

Dressing for Healthy Coleslaw
⅓ cup plain nonfat yogurt
1 tablespoon apple cider vinegar
2 tablespoons honey

Now, let's see how these recipes stack up when we compare the amounts of calories, fat, and cholesterol they each contain.

Recipe (per serving)	Calories	Grams of Fat	Percentage of Calories from Fat	Milligrams of Cholesterol
Traditional Coleslaw	225	20.2g	77	17 mg.
Cooking Without Fat Coleslaw	61	Fat-Free	0	0.3 mg.

And I can assure you that you don't have to sacrifice flavor when you prepare the *Cooking Without Fat* recipe for coleslaw.

To give you an idea of how much fat you can cut by using our recipes, here are a few more comparisons of the fat in traditional recipes and the amount in the recipes in this book:

Food (1 serving)	Calories	Grams of Fat	Percentage of Calories from Fat
Traditional Tuna Salad	383	19g	44
Cooking Without Fat version	218	1.4g	6
Traditional Potato Salad	360	14g	35
Cooking Without Fat version	108	Fat-Free	0
Traditional French Dressing	65	6g	83
Cooking Without Fat version	14	Fat-Free	0
Traditional Cheesecake	588	40g	61
Cooking Without Fat version	214	Fat-Free	0

Discovering the Terrible Secret of Granola

I soon discovered that coleslaw was just the tip of the "fat" iceberg, and that a number of other foods that seem "healthy" are actually sources of "hidden" fat.

Perhaps the biggest shock was granola.

For years, granola was one of my favorite breakfast foods. It is made with whole grains which provide plenty of B vitamins and fiber. Granola also contains dried fruit for energy, and nuts for protein. But here's the bad news. Until recently, most commercial granola contained coconut oil. And coconut oil is not only high in fat, most of the fat is saturated.

Once consumers became aware of the saturated fat in coconut oil, many companies simply replaced coconut oil with other forms of fat. Often, they use hydrogenated or partially hydrogenated oils. Hydrogenation is a process that artificially makes unsaturated fats more saturated. That's why many health conscious people avoid these fats.

But regardless of the type of oil, most granola is very high in fat.

For example, according to the label, a popular brand of "Natural" Granola Cereal contains over 32 percent fat and is made with partially hydrogenated cottonseed oil.

Many people eat as much as a cup of granola at a time. A cup of granola contains over 440 calories and almost 16 grams of fat!

I first discovered how much total fat and saturated fat are in granola when I was still a consumer, and not yet in the food business. But what appalled me even more than the amount of fat was the fact that the manufacturer didn't list the fat on the package. I believe that a company that makes healthy, nutritious products should have nothing to hide.

When I founded Health Valley, I vowed that we would always provide full nutritional information on all our labels.

I remember a few years ago, a snack food company had a slogan that said, "Bet you can't eat just one."

Well, today we know why. It's because many snack foods are loaded with fat, and fat can actually be addictive.

The Quest to Make Healthy, Good Tasting, Fat-Free Foods

As I said earlier, the whole reason I founded Health Valley was to improve my own diet by making the kinds of good tasting, nutritious foods I wanted to eat myself, but simply couldn't find from commercial sources.

And of all the many healthy, good tasting products Health Valley has developed over the years, the ones I'm proudest of are our Fat-Free foods.

That's because I believe Health Valley Fat-Free products represent a real breakthrough in healthy foods. In order to create them, we actually had to create something entirely new – a whole new method of baking!

Baking "experts" said it was impossible to make good tasting baked goods like cookies and tarts without shortening, or fat in the form of mono and diglycerides as processing agents.

That's because fat performs so many important functions in baking. It affects the texture of baked goods by helping to provide tenderness and moisture. It affects flavor by acting as a flavor carrier and by providing a smooth, creamy mouth feel. So it's not easy to make baked goods with the taste and texture people expect when you don't add fat.

I always believed that we could succeed. But it certainly wasn't easy.

Making The First Healthy Fat-Free Cookie
With Only <u>Half</u> the Calories

To give you an idea of the effort it took, let me describe the development of Health Valley's first Fat-Free cookie, our Raisin Oatmeal cookie.

Our goal was to make a moist, chewy, delicious cookie without any fat whatsoever. To do this, we had to carefully balance whole grains with fruit and fruit juice.

We tried dozens of different blends, and ended up with burnt cookies, cookies without shape, and cookies without flavor. We saw cookies that stuck to the pan, and cookies that were so hard you couldn't possibly take a bite out of them. But we didn't give up.

Finally, after over 100 trips to the oven, everything came together the way we knew it could, and we achieved what we set out to do–make baking history!

We became the first food company to introduce a delicious 35-calorie Fat-Free cookie made the healthy way: fat-free, cholesterol-free, high in fiber and low in sodium. And because this cookie is made without added fat, it contains <u>only half the calories of most cookies made with fat</u>. This was something that had never been done before.

In fact, when the ***Environmental Nutrition*** newsletter looked at 31 varieties of cookies and ranked them according to how "healthy" they are, based on the amount of fat they contain, the top cookies were Fat-Free Cookies from Health Valley with only four percent of calories from fat!

Many other varieties quickly followed the Raisin Oatmeal cookie. And then, we developed Fat-Free recipes for scones, crackers and granola bars–all much lower in calories than products made with fat. These were followed by Fat-Free soups and chilis, caramel corn puffs with only 2 calories, baked beans and Fat-Free versions of our Fast Menu® canned entrees.

All together, we've created over 100 new products that don't contain any fat, making Health Valley America's No. 1 Fat-Free Healthy Foods Company.

The Benefits You Can Enjoy By Using Our Fat-Free Foods

When we developed our first Fat-Free cookie, we knew that we had come up with something very special. It is what a cookie should be–fat-free, high in fiber, nutritious, with fruit you can taste in every bite.

And these cookies contain almost 40% fewer calories than many comparable cookies made with fat. For example:

Product/Size	Calories	Fat	% of Calories from Fat
Commercial Brand of Oatmeal Raisin Cookies (1.16 oz.)	160	6g	34%
Health Valley® Fat-Free Raisin Oatmeal Cookies (1.16 oz.)	100	0.0g	0%

Many of us at Health Valley discovered first hand what a difference the lower calories can make.

I lost 15 pounds just by eating our Fat-Free foods instead of comparable commercial products made with fat.

As our Fat-Free foods reached the market, our customers began to enjoy similar benefits. Here are just two of the many letters we received:

"I just love the new Health Valley Foods FAT-FREE products. By using the muffins, bars and cookies as part of the meal plan, I lost five pounds during the first week."

–Leisa Zarian, Montrose, CA

"Your cookies were a big help as I lost 25 pounds over the summer months. At an average of 25 calories per cookie, almost no fat and almost no sodium, I never felt "guilty" eating them, and they taste good! I reached my desired weight last September, but your low-fat and fat-free products are still part of my life because I like them."
  – Sue Modelski, West Wilmington, CT

Another important benefit is that we make our Fat-Free cookies from organically grown whole grains and real fruit. As a result they contain fiber from a variety of different sources, as well as the nutrients and micronutrients essential for good health.

We also "fortify" our Fat-Free foods naturally, by including ingredients that are especially rich sources of essential nutrients. For example, to many of our products we add natural beta carotene, a key nutrient of the 1990s because it is a natural antioxidant that is essential for good health.

So when you select Health Valley Fat-Free products, you get more than foods with no added fat whatsoever. You also get foods made the healthy way you want.

What Foods Should Be

It's ironic that so many people in this country are overfed, yet undernourished. It's because so much of the processed "fast" food they eat is too high in fat and fails to provide balanced nutrition.

At Health Valley, we're committed to preparing foods that have value. Our first requirement is that a product **must be nutritious.**

Our foods have been developed based on the latest scientific nutritional research. You always get the highest quality nutritious foods from Health Valley.

We define nutritious foods as those that are rich in vitamins, minerals, fiber and other natural nutrients from organic fruits, grains and vegetables that are grown without chemical pesticides or herbicides. Nutritious also means that they are made the healthy way–we cannot consider a food nutritious when the nutrients are being compromised by a lot of unhealthy fat, salt and empty calories. We create foods that will have a positive effect on the human body.

We take our food very seriously. We believe that preparing food is almost a sacred trust, because it nourishes the body and actually becomes part of it. In fact, according to the **Surgeon General's Report on Nutrition and Health,** diet plays a role in the diseases that cause about 70 percent of all the deaths in this country. So food has a significant impact on our overall health and well-being.

We believe that when a company really cares, you can tell the difference. That's why we're so gratified by the recognition of our customers. Here are a few examples:

> *"Health Valley has a genuine, humane concern for the health and well-being of its customers, and furthermore, shows a commitment and a sincerity almost entirely absent in today's marketplace."*
>
> –M. Correa, San Leandro, California

> *"It's so refreshing to see the personal interest that you take, not only in the care and production of your products, but also the relationship and interest you take in the concerns, needs and opinions of your consumers. It means a lot to the individual, especially in these times of mass-produced, fast foods, and corporate profiteering, that there are still some family-owned companies like yours that still have concern about proper nutrition, good health, and care about what is put into the human body. You are doing a great service to the public. Keep up the good work and thank you so much."*
>
> –J. Moore, Lexington, Virginia

Cooking without Fat

"I practice Internal Medicine...and my subspecialty is preventive cardiology. I have become increasingly impressed with the dedication of your company and the quality of the foods you produce to help preserve the health of the population. Usually something that is good for you tastes terrible. This is not the case with your products. Not only do my wife and I eat your products regularly, but I am also recommending them to my patients. The more we can influence people to eat properly, the longer they will live, and more importantly, the quality of their lives will improve."

— R.I. Hochman, M.D., Annapolis, Maryland

Health Valley Has Created a Food Facility That Is the Model for the Future

For over 25 years I have had a dream. That dream involved creating a food facility that would be a model for preparing healthy foods. The loyal support of our customers has helped me realize that dream.

Our modern facility is located in Irwindale, in the foothills of Southern California. It's the first facility to apply state-of-the-art technology to enhance the human skills of dedicated people with a real concern for food. This facility gave us the freedom to develop a revolutionary way of preparing foods with the same care and taste of homemade foods like mother made "from scratch," and still take advantage of the precision and the absolute cleanliness of the most modern facility.

What's the difference between our new facility and the typical automated plant of a giant food processor? There are many, but you see the most important one as soon as you walk in the door. There you see a sign that proclaims:

No refined sugar, No white flour, No hydrogenated oils,
No saturated fats, No artificial ingredients, and No chemical additives
will ever be allowed in Health Valley
products because we are genuinely concerned
about the health of our customers.

Another important difference is that our state-of-the-art equipment is under the full control of skillful bakers, rather than merely being monitored by technicians. This is not an automated plant where machines take the place of humans.

I believe that machines can never be quality oriented. Quality is strictly a human trait that comes from knowledge, personal pride and dedication.

The difference between Health Valley's equipment and that of food giants is one of fundamental focus and priorities. Food company technology is used because it can produce high output. That's why if you take a tour of a typical automated facility, you'll hear very impressive production capacity figures used to describe the equipment. At Health Valley, we don't measure success in terms of how much we produce, but rather in the quality of what we produce. In fact, we train our personnel to be concerned about quality, not profitability, because **we are obsessed with quality.**

We run our modern, state-of-the-art bakery as if it were a small, family bakery. We employ people with a sense of pride and positive energy because we believe that this results in positive products. That's why we believe that we have the finest employees anywhere.

Although Health Valley is blessed with a staff of very talented people who are skilled at food science, we still consider food preparation to be an art, rather than a science.

Our goal is to combine the best of old-fashioned food preparation with the efficiency and accuracy of state-of-the-art technology.

It is my personal belief that food prepared this way is truly the wave of the future. And we hope other companies will follow our lead.

The Health Valley Test Kitchen

An integral part of the quality control of our products involves our Health Valley kitchen. It isn't a cold, clinical laboratory like the test kitchens of many large food companies. Ours is a warm, inviting place where our food specialists can devote themselves to creating and improving our foods.

We set very stringent standards for the foods we prepare in our kitchen–no more than 15% of the total calories come from fat in any of the recipes we prepare or 3 grams of fat per serving in the new products we develop.

Just as a warm, friendly kitchen at home seems to draw everyone into it, so, too, our Health Valley kitchen is a place where people enjoy coming. You not only see skilled nutritionists and chefs working there, you're likely to find other employees, their families and friends, and even some celebrated nutrition experts visiting.

Health Valley's Commitment to Providing You with Nutritional Information

There is an old proverb that says, "Give someone a fish and you feed him for a day; teach someone to fish and you feed him for a lifetime."

To me, this adage illustrates the power of knowledge, and it's the reason Health Valley is so committed to providing you with information along with our products.

We view our customers as intelligent, enlightened individuals who want to be in control of their own health and well-being through informed choices–choices about which foods to eat and what kind of diet and lifestyle to select.

Unlike food companies that only view customers as "consumers" and sources of revenue, Health Valley thinks of its customers as friends and partners in the quest to make our society a healthier one. We're aware that our greatest tool is knowledge. That's why we were the first company to voluntarily list full nutritional information on all our packages. And it's the reason we provide you with a toll-free telephone number on our packages so you can use it to get nutritional information directly from us regarding any of our products or nutrition in general.

And Health Valley has added another source of information. We have opened the **Health Valley Education Center,** located at our headquarters in Irwindale, California. Here we conduct educational programs on subjects ranging from the latest nutritional research to new roles that private industry can play in conservation and environmental issues.

Since we built our Education Center to be at the vanguard of health and nutrition, we consciously used only environmentally safe materials. For example, we deliberately avoided using lead-based paints because lead is a toxic element that can accumulate in the body. Excess lead can lead to diminished brain capability, especially in small children. We also avoided such materials as resins and plastics that contain formaldehyde, because this chemical is an irritant to the respiratory system and can agitate allergies. The bonding materials we used included natural glues, and we installed the most efficient appliances that use the least amount of energy and water.

Our Education Center is located right next to our bakery, so you can actually look into the bakery from the Center. Because we have nothing to hide, we want you to be able to see the way we make our products, and to taste them fresh from the ovens.

The Health Valley Way of Doing Business

Every once in a while, I receive a letter from someone in business school who wants to use our company as a "case study." I'm always amused because I know that the way we do things violates all of the "accepted business practices" taught in most business schools.

To begin with, I made the commitment not to run Health Valley like a typical business. I would close the doors of the business before I'd allow Health Valley to make inferior-quality products in the interests of profitability.

From a marketing standpoint, we don't do marketing studies or conduct focus groups to find out what people want. We simply listen to what our customers tell us directly.

We also don't do cost analyses before we develop new products to determine if they will be profitable. We simply focus on making healthier products and trust that our customers will be concerned enough about their well-being to recognize the quality and value we offer.

Another difference between us and other companies is that we don't spend money on expensive media advertising. The reason is simple: We want to offer our customers the best value. At Health Valley, we think that you should pay for the quality of the product itself, not its fancy packaging or the expensive advertising to sell it.

We depend a lot on our existing customers telling their friends about our products to get new customers. So we ask you to do this for us.

We even do unheard of things like deciding not to make a product because it doesn't fulfill our nutritional standards, even though we know we can make money from it. As an example, we recently had a food broker tell us that we could make over a million dollars a year in additional revenue if we would produce a blue corn chip. But when we tried to make one, we found that it contained too much fat. When we couldn't make a blue corn chip with the right flavor and no added fat we simply decided not to make one at all. The fact that it might be profitable wasn't important to us. Our commitment to cutting fat is of the greatest importance.

Even the way our company is structured runs against the traditional standard. We don't have a hierarchy with different layers of management. There are no vice-presidents, or senior vice-presidents, or executive vice-presidents at Health Valley. We believe that having too many levels of management stifles creativity and encourages political maneuvering.

By eliminating the traditional management structure, we allow individuals to interact with each other directly, to work together as teams, and we encourage creativity. We probably have the leanest management structure of any company. We want to run more efficiently not so that we can make more profit, but because we want to offer our customers greater value for their money.

Only a company with an outstanding customer satisfaction department would dare make changes the way we do. We're proud that we've developed what we feel is the best customer service in the entire food business. Unlike other companies, we expect our customer service people to serve you, not to defend the company. We believe that our job isn't just to provide you with healthy food, but to continue to serve after you've purchased our products. Our goal is to give you service that isn't just good, but legendary. That's why we're so pleased by comments such as this:

"You and your company are certainly the ultimate in service to your customers… you should be voted as the President of the Year, and your company in the same top category for outstanding attention to your customers."

—Lonnie Wurn, Jacksonville, Florida

Health Valley's Vision is to Help Make the World a Better, Healthier Place.

At Health Valley, we have a vision of a healthier world where people enjoy longer, richer, more fulfilling lives by taking control over their own health.

A world where food is grown and handled with care. Where food companies prepare and package their foods with a passion for quality. Where everyone works together to protect and enhance the environment.

A world where the relationship between companies and their customers is based on mutual trust and genuine concern for each other, not on exploitation.

At the very core of this vision is caring: for the individual, for the earth, for the seas, and for the air. We believe a vision should express our fondest hopes, and should challenge and inspire us to reach beyond what we would ordinarily expect to accomplish.

In the most fundamental sense, our vision is based on the power of doing good and on caring.

This idealism forms the basis for the way we run our company. It was my vision when I founded Health Valley, and it remains the vision that drives the company today.

Health Valley's Concern for the Future of Our Planet

If you're truly concerned about health, you must be concerned about more than your own personal health. You must be concerned about the health of your community, your country, and the entire planet.

That's why I believe that food, health, recycling and the environment are all tied together.

I have been concerned that we leave a better world for our children since long before it became fashionable to do so.

All of us at the company look to the future and realize that we must continue to improve our products in response to your changing needs. That's why I feel it is important to share my vision of the future with you.

I believe companies, like individuals, should have well defined moral and ethical values, and that they should abide by them.

People around the world now realize how small and fragile our planet is. Instead of viewing Mother Earth as a limitless supplier of natural resources, we recognize the responsibility we all have to conserve and recycle the precious materials we have been given.

At Health Valley, we believe that food companies have a social responsibility to give something back to the land, rather than just reaping the harvests. That's why we have our "Save The Earth" Policy.

We implement it in a variety of ways: We don't do any testing with animals and we actively support sustainable farming methods by providing both financial and moral support to farmers who grow foods without chemical pesticides, herbicides or fumigants.

We support farmers who develop organic fields, and we continue to support them by creating an ongoing market for their crops. In 1996,

*Cooking
without
Fat*

Health Valley will purchase over 50 million pounds of organic ingredients. That means we use more organic ingredients than any other company in the world!

I personally believe that organic crops are safer, more nutritious and better tasting. Equally important, I am alarmed by the amount of chemicals used in agriculture.

Each year, U.S farmers spray 750 million pounds of pesticides on their crops. And they use 22 billion pounds of synthetic fertilizers a year. In fact, the total weight of the chemicals used in farming each year is greater than the combined weight of our population!

This poses not only a great threat from chemical contamination to the nation's ground water, but erosion of our country's valuable topsoil. Chemical fertilizers make topsoil more vulnerable to erosion than using natural fertilizers and practicing crop rotation. This is clear in the reports issued by the Soil Conservation Service of the U.S. Department of Agriculture. They tell us that 200 years ago, the farmland in this country averaged 21 inches of topsoil. Today, the average is down to 6 inches of topsoil. We have lost 4 million acres of cropland through erosion.

That's why Health Valley's goal is to use organically grown ingredients exclusively in all our products. We are well on our way to achieving that goal.

Another way we fulfill our commitment is by recycling: our boxes are made from recycled materials. And along with the plastic trays and bags inside, they are recyclable. Our cans and labels are all recyclable.

Health Valley was the first company in the country to use soy-based inks exclusively for printing our packages and labels. The EPA commends these inks as environmentally safe, while regular petroleum-based inks can result in toxic by-products.

Locally, Health Valley encourages fuel conservation at our manufacturing facility.

We have the most energy-efficient equipment in the food industry.

Through incentives, such as preferred parking and cash subsidies, we encourage employees to rideshare and to use mass transportation.

We've installed a recycling center at our headquarters in Irwindale to encourage employees and the community to conserve natural resources.

Because we realize that even little things count, we provide our employees with beverage mugs that are reusable, rather than disposable cups. For guests and visitors, the cups are paper, rather than styrofoam.

We also express our concern for the health and well-being of our society by supporting such organizations as the American Cancer Society, the American Heart Association, and Bastyr College of Natural Health Sciences. Each year, we make financial contributions to support these and other health-promoting organizations.

There's another kind of environment we're concerned about at Health Valley—that's the emotional environment.

Visitors have asked me how I keep that environment so positive. The answer is simple: At Health Valley, everyone is an individual and is treated as such. And we demonstrate our concern for our employees in a number of ways, such as the Wellness Program. Consequently, everyone wants to contribute to the process of making this a better, healthier world for all of us.

We still take pride in what we do. Together.

chapter two

Why You Should Cut Down on Fat

Are You Eating Too Much Fat?

The average American consumes 135 pounds of fat each year! This alarming statistic is why the American Heart Association, the American Cancer Society and the United States Surgeon General all recommend that you cut down dramatically on fat. Too much fat in the diet is America's #1 nutrition hazard since it contributes to developing:

1. Obesity
2. Heart disease
3. Several forms of cancer.
4. Diabetes

In fact, statistics show that if you're an average American, you have a 50-50 chance of dying of stroke or heart disease. But there is something you can do about it – you can start cutting down on fat now. The good news is that you can cut fat enough to actually reverse some of the conditions that contribute to cardiovascular heart disease and stroke.

That means you can actually prevent disease, rather than having to treat it later. You will be in a position to fulfill the promise of the **Center for Science in the Public Interest** that stated:

"As a nation, it's within our grasp to cut the rates of diet-related diseases by at least 50 percent before the year 2000. Half as much heart disease, half as much hypertension, even half as much constipation and tooth decay."

Just as importantly, you can control your weight without dieting, have more energy, and just plain feel better and look better.

Eating Too Much Fat Can Make You Fat

Several years ago, I discovered from my own experience that eating too much fat makes you fat. And now there is extensive clinical research verifying that fact.

The American Journal of Clinical Nutrition stated that, on the average, lean people get 29 percent of their calories from fat, while overweight people eat 35 percent or more fat.[1]

Fat is the single most important dietary factor when it comes to weight control. So if you want to lose weight, you should count fat, not calories.

You may already know that fat contains more than twice as many calories as the same amount of protein and carbohydrates. But did you know that your body is much more efficient at turning fat from food into body fat than it is at turning protein and carbohydrates into body fat? That's because your body uses only 3 percent of the energy that's in fat to store it in fat cells in the body, while it takes 25 percent to convert protein or carbohydrates into stored body fat.

But there's more: recent studies have shown that not all calories are created equally. Calories from fat are more likely to make you fat than calories from protein or carbohydrates.

The evidence to support the dual disposition of calories comes from a variety of studies. A long-term study, which was conducted by the Chinese Academy of Preventive Medicine, investigated the eating habits of 6,500 Chinese. Perhaps the most striking finding was that the average Chinese consumes 30 percent more calories with 60 percent less calories from fat than we do in America. That's because of the kinds of foods they eat – low in fat, high in carbohydrates. As a result, the average Chinese weighs less than the average American (adjusted for height differences). The study showed that the Chinese also enjoy a much lower rate of heart disease and several forms of cancer.[2]

1. The American Journal of Clinical Nutrition – 1990; 52:426-30
2. Ibid., 52:1027-36. Also Chen J., Campbell T.C., Li J., Pato R., "Diet, Lifestyle and Mortality in China: A Study of the Characteristics of 65 Chinese Counties." Oxford: Oxford University Press

The Danger in Combining Fat and Sugar

Even though the average American actually consumes fewer total calories than the average Chinese, it's no wonder that we're fatter. Not only do we consume a much higher percentage of fat, but we eat a lot of highly processed foods that are made almost entirely from fat and refined sugar. Some of the biggest offenders are ice cream, doughnuts, and many packaged baked goods, such as sweet rolls and danishes. Mixing fat and sugar in the same food presents a particular problem if you're trying to control your weight: sugar stimulates the release of insulin, which, in turn, activates enzymes that promote fat storage.

A Cornell University Weight Loss Study

If you've ever had trouble losing weight, there's good news.

A recent study at Cornell University found that women who ate a low-fat diet lost an average of one-half pound a week while eating as much food as they wanted.

At Cornell, women ate either a typical diet with 37 percent of calories from fat or a 25 percent fat diet. Both groups were allowed to eat as much as they wanted. The low-fat group could even eat foods like pizza and ice cream prepared with reduced-fat ingredients. The women who ate the low-fat diet lost what most experts consider to be the ideal amount each week for permanent weight loss, and they did it without being concerned about how much they ate or counting calories.[3]

In a similar study in Seattle, 303 women participated in a study in which half were put on a menu that averaged about 21 percent of calories from fat, while the other half ate a menu that averaged 39 percent fat. Without any thought of eating less, the low-fat group lost weight and kept it off. The authors of the study calculated that for every percentage point of fat they cut from their diet, one-quarter to one-half pound of body fat came off their bodies.[4]

3. The American Journal of Clinical Nutrition – 1991; 53:1124-9
4. Ibid., 54:821-8

This study also showed that not all calories are equal when it comes to losing weight. Women who ate less fat lost more weight than those who ate fewer calories, but a higher percentage of fat.

So although the number of calories you consume is important, it is equally important to count the grams of fat you eat everyday. The recipes in this book prove it can be just as easy to eat whole foods that are low in fat or are fat-free without compromising convenience or taste.

Overcoming the Fear of Eating

It is sadly ironic that in a society where there is such an abundance of food, eating disorders afflict so many people. Some of these disorders have psychological roots. I can't help but think that the high fat content of so many packaged and prepared foods is a contributing factor. With so much fat being used in processed foods, it is no wonder some people begin to feel that there's nothing they can eat that doesn't cause them to get fat.

This fear has led to the enormous growth of meal replacements. I think these "diet" drinks are a poor substitute for healthy low-fat foods that provide all the carbohydrates, protein, fat, and natural vitamins and minerals necessary for good health.

How Much Fat Is the Right Amount?

When I was eating too many fatty foods, I not only gained weight, I didn't really feel healthy. Since then, I discovered the reason. Eating excess fat can lead to impaired blood circulation, which can leave you feeling tired and run down. Furthermore, an excess of fat can actually affect normal immune functions, making you more vulnerable to becoming ill.

The Dangers of Eating More Than 30% of Calories from Fat

If you eat a diet that supplies more than 30 percent of calories from fat, you may wind up with clogged arteries, and you dramatically increase your risk of developing serious degenerative diseases, including cancer and diabetes.

That's why the leading health-promoting organizations all recommend that you reduce fat intake to no more than 30% of calories.

Cutting Fat to 25% of Calories is Better

The Journal of The American Medical Association published the results of research that showed that a diet which provides 30 percent of calories from fat helps prevent new arterial blockages from forming, but in patients with existing heart disease, it does not prevent clogged arteries from getting even worse. To effectively stop blockages from getting worse, fat intake has to be reduced to 25 percent of calories or less.[5]

Cutting Fat to 15% of Calories or Less is Best

The really exciting news about preventing heart disease comes from the research by Dr. Dean Ornish, which was published in the British Medical Journal, *Lancet.*[6]

Dr. Ornish's research showed that **a diet with essentially all added fat removed could actually help unclog blocked arteries** as part of a total program of diet, exercise and stress management. What is significant is that Dr. Ornish's program did not involve any drugs or invasive techniques.

We have created over 100 wholesome recipes with absolutely no added fat or high-fat ingredients. As a result, all of the recipes provide less than 15 percent of calories from fat.

5. Journal of the American Medical Association 1990; 263:1646-52
6. Lancet 1990; 336:129-33

Cooking
without
Fat

A Simple Way to Calculate
How Much Fat You Should Eat

There is an easy way to calculate the amount of fat in your diet. Most of us know approximately how many calories we'd like to eat each day. Simply calculate 15 percent of that number.

Here's an example: if you normally eat 1,500 calories a day, 15 percent of that is 225. Next, convert this figure into the number of grams of fat you can eat each day. To do this, divide the number of calories by nine (because there are nine calories in every gram of fat). In our example, you end up with 25. That means your maximum fat intake should be no more than 25 grams of fat if you want to hold your fat level to 15 percent of your total calories.

To make it even simpler for you, here are charts that show the number of grams of fat you can eat for a variety of different calorie levels:

Grams of Fat Equal to 30% of Calories and to 15% of Calories

Calories Per Day	Grams of Fat Equal to 30% of Calories	Grams of Fat Equal to 15% of Calories
1000	33 gm	16 gm
1200	40 gm	20 gm
1500	50 gm	25 gm
1800	60 gm	30 gm
2000	67 gm	33 gm
2200	73 gm	36 gm
2600	87 gm	43 gm
2800	93 gm	46 gm
3000	100 gm	50 gm
3500	117 gm	58 gm

To give you a point of reference about how much fat you can consume based on actual foods, rather than on numbers of grams, here is a list of the grams of fat found in some popular foods versus Health Valley Fat-Free foods:

Food/Quantity:	Amount of Fat:
Vegetable oil (1 tablespoon)	14 gm
Beef Hot Dog (2 oz.)	17 gm
Regular Ice Cream (4 oz.)	18 gm
Hamburger, Fries & Milk Shake	64 gm
Potato Chips (8 oz. bag)	80 gm
Health Valley Fat-Free Foods	**0 gm per serving**

Your Fat Budget

One of the most important things you can do to ensure that you'll enjoy a long, healthy life is to cut fat from your daily diet. That's why **all the recipes in this book contain no more than 15 percent of calories from fat.**

Being realistic, I know that there will be times when you can't use these recipes. It may be because you're severely pressed for time, or because you're out with friends at a restaurant.

When you do eat meals with more than 15 percent of the calories from fat, you don't have to feel bad, as long as you try to balance a high fat meal with one that is even lower than 15 percent fat.

The best analogy I can offer is your budget. To stay financially solvent, you have to balance your income and your expenses. When you have an unusually large expense in one area, you need to balance it by saving money in other areas.

Using this same principle, it's all right to eat high fat foods occasionally, but you should try to maintain a balanced "fat budget."

To make it easier for you to do this, **Health Valley has developed a line of Fat-Free foods that contain no added fat or oil.**

So when you "cheat" by eating a high fat food you enjoy and go over your fat budget, you can use our Fat-Free foods to help "balance your fat budget."

Is There Any Danger in Cutting Back on Fat?

Since I am such a strong advocate of cutting back on fat as part of a healthier way of eating, I'm often asked to address groups of nutrition-minded people. One of the questions I'm asked most concerns how safe it is to cut fat dramatically.

I remind people that virtually all natural foods contain some fat, so it really isn't necessary to add fat to any food if you eat a balanced diet that includes a variety of foods.

The only essential nutrients associated with fats are two fatty acids, linolenic and linoleic acid, which our bodies can't make. These two essential fatty acids are usually found in the form of Omega-3 and Omega-6 fatty acids.

Omega-6 fatty acids are found in most whole grains such as cereals and baked goods made from whole wheat, so most people don't have a problem getting them.

People are more likely to be deficient in Omega-3 fatty acids, which are the kind most commonly associated with cold water fish, such as salmon. But there are also some rich vegetable sources, especially golden flax seed, which actually contains 10 times more Omega-3 than a comparable amount of salmon. That's why Health Valley prepares both cereals and bars made with golden flax seed. Our Omega-3 bars, Omega-3 cereal and Golden Flax cereal all provide 1,000 milligrams of Omega-3 in each serving, yet they are all low in fat.

So if you're concerned about getting enough Omega-3, make our products made with golden flax seed a regular part of your diet.

chapter three

The Cooking Without Fat Method

What You Need to Know to Make This Method of Cooking Work

We've made it easy for you to get the results you want quickly and easily. Remember these three steps:

1. **Follow recipes to enjoy good tasting, satisfying, convenient meals with no added fat.**
2. **Consult the charts when shopping so you bring only low-fat foods into your home.**
3. **Try cutting fat for 5 days using our "Kick the Fat Habit" Meal Plan.**

What Makes This Method of Cooking So Revolutionary

This is the first cookbook that actually explains how to cook without **adding any fat.**

Unlike low-fat cookbooks, we haven't simply reduced the amount of fat in our recipes from three tablespoons of butter to one tablespoon of olive oil, for example.

What distinguishes these recipes is that they contain no added fat at all. **Nor do we add high fat ingredients like cheese or avocados.**

The experts said it couldn't be done. They said that there was no way a chef could get away with cooking without butter, oil, margarine or lard. I am absolutely delighted that we could prove them wrong. We've taken some of the world's most popular traditional recipes, and recreated them—without the fat.

Cooking without Fat

Why You Don't Need Fat for Flavor

Whenever I'm invited to talk about the benefits of low-fat eating, I finish my presentation by opening the meeting up for questions. Someone invariably points out that fat is necessary for flavor and asks how it's possible to cook without fat and still prepare flavorful meals.

I explain that there are many misconceptions about fat and flavor.

First of all, **fat itself isn't a flavor.**

Fat simply acts as a "carrier" for many flavor elements and it lends a distinctive "creamy" texture to foods.

Virtually all whole foods contain fat, sometimes in very minute amounts. But one thing that is not seen in nature is pure fat in any form. So it would only seem logical that we should be able to cook without fat, since fat doesn't occur alone in nature.

Recent research indicates that the sense of taste results from a complex interaction among the taste buds, which are dense nerve fibers located on the tongue, together with nasal senses and the trigeminal system, which are branches of nerves running between the brain, the nose and the mouth.

There are really only four "tastes" that your tongue can sense: sweet, sour, salty and bitter.

Of these, the abilities to sense bitter and salty tastes serve mainly a protective function. Many deadly toxins taste bitter. This unpleasant sensation usually causes us to spit out the offending substance before any harm is done. This ability undoubtedly protected our ancestors from swallowing many poisonous foods.

Since water is the most primary nutrient of all, the ability to distinguish fresh from salt water also was a key element in the survival of early humans.

The remaining two sensations, sweet and sour, are really the only two that serve us in sensing the unique flavors of the foods we eat. So the secret to creating delicious foods without added fat lies in amplifying, enriching and balancing these two sensations.

It's also important to understand that many taste preferences are acquired rather than being something that we are born with. It's easy to demonstrate this fact just by looking at the items different cultures consider to be gourmet delicacies.

For example, in Hawaii the indigenous people consider poi, or mashed taro root, to be a tasty and festive treat, while mainlanders find it to be little more than an unappealing paste.

To successfully cut down on fat, you should educate your palate to appreciate the natural flavors of foods without added fat.

The Two Basic Principles of the Cooking Without Fat Method

The last time I was asked about my *Cooking Without Fat Method,* I explained that it was a lot like following the Ten Commandments: It's simple to understand, but not always so easy to practice on a daily basis.

There are really only two basic principles to cooking without fat:

1. Substitute fat-free or low-fat ingredients for high-fat ingredients.
2. Highlight the natural flavors of foods.

How to Substitute Low Fat Ingredients for High Fat Ones

The first and most obvious way to maintain the familiar flavors of foods is by simply substituting fat-free or low-fat ingredients for analogous high-fat ones.

For example, nonfat yogurt has the same nutritional value of full-fat yogurt, as well as the same mildly tangy flavor and creamy texture, but without all the fat.

*Cooking
without
Fat*

Another important substitution you can make is to use chicken broth instead of oil, butter or margarine for sauteing such ingredients as chicken, ground turkey, onions, garlic and most vegetables.

Finally, you can cut fat merely by being selective. For example, a breast of chicken without the skin is much lower in fat than the leg and thigh meat with the skin on.

Take a look at this chart for more tips:

Low-Fat Substitutions

Ingredient (size)	Calories	Percentage of Calories from fat	Grams of Fat	Savings in Grams
Yogurt (1 cup)	139	48	7.4	
Nonfat Yogurt	**127**	**0**	**Fat-Free**	**7**
Mayonnaise (1 Tbsp.)	99	100	11	
Nonfat Yogurt	**8**	**0**	**Fat-Free**	**11**
Cream Cheese (½ oz.)	50	90	5	
Nonfat Yogurt	**8**	**0**	**Fat-Free**	**5**
Sour Cream (1 cup)	415	85	39	
Nonfat Yogurt	**127**	**0**	**Fat-Free**	**38.6**
Oil (1 Tbsp.)	126	100	14	
Fat-Free Chicken Broth	**3**	**0**	**Fat-Free**	**14**
Chicken Leg (4 oz.)	265	52	15.4	
Skinless Chicken Breast	**187**	**19**	**4**	**11.4**
Ground Beef (4 oz.)	325	65	23.5	
Ground Turkey Breast	**153**	**5**	**.8**	**22.7**
Whole Egg (1)	79	64	5.6	
Egg Whites (2)	**32**	**0**	**Fat-Free**	**5.6**

How to Highlight Natural Flavors

I have traveled extensively throughout my life, and because of my love for food, I have always observed the way different cultures prepared and seasoned their foods.

So when I began to develop the *Cooking Without Fat Method,* I had a wide variety of different sources to draw upon.

One of the important concepts that I had discovered was combining sweet ingredients, such as fruit, with tangy or spicy ingredients, such as mustard, vinegar or chilis.

For example, in Thailand, they combine small bits of hot, spicy sausage with cool pieces of sweet melon to make a wonderful salad.

In Mexico, the classic mole sauce combines the sweetness of chocolate with the spiciness of chilis to set off the flavors of chicken.

Although we Americans have not extensively explored the use of fruit and other sweet ingredients with tangy or spicy ingredients, I found that this technique provides strong flavor definition for poultry, fish and vegetable dishes without adding fat.

Nature has given us an abundant storehouse of ingredients to work with. Just think about the wonderfully sweet, succulent taste of a peach in the summer, or the incomparable sweet tangy flavor of vine-ripened raspberries. There's also the rich, mellow texture of a perfectly ripe banana and the crisp bite of a cool apple that tastes like fall feels. Each season provides its own bounty of fruits, and each fruit has its own distinctive flavor and texture for us to savor.

Fruit is a key ingredient in highlighting natural flavors.

Besides fruits, we have spices to help celebrate flavors. There's everything from ginger to cinnamon to nutmeg. We also have herbs, which can work subtly or boldly. To understand what I mean, just grab a handful of sweet basil and inhale its fragrance. Then tell me you need fat to give your foods character and flavor.

Key Ingredients for Highlighting Natural Flavors

As you use the recipes in this book, you'll notice that there are some ingredients we specify regularly. I'm listing these ingredients, along with some comments about them.

Even if you're only planning to follow the recipes as they are, you may find it helpful to glance at the list so you'll know the kinds of basic ingredients you'll be using.

I've already mentioned how important fruit can be. I realize that using fruit in recipes other than desserts may sound strange at first, but I urge you to try it for yourself. Start with the Orange Honey Baked Chicken recipe on page 151, or the Orange Roughy in Citrus Sauce on page 181.

Nonfat Yogurt and Nonfat Yogurt Cheese are two important ingredients used in this book because they're really versatile. They provide a pleasantly tart dairy flavor that contrasts well with the sweetness of fruits and fruit juices. They work well with poultry and vegetables, and they have a creamy texture without much fat, so they're the basis for our cheesecake recipes. Nutritionally, they provide the same vitamins and calcium as full-fat yogurt, but without all the fat.

Chicken Broth is also wonderfully versatile. I use it for sauteing foods, instead of using oil. A tablespoon of olive oil contains about 14 grams of fat, while a tablespoon of Health Valley chicken broth is fat-free! I also use chicken broth instead of water when making rice because it gives the rice more flavor without any extra fat.

Lemon Juice is a wonderful substitute for salt in highlighting flavors. I also like its clean, fresh aroma and use it as a natural deodorant in my kitchen.

Orange Juice has a sweet, slightly acidic flavor that combines especially well with chicken and fish.

Honey is what I use when I need a natural, yet concentrated sweetener. Clover honey works best in these recipes because its mild flavor doesn't intrude on the other ingredients. But one of the glories of honey is the fact that there are so many varieties that reflect the sources of the pollen used to make them. So, if I were drizzling a little honey over fresh berries and nonfat yogurt, I might select a honey made from the blossoms of a fruit tree to add an extra touch of flavor. Many home cooks consider honey too sticky and messy to use, but I keep mine in a handy squeeze bottle with a pop-off cap, so it stays neat and ready-to-use.

Mustard doesn't have to come on strong if you blend it with other ingredients. For example, in my Chicken Dijon recipe, it adds wonderful flavor definition without being hot. Incidentally, the kind you should use in these recipes is Dijon or spicy style, rather than the kind you find at the ball park.

Vinegars are another of nature's gifts to us for enhancing flavors without fat. I like to use apple cider, wine and balsamic vinegars, each for its own distinctive characteristics. Apple cider vinegar is lively and tangy, while wine vinegar can be full-flavored and intense. Balsamic is a wine vinegar that has been aged in different-sized barrels made of various woods for several years to give it a rich, mellow flavor. I sometimes like to combine different varieties to achieve a balance that is especially complex.

Celebrating Natural Flavors in *Cooking Without Fat* Recipes

There are three elements necessary to enjoying a meal:

1. The foods must have excellent flavor.
2. They must be visually appealing.
3. The ambience must be attractive.

It's also important that you get up from the table feeling satisfied physically and emotionally.

We took all three factors into account when we created these recipes that we're sharing with you.

These recipes are the culmination of over 25 years of effort. They are recipes that we have refined and improved after preparing them countless times. All of them have been changed at least a dozen times. Many others simply didn't meet our standards, so they aren't included in this book. The recipes in this book are the best of the best.

They're not only good tasting and satisfying, they all contain 15% or less of calories from fat, they're rich in nutrients and complex carbohydrates, and most are excellent sources of fiber.

Cut the Fat for a Day Meal Plan

Here is your guide for eating *healthier* with Health Valley. It's easy to follow because it includes the entire day's meals, including breakfast, lunch, and dinner, plus three energy breaks. And it's fast and convenient because there's no cooking. All you have to do is add hot water to the Healthy Fat-Free Soup in a Cup at lunch, and heat a can of Fat-Free Soup and a can of Fat-Free Chili at dinner. All the other Health Valley products are ready to enjoy right from the package.

By following this sample day, **you'll save 600 calories and 67 grams of fat!**

Another benefit is that you won't be hungry, because there's plenty to eat. In fact, many women find they can't even eat everything on the plan. However, if you're a larger person, or someone who is very active, you can have a turkey breast sandwich, which adds 212 calories. At dinner, you can add or substitute 4-ounces of broiled chicken or fish for an additional 180 calories. For energy breaks, you can substitute Health Valley Omega-3 Bars. Although, these bars are not Fat-Free, each one supplies 1,000 milligrams of essential Omega-3 fatty acids, which is lacking in the typical American diet. Or, if you're a chocolate lover, try substituting Health Valley Fat-Free Healthy Chocolate Flavor Sandwich Bars for a snack. The beauty of this organizer is that it's flexible, so you can tailor it to your own tastes and convenience. Try a day this way–and then do it your own way, selecting the Health Valley products you like best. No matter what you choose from Health Valley, you'll be saving lots of calories, cutting lots of fat, and eating 100% healthy.

Please remember that although this is a healthy way of eating, you are advised to consult your physician before making any changes to your diet.

MEAL	CALORIES / FAT	COMPARE	CALORIES / FAT
BREAKFAST			
Health Valley Fat-Free Breakfast Bar			
(Raspberry, Blueberry and other flavors) or Health Valley Cereal Bar 110 / 0g		Kellogg's®	
8 oz. nonfat milk .... 86 / 0g		Nutri-Grain® Cereal Bar ..140 / 4g	
1 banana (or 8 oz. orange juice) .... 105 / 0g			
10:00 AM ENERGY BREAK			
Health Valley Fat-Free Healthy Tart			
(Try Mountain Blueberry, Cherry or other flavors) .... 150 / 0g		Nabisco® Toastettes® .... 206 / 5g	
½ cup nonfat yogurt .... 63 / 0g			
LUNCH			
Health Valley Fat-Free Healthy Soup in a Cup			
(1 serving)		Fantastic Foods® Rice &	
(Try Zesty Black Bean with Rice, Pasta Italiano or other varieties) ..100 / 0g		Beans Tex-Mex Soup ..... 110 / 1g	
Health Valley Fat-Free Crackers			
(7 cracker serving) .... 50 / 0g		Nabisco® Wheat Thins® ..... 140 / 6g	
Mixed green salad with 2 Tbs fat-free salad dressing .... 55 / 0g			
3:00 PM ENERGY BREAK			
Health Valley Fat-Free Granola Bar			
(Chocolate Chip or Strawberry) .... 140 / 0g		Nature Valley® Granola Bar..188 / 7g	
5:00 PM ENERGY BREAK			
Health Valley Fat-Free Healthy Scone			
(muffin of the '90's)		Hostess®	
(Enjoy Cranberry Orange, Raisin Cinnamon and other flavors) ......180 / 0g		Blueberry Mini Muffins .253 / 14g	
DINNER			
Health Valley Fat-Free Soup			
(1 serving 14 Garden Vegetable) .... 80 / 0g		Healthy Choice® .... 120 / 1g	
Health Valley Fat-Free Cheese Flavor Puffs .... 110 / 0g		Frito-Lay® Chee-tos® .... 154 / 10g	
Mixed green salad with 2 Tbs fat-free dressing .... 55 / 0g			
Health Valley Fat-Free Black Bean Chili		Dennison's® Chunky Chili	
(8 oz.) .... 160 / 0g		Con Carne with Beans ..330 / 15g	
Health Valley Fat-Free Healthy Marshmallow Bars ..90 / 0g		Quaker® Chewy	
		Granola Bar S'mores ..... 129 / 4g	
You save over 600 calories	**TOTAL 1,534 / 0g**	**TOTAL**	**2,134* / 67g**

*Total calories include the fruit, dairy and salads listed on the Health Valley side of the chart.

You get <u>12 Healthy Benefits</u> from Health Valley.

Only Health Valley always offers you more healthy benefits when you use this organizer:

1. **Over 30,000 *IU* of the natural antioxidant, beta carotene,** so you get over 100% of the daily value for vitamin A.

2. **Over 35 grams of fiber,** which is 100% of the daily amount most often recommended by the leading health-promoting organizations.

3. **100% of the daily value for Folic Acid,** an important B vitamin that is especially important for women of child-bearing age.

4. **Five Servings of Fruit & Vegetables** as recommended by the National Cancer Institute. Fruits and vegetables contain **Phytochemicals** which exhibit a unique potential to reduce the occurrence of many degenerative diseases.

5. **Fulfillment of the Dietary Guidelines** of the American Cancer Society, the American Heart Association and the U.S. Surgeon General.

6. **Fat reduction** by over 60 grams of fat a day compared with eating the same amount of similar foods made with fat.

7. **Calorie reduction** of over 600 calories a day compared with similar foods made with fat.

8. **Cholesterol reduction** to less than 10 milligrams per day from nonfat milk and yogurt only.

9. **Sodium reduction** to fewer than 1,500 milligrams a day.

10. **Over 25 certified organic ingredients** grown without chemical fertilizers, herbicides or pesticides because Health Valley is a leader in protecting our planet and uses more organic ingredients than any other company.

11. **Superior service from Health Valley health professionals** who are available to answer your questions about how to enjoy a healthier lifestyle using Health Valley Fat-Free foods. Call **(800) 423-4846,** Monday-Friday between 7:00 AM and 5:00 PM West Coast time.

12. **Health Valley's Total Guarantee** that assures your complete satisfaction with all Health Valley products you buy. So <u>Health Valley offers you more value than any other company</u>.

A Quick Alternative to Making Yogurt Cheese

The technique for turning nonfat yogurt into yogurt cheese that is illustrated on the facing page produces a very versatile and nutritious ingredient that is specified in a variety of recipes, especially the ones for cheesecake.

However, you have to let the nonfat yogurt drain for several hours in the refrigerator to make yogurt cheese, and we recognize there are times when you want to make one of our cheesecake recipes in a hurry or at the last minute.

A fat-free alternative to making yogurt cheese is to substitute a blend of two-thirds fat-free ricotta cheese with one-third fat-free sour ceam.

Here are the exact amounts and directions:

Recipes that call for 4 cups of yogurt cheese

2⅔ cups fat-free ricotta cheese
1⅓ cups fat-free sour cream

Substitute for yogurt cheese in cheesecake recipe and follow the rest of the directions as written.

Recipes that call for 2 cups of yogurt cheese

1⅓ cups fat-free ricotta cheese
⅔ cup fat-free sour cream

Substitute for yogurt cheese and follow the rest of the recipe as written.

yogurt cheese

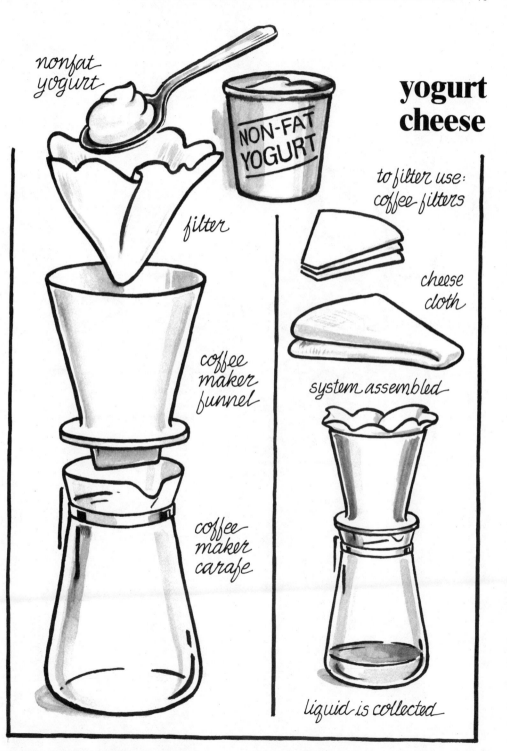

nonfat yogurt

NON-FAT YOGURT

filter

coffee maker funnel

coffee maker carafe

to filter use: coffee-filters

cheese cloth

system assembled

liquid is collected

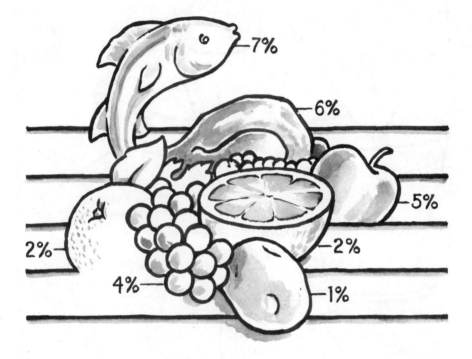

chapter four

How to Shop for Low Fat Foods

2 grams of fat per serving

90 calories per serving

$$
\begin{array}{r}
2\ grams \\
\times\ 9 \\
\hline
18
\end{array}
$$

$$
90\overline{)18.00}
$$
$$
\underline{180}
$$
$$
0
$$
.20

20%

1. Don't buy anything with more than 30% of calories from fat

2. Don't buy anything with more than 3 grams of fat per serving

3. Check the serving size make sure it's realistic for you

Nutrition Facts
Serving Size 1 Bar (42g)
Servings per Container 6

Amount Per Serving

Calories 140   Calories from Fat 81

% Daily Value*

Total Fat 9g   5%

Saturated Fat 1g   0%

Cholesterol 0mg

Sodium 90r

The 3 Golden Rules for Cutting Hidden Fat

The most effective way to cut down on fat is to bring only low-fat foods into your home. That means reading the labels of packaged foods before you buy them to avoid "hidden" fat. To help you do this, I've developed these 3 Golden Rules for Cutting Hidden Fat from your diet:

1. Don't buy anything with more than 30 percent of calories from fat.
When a percentage of fat is listed on the label, be sure it is the percentage of fat by *calories,* not by the *weight* of the product.

2. Don't buy anything with more than 3 grams of fat per serving.

3. Check the serving size to make sure it's realistic for you.
If it's not, recalculate the amount of fat per serving based on the serving size you will be using.

Here are some tips to make these 3 Golden Rules easy to follow.

Rule 1:
Don't Buy Anything with More Than 30 Percent of Calories From Fat.

How to calculate the percentage of calories from fat.

The first question people ask when they hear this rule is, "How do I calculate the percentage of calories from fat when the label doesn't list that information?"

It's really quite easy.

Cooking without Fat

Most labels list the total number of calories in a serving. They also list grams of fat per serving. Here's how to calculate the percentage of calories from fat:

1. Multiply the grams of fat by 9.

2. Divide that figure by the total number of calories.

The resulting number is percentage of calories from fat. Here's an example:

A popular brand of cheese-flavored puffs lists the calories per serving as 290, and the fat per serving as 18 grams.

First, multiply the 18 grams of fat by 9. The reason we do this is because there are 9 calories in every gram of fat and we want to convert the amount of fat in grams into the number of calories supplied by fat. In this case, the total is 162. So we know that in every serving, 162 of the calories come from fat.

Next, we divide 162 by the total calories in a serving, which in this example is 290.

The resulting total is .558, which means that 55.8% of the calories in this product are supplied by fat.

If you are in a store and don't want to take the time to do a precise calculation, you can simply multiply the grams of fat by 9 to get the total number of calories supplied by fat. Then compare that figure with the total number of calories in a serving. The fat figure should be less than one-third the amount of the total calories.

Using our cheese puffs example again, we can easily see that 162 is more than half the amount of 290, which means that more than half the calories in the product come from fat.

Beware of Packages That List the Percentage of Fat by Weight

Today, more and more packages proclaim that they are "X percent fat-free." This claim can be deceptive. A label worded in this way measures fat as a **percentage of the total weight of the product, rather than as the percentage of total calories.**

What's the difference? When the leading health-promoting associations advise you to lower your fat consumption to no more than 30 percent, they are referring to the total number of calories you consume. A product that is only 3 or 4 percent fat by weight like so-called lowfat yogurt can still supply 30 percent of its total calories from fat! That's because much of the weight in the product can be from water, which contains no calories.

A good example is "lowfat" frozen yogurt that claims to be "96% fat-free." The nutrition panel lists the amount of fat in a 3-ounce serving as 3 grams, and the number of calories as 90. That means **the percentage of calories from fat is actually 30 percent.**

Another example is a brand of soup sold in many health food stores. The label says "99% Fat Free Soup," which would lead you to think that only 1% of the calories are from fat. But the nutrition panel shows that there are 150 calories in a serving and 2 grams of fat. Multiplying the 2 grams by 9 calories totals 18. When this number is divided by 150, the total is .12 or 12% of calories from fat. Of course, this is a very low fat figure, but it is still considerably more than the label claim of "99% Fat Free" would lead you to believe.

Don't be fooled by these label claims. A good rule of thumb: if fat or a high-fat ingredient is listed among the first three ingredients, the product is probably high in fat, despite claims to the contrary.

Cooking without Fat

What Does "Fat-Free" Mean?

The U.S. Food and Drug Administration has finalized its proposal on what the term "Fat-Free" means on food packages. The definition of "Fat-Free" means that a food contains less than 0.5 gram of fat in a serving.

All Health Valley Fat-Free foods meet this definition.

Rules 2 and 3:
Don't Buy Anything With More Than 3 Grams of Fat Per Serving, and Check the Serving Size to See If It's Realistic.

The current labeling laws require food manufacturers to list the total amount of fat per serving on the panel called "Nutrition Facts." So one of the ways to ensure that you avoid high fat products is to avoid any packaged food product that contains more than 3 grams of fat in a serving.

The label laws also stipulate the size of a serving. For example, a serving of granola cereal is 55 grams or about ⅔ of a cup. However, it's very possible that these "official" sizes don't accurately reflect the amount *you* actually eat. So it's important that you take that into consideration when you buy and use a product.

I know fat-conscious people who used to eat ice cream only occasionally, but who now eat huge servings of nonfat yogurt every day and think they are eating healthier. In most cases, these people are consuming a lot more total calories than they were before, without getting much additional nutrition.

It's important to remember that according to government labeling laws, the term "fat-free" does not necessarily mean the food is literally free of all fat, but that it contains less than half a gram of fat in a serving. But if the amount you eat is the equivalent to several "official" servings, you could be consuming more fat and calories than you realize.

Shopping for Whole Foods with the Lowest Fat

Most unprocessed, whole foods are lower in fat than the processed versions of the same foods. But some whole foods are better low-fat choices than others. Here are some charts to consult before buying:

Meat & Poultry

LESS THAN 15% OF CALORIES FROM FAT

FOOD–SERVING SIZE	CALORIES	FAT (g)	% OF CALORIES FROM FAT
Turkey Breast,* no skin, 3.5 oz.	144	1.8	11

*Note: When buying ground turkey meat, be sure to check with the butcher to determine whether or not the skin has been included and whether both light and dark meat have been used. As you can see from the chart below, turkey breast with the skin has four times as much fat as turkey breast without the skin.

15% TO 30% OF CALORIES FROM FAT

FOOD–SERVING SIZE	CALORIES	FAT (g)	% OF CALORIES FROM FAT
Turkey, light, w/skin, 3.5 oz.	210	7	30
Chicken Breast, no skin, 3.5 oz.	165	4.5	25
Veal, leg, sliced, 3.5 oz.	150	3.4	20

GREATER THAN 30% OF CALORIES FROM FAT

FOOD–SERVING SIZE	CALORIES	FAT (g)	% OF CALORIES FROM FAT
Bacon, 3 strips	109	9.4	78
Beef Hot Dog, 1	180	16.3	82
Chicken, dark, no skin, 3.5 oz.	205	9.7	43
Duck, no skin, 3.5 oz.	201	11.2	50
Ground Beef, extra lean, 3.5 oz.	250	16.1	58
Ground Beef, regular, 3.5 oz.	287	20.9	66
Ham, roasted, 3.5 oz.	178	9	46
Turkey, dark, no skin, 3.5 oz.	221	11.5	47
Beef, Tenderloin 3.5 oz.	244	14.3	53

Fish

LESS THAN 15% OF CALORIES FROM FAT

FOOD–SERVING SIZE	CALORIES	FAT (g)	% OF CALORIES FROM FAT
Cod, Cooked, 3 oz.	89	.7	7
Orange Roughy, Cooked, 3 oz.	75	.8	10
Perch, Cooked, 3 oz.	99	1	9
Pike, Cooked, 3 oz.	96	.8	8
Scallops, Cooked, 3 oz.	75	.6	7
Snapper, Cooked, 3 oz.	109	1.5	12
Tuna, light, in water, 3 oz.	99	.7	6

15% TO 30% OF CALORIES FROM FAT

FOOD–SERVING SIZE	CALORIES	FAT (g)	% OF CALORIES FROM FAT
Halibut, Cooked, 3 oz.	119	2.5	19
Trout, Cooked, 4 oz.	129	3.7	26

GREATER THAN 30% OF CALORIES FROM FAT

FOOD–SERVING SIZE	CALORIES	FAT (g)	% OF CALORIES FROM FAT
Mackerel, Cooked, 4 oz.	171	8.6	45
Salmon, pink, canned, 4 oz.	196	11.4	52
Shark, 3 oz.	194	11.8	55

Note: Salmon and Mackerel are a rich source of Omega-3 fatty acids which are considered a beneficial part of a healthy diet.

Dairy & Eggs

LESS THAN 15% OF CALORIES FROM FAT

FOOD–SERVING SIZE	CALORIES	FAT (g)	% OF CALORIES FROM FAT
Cottage Cheese, nonfat, ½ cup	90	0.4	4
Cottage Cheese, 1%, ½ cup	164	2.3	13
Milk, nonfat, 1 cup	86	0.4	4
Ricotta cheese, fat-free, ½ cup	81	0.4	4
Sour Cream, fat-free, 1 cup	121	0.4	3
Yogurt, nonfat, 1 cup	127	0.4	3

15% TO 30% OF CALORIES FROM FAT

FOOD–SERVING SIZE	CALORIES	FAT (g)	% OF CALORIES FROM FAT
Buttermilk, 1 cup	99	2.2	20
Milk, 1%, 1 cup	99	2.6	23
Yogurt, lowfat, 1 cup	140	4.0	26

GREATER THAN 30% OF CALORIES FROM FAT

FOOD–SERVING SIZE	CALORIES	FAT (g)	% OF CALORIES FROM FAT
American Cheese, 1 oz.	106	8.9	76
Cream Cheese, 1 oz.	98	9.5	87
Eggs, whole, each	75	5.0	60
Heavy Cream, 1 Tbsp.	52	5.6	97
Ice Cream, premium, ½ cup	220	14.0	57
Milk, whole, 1 cup	150	8.2	49
Parmesan Cheese, 1 Tbsp.	23	1.5	59
Sour Cream, 1 Tbsp.	26	2.5	87
Swiss Cheese, 1 oz.	107	7.8	66

Cooking without Fat

Fruits

LESS THAN 15% OF CALORIES FROM FAT

FOOD–SERVING SIZE	CALORIES	FAT (g)	% OF CALORIES FROM FAT
Apple, 1 medium	81	0.5	6
Apricots, 3 medium	51	0.4	7
Banana, 1 medium	105	0.6	5
Blackberries, ½ cup	37	0.3	7
Blueberries, 1 cup	82	0.6	7
Cantaloupe, 1 cup	57	0.4	6
Cherries, 10 cherries	49	0.7	13
Dates, 10 dried	228	0.4	2
Figs, 10 dried	477	2.2	4
Grapefruit, ½ medium	37	0.1	2
Grapes, 1 cup	58	0.3	5
Kiwi, 1 medium	46	0.3	6
Nectarine, 1 medium	67	0.6	8
Orange, 1 medium	59	0.4	6
Peach, 1 medium	37	0.1	2
Pear, 1 medium	98	0.7	6
Pineapple, fresh, 1 cup	77	0.7	8
Plum, 1 medium	36	0.4	10
Prunes, 10 dried	201	0.4	2
Raisins, ⅔ cup	300	0.5	2
Raspberries, 1 cup	61	0.7	10
Strawberries, 1 cup	45	0.6	12
Tangerine, 1 medium	37	0.2	5
Watermelon, 1 cup	50	0.7	13

GREATER THAN 30% OF CALORIES FROM FAT

FOOD–SERVING SIZE	CALORIES	FAT (g)	% OF CALORIES FROM FAT
Avocado, 1 medium	306	30	88

Vegetables

LESS THAN 15% OF CALORIES FROM FAT

FOOD–SERVING SIZE	CALORIES	FAT (g)	% OF CALORIES FROM FAT
Artichoke hearts, ½ cup	37	0.1	2
Beans, Snap, 1 cup	44	0.4	6
Beets, cooked, ½ cup	26	0.0	0
Broccoli, cooked, ½ cup	22	0.3	12
Brussels Sprouts, ½ cup	30	0.4	12
Carrot, raw, 1 medium	31	0.1	3
Cauliflower, ½ cup	12	0.1	8
Celery, 1 stalk	6	0.1	15
Corn, cooked, ½ cup	89	1.1	11
Cucumber, ½ cup	7	0.1	13
Eggplant, cooked, ½ cup	13	0.1	7
Kale, cooked, ½ cup	21	0.3	13
Onions, chopped, ½ cup	30	0.1	3
Peas, cooked, ½ cup	58	0.3	5
Peppers, Sweet, raw, ½ cup	13	0.1	14
Potato, baked, 1 medium with skin	220	0.2	1
Squash, Summer, raw, ½ cup	13	0.1	7
Sweet Potatoes, baked, 1 medium	118	0.1	1
Tomato, raw, 1 medium	26	0.4	14

Cooking without Fat

Legumes

LESS THAN 15% OF CALORIES FROM FAT

FOOD–SERVING SIZE	CALORIES	FAT (g)	% OF CALORIES FROM FAT
Black Beans, cooked, 1 cup	225	1.0	4
Garbanzo Beans, boiled, 1 cup	269	4.3	14
Great Northern Beans, cooked, 1 cup	210	0.8	3
Kidney Beans, cooked, 1 cup	225	0.9	4
Lentils, cooked, 1 cup	231	0.7	3
Lima Beans, cooked, 1 cup	217	0.7	3
Navy Beans, cooked, 1 cup	259	1.0	3
Pinto Beans, cooked, 1 cup	270	0.8	3
Split Peas, cooked, 1 cup	231	0.8	3

GREATER THAN 30% OF CALORIES FROM FAT

FOOD–SERVING SIZE	CALORIES	FAT (g)	% OF CALORIES FROM FAT
Soybeans, cooked, 1 cup	255	11.5	38

Grains

LESS THAN 15% OF CALORIES FROM FAT

FOOD–SERVING SIZE	CALORIES	FAT (g)	% OF CALORIES FROM FAT
Barley, cooked, 1 cup	193	0.7	3
Brown Rice, cooked, 1 cup	216	1.8	8
Bulgar Wheat, cooked, 1 cup	152	0.4	2
Whole Wheat Pasta, cooked, 1 cup	174	0.8	4
Wild Rice, cooked, 1 cup	166	0.6	3

Nuts & Seeds

LESS THAN 15% OF CALORIES FROM FAT

FOOD–SERVING SIZE	CALORIES	FAT (g)	% OF CALORIES FROM FAT
Chestnuts, roasted, 1 oz.	70	0.6	8
Water Chestnuts, raw, 1/2 cup	66	0.1	1

GREATER THAN 30% OF CALORIES FROM FAT

FOOD–SERVING SIZE	CALORIES	FAT (g)	% OF CALORIES FROM FAT
Almonds, dry roasted, 1 oz.	167	14.7	79
Cashews, dry roasted, 1 oz.	163	13.2	73
Hazelnuts, dry roasted, 1 oz.	180	18	90
Macadamia, oil roasted, 1 oz.	204	21.7	96
Peanuts, oil roasted, 1 oz.	163	13.8	76
Pecans, 1 oz.	190	19.2	91
Pinenuts, 1 oz.	161	17.3	97
Pistachios, 1 oz.	164	13.7	75
Sesame Seeds, 1 Tbsp.	47	4.4	84
Sunflower Seeds, 1 oz.	162	14.1	78
Walnuts, 1 oz.	172	16.1	84

Note: Nuts, especially walnuts, are a rich source of Omega-3 fatty acids which are an essential part of a healthy diet.

chapter five

How to Kick The Fat Habit

My Personal Experience

When I began eating natural foods in the late 1960's, I ate foods that were considered healthy at that time, like granola, nuts, seeds, raw milk cheeses, baked goods made with butter, and avocados. Of course, I ate vegetables and fruits, too.

The nutritional information available at that time told us that we should eliminate artificial ingredients and chemicals from our diet, and eat whole foods.

It wasn't until years later that nutritional research revealed that the biggest threat to good health is too much fat in our diets.

And as I became more conscious of fat, I realized how much of it is "hidden" in processed and packaged foods.

So it's no wonder that the typical American diet has nearly 40 percent of calories from fat.

Once I became aware of the dangers of eating too much fat, I attempted to cut down, but discovered it was a lot harder to do than I thought.

First of all, I discovered that when I tried to cut back on fat, my body seemed to crave it even more. That's because eating fat can actually become an addiction.

Cutting down on fat became a personal challenge to me. And the first step was breaking my own addiction to fat. At the time, there was virtually no literature on fat addiction, so I did my own study using myself as the subject. I found through personal experience that the most effective way to kick the fat habit is not to try and cut down gradually, but to eliminate all added fat and to reduce the percentage of calories from fat to 5 percent or less. I found that after about five days of eating this way, the craving for fat went away.

Since then, I've helped many of my friends and colleagues kick the fat habit the same way. Although it can be different for each individual, most people find that five days is the average amount of time it takes to kick their fat habit.

Are You Addicted to Fat or Fat Sensitive?

Researchers at the University of Michigan suggest that the craving for sugar or what has been called a "sweet tooth" may actually be a craving for fat, or, more accurately, for sweetened fat. They found that the sweet foods people tended to crave, such as ice cream, chocolate, or pastries, were actually as high or higher in fat than in sugar.

Indeed, studies have shown that strong fat cravings may be triggered by the physiological mechanism that is responsible for drug addiction.

So for some people fat can be addictive, but other people are fat sensitive.

In people who are fat sensitive, eating even a small amount of fat can result in becoming fat. That's because their bodies are especially prone to converting dietary fat into stored body fat.

Fat and the American Diet

Kicking the fat habit is difficult because eating fatty foods is such an integral part of the American way of life.

Fat is in the hot dogs we enjoy at baseball games, the hamburgers we barbecue at family picnics, and the cool refreshing ice cream we relish on a hot summer afternoon. It's on the buttered popcorn at the movie theater, and the french fries we munch at fast food restaurants.

And because most of the fat in our diets is "hidden" in processed foods, it's easy to underestimate the amount you actually consume. To see exactly where you can cut fat out of your diet, take a moment to fill out this questionnaire:

Answer Yes or No

1. I eat fish or poultry more often than red meat.
   yes_____no_____

2. When buying red meat, I choose the leanest cut available with little visible fat.
   yes_____no_____

3. I use low-fat or fat-free salad dressing and apply it sparingly.
   yes_____no_____

4. I eat fewer than 4 ounces of cheese per week and select lower-fat cheeses.
   yes_____no_____

5. I use chicken and turkey breast most often and remove the skin before eating it.
   yes_____no_____

6. I use the full fat version of butter, margarine and mayonnaise less than 3 times per week and use one tablespoon or less per serving.
   yes_____no_____

7. I eat fruit for a snack at least once every day and choose ice cream, cookies or cake no more than 2 times per week.
   yes_____no_____

8. When cooking, I steam, boil, broil or bake foods rather than oil-sauteing or deep-frying.
   yes_____no_____

9. I use low-fat or nonfat dairy products instead of full fat varieties.
   yes_____no_____

10. I order popcorn without butter at the movies.
    yes_____no_____

Add up your total number of "yes" answers. If your score is:

0 - 3 Study this book, you can make great improvements

4 - 7 Not bad, but there's still room for improvement

8 - 10 Good work. You're doing a lot of things right, but study this book to do even better.

Kick the Fat Habit in Just Five Days and Feel Terrific

Now that you have filled out our questionnaire, and have a better idea of how fat fits into your lifestyle, I suggest you virtually eliminate fat from your diet for five days: follow the meal plan in this chapter, and kick the fat habit. You'll feel terrific – almost like a new person. Plus, your vitality will increase tremendously.

Other benefits can be substantial as well, since a high consumption of fat may lead to indigestion, bloating and sluggishness.

Why This Meal Plan Will Give You Plenty of Energy on Fewer Calories

The meal plan you'll find on the next few pages is one of the most exciting parts of this book! It's meant to be followed for one or two weeks to curb your body's craving for fat.

By following this plan, you'll be able to do wonderful things for your body.

You may be able to kick the fat habit in only five short days.

You'll be well on your way to controlling your weight without ever feeling hungry because each day's plan provides plenty of good tasting, satisfying food with **under 1,200 calories,** and with 5 percent or less of calories from fat.

You'll be fulfilling the guidelines for healthier eating because you'll be eating five servings of fruits and vegetables a day, something that is missing from most diets today.

You'll be getting plenty of fiber, both the kind that helps keep your digestive system healthy and the kind that can help control your cholesterol level.

Let me assure you that this isn't some sort of rigid diet that's going to leave you feeling hungry. I guarantee that there is no suffering involved. That's because there's plenty of fiber and complex carbohydrates in each day's menu. Fiber is filling without adding any calories. Carbohydrates are your body's best source of energy. They can actually help speed up your metabolism, which makes you feel energized.

What I've developed for you is a system that breaks the fat habit.

To Eat a Healthy Meal Plan, You Need	Health Valley Meal Plan has
Per Day	*Per Day*
less than 30% calories from fat	4-5% calories from fat
less than 300 mg. cholesterol	less than 100 mg. cholesterol
less than 2,400 mg. sodium	less than 1,500 mg. sodium
at least 25 gms. fiber	at least 35 gms. fiber
5 servings of fruit and vegetables	5 servings of fruit and vegetables

Use Health Valley Products to Enjoy Delicious, Fat-Free Meals with No Cooking

You want to cut down on fat, but you don't want to give up convenience or flavor. The answer is simple: Use Health Valley Fat-Free foods as part of this 5-Day "Kick the Fat Habit" Meal Plan.

Health Valley Fat-Free foods are either ready to eat right from the package, or simply need to be heated, so you can enjoy them in minutes with no real cooking. And because they're made the healthy way, they're not only fat-free, they're also full of the vital nutrients and fiber your body needs every day for energy, vitality and just plain feeling great.

For example, the Health Valley Fat-Free 14 Garden Vegetable Soup recommended in this meal plan is made with more than 12 different organically grown vegetables and herbs. Yet a serving contains only 80 calories.

You can also use Health Valley Fat-Free foods to snack on whenever you're hungry and you don't have to worry about fat or calories.

For example, Health Valley Fat-Free Crackers contain only about 50 calories and no fat in a ½-ounce serving, compared to about 70 calories and 3 or 4 grams of fat in most commercial crackers. And Health Valley Fat-Free Caramel Corn Puffs contain only 2 calories per puff.

Today, nutritionists are urging people to include at least five servings of fruits and vegetables in their daily diets.

Health Valley Fat-Free Cookies are a delicious way to get the fruit you need because they contain more than 50 percent fruit and fruit juice. And each cookie contains just 33 calories.

Cooking without Fat

Kick the Fat Habit 5-Day Meal Plan

Monday

Breakfast
1 cup berries or melon
1 oz. Health Valley Fat-Free Cereal
¾ cup nonfat milk

Snack
1 Health Valley Fat-Free Healthy Tart

Lunch
1 cup Health Valley Fat-Free 5 Bean Vegetable Soup
tuna sandwich
⅓ cup Tuna Sandwich Spread,
lettuce, tomato, fat-free whole wheat bread

Snack
1 apple

Dinner
3 oz. Orange Honey Baked Chicken
½ cup Healthy Coleslaw
⅓ cup Spanish Rice
½ cup green vegetable

Snack
1 Health Valley Fat-Free Bar
½ cup nonfat milk

Nutritional Analysis:
Calories 1,161   Fat/grams 7.3   Percentage Cal./Fat 5%   Sodium 1,101 mg.

Remember to drink plenty of fluids – water, herbal tea,
sparkling water with lemon or lime wedge

Tuesday

Breakfast

¾ cup nonfat milk
1 Health Valley Fat-Free Breakfast Bar
quartered orange

Snack

Health Valley Jumbo Fat-Free Cookie

Lunch

1 serving Health Valley Fat-Free
Healthy Soup in a Cup, Pasta Italiano
turkey sandwich
*2 oz. turkey (breast meat), tomato, mustard, lettuce,
fat-free whole wheat bread*

Snack

2 Health Valley Fat-Free Cookies
½ cup nonfat yogurt

Dinner

7.5 oz. Health Valley Fat-Free Chili
½ cup steamed broccoli
½ cup steamed brown rice

Snack

1 pear

Nutritional Analysis:

Calories 1,093   Fat/grams 5.4   Percentage Cal./Fat 4%   Sodium 1,402 mg.

*Remember to drink plenty of fluids – water, herbal tea,
sparkling water with lemon or lime wedge*

Cooking without Fat

Wednesday

Breakfast

1 banana
1 oz. Health Valley Fat-Free Cereal
¾ cup nonfat milk

Snack

1 Health Valley Fat-Free Granola Bar

Lunch

1 cup Health Valley Fat-Free Real Italian Minestrone Soup
tuna sandwich
⅓ cup Tuna Sandwich Spread,
lettuce, tomato, fat-free whole wheat bread

Snack

1 apple

Dinner

3 oz. Chicken Dijon
½ cup steamed carrots
1 small potato, steamed

Snack

1 Health Valley Fat-Free Healthy Marshmallow Bar
½ cup nonfat milk

Nutritional Analysis:

Calories 1,180   Fat/grams 7.2   Percentage Cal./Fat 5%   Sodium 1,303 mg.

Remember to drink plenty of fluids – water, herbal tea,
sparkling water with lemon or lime wedge

Thursday

Breakfast

¾ cup nonfat milk
1 Health Valley Fat-Free Healthy Tart
quartered orange

Snack

Health Valley Healthy Chocolate Sandwich Bar

Lunch

1 serving Health Valley Fat-Free Healthy Soup in a Cup,
Corn Chowder with Tomatoes
turkey sandwich
*2 oz. turkey (breast meat), tomato, mustard, lettuce,
fat-free whole wheat bread*

Snack

2 Health Valley Fat-Free Cookies
½ cup nonfat yogurt

Dinner

7.5 oz. Health Valley Fat-Free Chili
½ cup steamed brown rice
1 cup green salad with 1 tablespoon fat-free dressing

Snack

1 apple

Nutritional Analysis:

Calories 1,079   Fat/grams 5.2   Percentage Cal./Fat 4%   Sodium 1,426 mg.

*Remember to drink plenty of fluids – water, herbal tea,
sparkling water with lemon or lime wedge*

Friday

Breakfast

1 banana
1 oz. Health Valley Fat-Free Cereal
¾ cup nonfat milk

Snack

1 Health Valley Fat-Free Healthy Tart

Lunch

1 cup Health Valley Fat-Free Real Italian Minestrone Soup
tuna sandwich
⅓ cup Tuna Sandwich Spread,
lettuce, tomato, fat-free whole wheat bread

Snack

1 apple

Dinner

3 oz. Orange Roughy in Citrus Sauce
½ cup Healthy Coleslaw
1 small potato, steamed

Snack

1 Health Valley Fat-Free Bar
½ cup nonfat milk

Nutritional Analysis:

Calories 1,180   Fat/grams 5.3   Percentage Cal./Fat 4%   Sodium 1,058 mg.

Remember to drink plenty of fluids – water, herbal tea,
sparkling water with lemon or lime wedge

How Health Valley Can Help Make It Easy to Cut Fat.

Health Valley is the only company that prepares only healthy foods that are appropriate to meet your needs throughout the day on an ongoing basis. We have foods that are good tasting and convenient, as well as healthy, that you can use at breakfast, lunch, dinner and snacks. So using a variety of our products on a regular basis makes it easier to make healthy eating your regular way of eating.

Here is a list of our foods with suggestions for when and how you can use them:

BREAKFAST:
Cereals
98% Fat-Free Granola
Omega-3 Cereal
Fat-Free Healthy Fiber Flakes
Golden Flax Cereal
Fat-Free Honey Clusters & Flakes

Breakfast Bakes
Fat-Free Breakfast Bakes in 4 fruit flavors

Cereal Bars
Fat-Free Cereal Bars in 3 fruit varieties

Scones
Fat-Free Healthy Scones in 5 fruit flavors

LUNCH:
Canned Soups
Fat-Free Soups in 9 different varieties
Fat-Free Healthy Pasta Soups in 6 varieties

Fat-Free Healthy Soup in a Cup
Fat-Free Soup in a Cup in 8 varieties

Crackers
Fat-Free Wheat Crackers in 5 varieties
Fat-Free Healthy Pizza Crackers in 3 varieties

Cookies
Fat-Free Cookies in 8 varieties
Fat-Free Healthy Chips cookies in 3 varieties

DINNER:
Canned Soups
Fat-Free Carotene Soups in 3 varieties

Chili
Fat-Free Chili in 6 varieties

Fast Menu Canned Entrees
Fat-Free Fast Menu in 6 varieties

Tarts
Fat-Free Healthy Tarts in 7 varieties

HEALTHY SNACKS
Sandwich Bars
Fat-Free Healthy Chocolate Flavor Sandwich Bars in 4 varieties

Marshmallow Bars
Fat-Free Healthy Marshmallow Bars in 3 varieties

Granola Bars
Fat-Free Granola Bars in 6 fruit flavors

Omega-3 Bars
Omega-3 Bars in 3 varieties

Graham Crackers
Graham Crackers in 3 varieties

Puffs and Crisp Snacks
Fat-Free Healthy Hot Potatoes in 3 varieties
Organic Cheddar Lites in 2 varieties
Fat-Free Caramel Corn Puffs in 2 varieties

chapter six

The Recipes

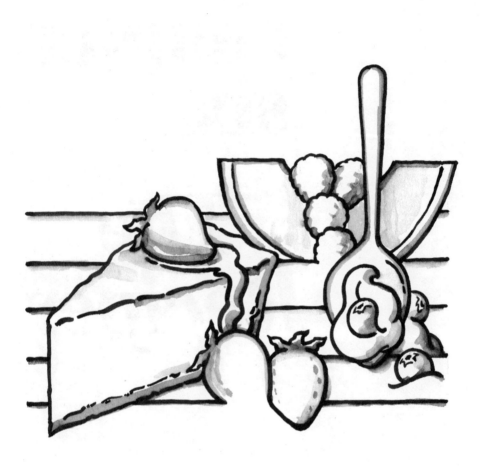

Cooking without Fat DESSERTS

When you crave something special for dessert or want to serve something fancy, it can be done the healthy way. Our cheesecake recipes are as elegant a party dessert as you could wish for. Frozen Fruit Cremes are a refreshing frozen dessert, and you won't find any fat in them at all. They are, however, a superior source of protein, calcium, and vitamins A, C, riboflavin and B12. Our Old Fashioned Rice Pudding and Apple Banana Bread Pudding compare well with heirloom recipes, and they win hands down where nutrition is concerned. If you don't believe us, take a look at the figures below and see how our desserts compare to the traditional fare. Then try some of these recipes and see if you're not pleasantly surprised.

| Food | Cooking Without Fat | | | Traditional Recipes | | |
	Calories	Fat	% Cal Fat	Calories	Fat	% Cal Fat
New York Cheesecake	214	Fat-Free	0	588	43.0g	66
Frozen Fruit Creme	193	Fat-Free	0	324	25.0g	69
Old Fashioned Rice Pudding	200	0.8g	3	270	7.0g	23
Apple Banana Bread Pudding	247	1.5g	5	322	13.0g	36

Cooking without Fat

After you've mastered the recipes in this section, use them as blueprints for making all of your dessert recipes healthier. For example, try using more fruit and fruit juice as sweeteners instead of sugar; or reduced amounts of honey instead of the large amounts of sugar that many recipes call for. Use plain nonfat yogurt with a dash of vanilla instead of butter and cream.

A Healthy Alternative for Extra Convenience

At Health Valley, we believe that dessert doesn't have to be the part of your meal you always feel guilty about eating. That's why we make a wide variety of packaged fat-free cookies, bars and tarts that are made using the finest fruits and whole grains as ingredients, and sweetened with pure fruit juices or a touch of honey.

So, when you're in a hurry and don't have time to prepare a recipe from scratch, try Health Valley Fat-Free Cookies, or Fat-Free Healthy Chocolate Flavor Sandwich Bars, or Omega-3 Bars, or one of our satisfying Fat-Free Healthy Tarts, or any other of the many Health Valley healthier baked goods. They're as good tasting as they are good for you.

Fat-Free Crusts for Pies and Cakes

Health Valley makes fat-free cookies that work extremely well for preparing healthy foolproof crusts for your favorite desserts. They are available in regular dessert size (Date Delight, Apple Spice, Raisin Oatmeal, Apricot Delight, and Hawaiian Fruit) and in jumbo sizes (Raspberry Jumbo, Apple Raisin Jumbo, and Raisin-Raisin Jumbo). Using a blender or food processor, grind a few cookies at a time until processed into uniform crumbs. Unlike conventional crumb crusts, Health Valley cookie crusts do not need any added fat or sweetener. Simply press into the pan using damp fingers to prevent sticking.

Use 1¼ cups of crumbs to cover the bottom of an 8- or 9-inch spring-form pan. For a small lip extending up the sides increase by ¼ cup. For a full crust covering the bottom and sides of an 8- or 9-inch pie plate you will need 1¾ cups of crumbs. This amount also will cover the bottom and go a little ways up the sides of a 10-inch springform. One package (or less) of Health Valley fat-free cookies is sufficient to prepare all of the pie crusts for the recipes in this chapter.

If possible, chill crust-lined pan while you prepare the filling. Even a short time in the refrigerator will improve the way the crust holds together.

When the filling is not cooked inside the crust, bake the empty crust in a 375°F. oven for about 8 minutes, until it just begins to darken. Where filling bakes inside the crust, prebaking is not necessary. However, partial baking before filling does make the final result crisper. To partially pre-bake, place the empty shell in a 375°F. oven for 4-5 minutes. Let cool at room temperature for about 10 minutes before filling.

Your choice of cookie will influence the taste of the finished dish. Pick one that seems most compatible with the filling. Health Valley Fat-Free Apple Raisin Jumbo, Fat-Free Date Delight and the apple flavored varieties work well with such winter fruits as apple, pear, and pumpkin. More commanding cookies like Health Valley Fat-Free Raspberry Jumbo, Fat-Free Hawaiian Fruit, and Fat-Free Apricot Delight have greater impact on flavor. Since their rich essence will permeate the filling, these varieties should be selected with greater consideration for balance.

We also have included a recipe for Fat-Free Crust on page 107. This is an excellent crust, based on our fat-free granola, for all of our cheesecake recipes. The entire crust contains only 629 calories and is Fat-Free!

quick cheesecake filling

The technique for turning nonfat yogurt into yogurt cheese on page 139 produces a very versatile and nutritious ingredient that is specified in all the cheesecake recipes.

However, you have to let the nonfat yogurt drain for between 12 and 24 hours in the refrigerator to make yogurt cheese, and we recognize there are times when you want to make one of our cheesecake recipes in a hurry or at the last minute.

A fat-free alternative to making yogurt cheese is to substitute a blend of two-thirds fat-free ricotta cheese with one-third fat-free sour cream.

Here are the exact amounts and directions:

Recipes that call for 4 cups of yogurt cheese

2⅔ cups fat-free ricotta cheese
1⅓ cups fat-free sour cream

Substitute for yogurt cheese in cheesecake recipe and follow the rest of the directions as written.

Recipes that call for 2 cups of yogurt cheese

1⅓ cups fat-free ricotta cheese
⅔ cup fat-free sour cream

Substitute for yogurt cheese and follow the rest of the recipe as written.

fat-free crust

prep time: 5 minutes

cooking time: 12-15 minutes

ingredients: 1½ cups No Fat Added granola (without fruit added)

1 tablespoon frozen apple juice concentrate (defrosted)

1 tablespoon honey

1 egg white, unbeaten

directions: Preheat oven to 325°F. Grind granola in food processor for 2 minutes. Add juice concentrate, honey and egg white. Process minimally to blend ingredients, approximately 30 seconds.

Press granola mixture over bottom of 8- or 9-inch nonstick springform pan. Bake for 12-15 minutes at 325°F. Let cool while preparing filling.

yield: 1 8- or 9-inch crust (8 servings)

We developed this recipe using Health Valley 98% Fat-Free Granola with Date and Almond Flavor.

Nutrition Information Per Serving

Calories	79
Fat	Fat-Free*
Cholesterol	0 milligram
Sodium	33 milligrams
Dietary Fiber	2 grams

All foods contain some fat. Less than .5 gram of fat per serving is nutritionally insignificant and considered to be "Fat-Free."

Cooking without Fat

YOU SAVE 374 CALORIES
This recipe contains 214 calories per serving
Typical recipe contains 588 calories per serving

creamy new york cheesecake

A variety of recipes have been developed for cheesecake lovers who may be wondering how they can remain loyal to the tenets of good nutrition without forswearing this treasured pleasure. (One serving of typical cheesecake contains a hefty 588 calories and 43 grams fat, adding up to a walloping 66% of calories.) As you will soon discover, when it comes to cheesecake, flavor and nutrition can go hand in hand.

If this is your first foray into cheesecake making, you may be surprised (and intimidated) by what seem to be very imprecise baking instructions. Cheesecake is extremely variable when it comes to baking time. This is because baking takes place at such a low temperature that even slight variations in ovens have great impact. It is best to check frequently near the end and gauge time visually; cheesecake is deemed "done" when the filling no longer jiggles in the center and the top is lightly colored. All cheesecakes shrink a little as they become firm, so don't be alarmed by some cracking on the surface.

This first recipe for Creamy New York Cheesecake produces a dessert that is dense and full flavored, in the tradition of the finest cream cheesecakes for which the Big Apple is justly famous.

We developed this recipe using Health Valley Fat-Free Date Delight Cookies.

Nutrition Information Per Serving

Calories	214
Fat	Fat-Free*
Cholesterol	2.7 milligrams
Sodium	156 milligrams
Dietary Fiber	1.3 grams

All foods contain some fat. Less than .5 gram of fat per serving is nutritionally insignificant and considered to be "Fat-Free."

creamy new york cheesecake

prep time: 15 minutes

cooking time: 60 minutes

chilling time: 7 hours

ingredients: 4 cups yogurt cheese (see page 139. Drain yogurt 24 hours in advance)

1 recipe Fat-Free Crust (see page 107) or 1½ cups fat-free cookies, ground into fine crumbs

⅔ cup honey

⅓ cup frozen apple juice concentrate (defrosted)

2 teaspoons vanilla

¾ teaspoon lemon extract

¼ cup whole wheat pastry flour

3 tablespoons arrowroot

5 egg whites

directions: 1. Prepare crust for 9-inch nonstick springform pan, OR moisten fingers with water and press cookie crumbs over bottom and slightly up sides of 9- inch springform pan. Chill while preparing remaining ingredients.

2. Preheat oven to 300°F.

3. For filling, in large bowl, with electric mixer on high, beat yogurt cheese, honey, apple juice concentrate, vanilla and lemon extracts, flour, arrowroot and egg whites until thoroughly blended.

4. Pour filling into prepared nonstick springform pan.

5. Bake at 300°F. for 60-70 minutes, or until done. Cheesecake is done when center appears set but jiggles slightly when shaken.

6. Remove cheesecake from oven and loosen edges with knife to prevent cracking. Cool on wire rack for 1 hour and then refrigerate for 6 hours or until chilled and set.

yield: 12 Servings

note: You may wish to try this with Fresh Berry Topping (see recipe in this section, page 137).

Cooking without Fat

YOU SAVE 197 CALORIES
This recipe contains 213 calories per serving
Typical recipe contains 410 calories per serving

raspberry cheesecake

If you prefer a lighter cheesecake than the classic New York try this Raspberry Cheesecake.

The fruit juice sweetened preserves make a light fruit glaze on top and pop up in the filling every few bitefuls. The tangy raspberry preserves provide a pleasingly fruity contrast to the smoothness of the filling.

Over two centuries ago, cheesecake recipes were standard fare in family cookbooks. Cheesecake has grown so popular that it now rivals apple pie as an American favorite. What is different today is the creation of a cheesecake that is low in fat.

We developed this recipe using Health Valley Fat-Free Raspberry Jumbo Cookies.

Nutrition Information Per Serving	
Calories	213
Fat	Fat-Free*
Cholesterol	2 milligrams
Sodium	151 milligrams
Dietary Fiber	2 grams

All foods contain some fat. Less than .5 gram of fat per serving is nutritionally insignificant and considered to be "Fat-Free."

raspberry cheesecake

prep time: 15 minutes

cooking time: 50 minutes

chilling time: 7 hours

ingredients: 2 cups yogurt cheese (see page 139. Drain yogurt 24 hours in advance.)

1 recipe Fat-Free Crust (see page 107) or
1½ cups fat-free cookies, ground into fine crumbs

½ cup honey

¾ teaspoon vanilla

2 tablespoons and 1 teaspoon arrowroot

3 egg whites

¼ cup + ¼ cup fruit-juice-sweetened raspberry preserves

directions:

1. Prepare crust for 8-inch nonstick springform pan, OR moisten fingers with water and press cookie crumbs over bottom and slightly up sides of 8-inch springform pan. Chill while preparing remaining ingredients.

2. Preheat oven to 325°F.

3. For filling, in large bowl, with electric mixer on high, beat yogurt cheese, honey, vanilla extract and arrowroot until thoroughly blended.

4. Beat egg whites to soft peak stage. Fold egg whites into cheese mixture and beat until well blended.

5. Pour half of filling into prepared nonstick springform pan. Spread ¼ cup jam on top; pour remaining filling on top. With knife cut through cheesecake to form a swirl. Smooth top with spatula.

6. Bake at 325°F. for 50 minutes, or until done. Cheesecake is done when center appears set but jiggles slightly when shaken.

7. Remove cheesecake from oven and loosen edges with knife to prevent cracking. Cool on wire rack for 1 hour and then refrigerate for 6 hours or until chilled and set.

8. Spread remaining ¼ cup preserves over top of cheesecake and serve.

yield: 8 Servings

Cooking without Fat

YOU SAVE 232 CALORIES
This recipe contains 188 calories per serving
Typical recipe contains 420 calories per serving

creamy peach cheesecake

Peaches and cream are traditional partners. In this dessert, peaches team up with yogurt cheese and tapioca to create a cheesecake with a delicate fruit flavor and the homey texture of tapioca. Tapioca is a natural starch found in cassava roots and traditionally used in thickening puddings.

The peach decorated cheesecake top makes a colorful presentation for a holiday or company meal. Its excellent nutritional profile includes fiber and beta carotene.

We developed this recipe using Health Valley Fat-Free Date Delight Cookies.

Nutrition Information Per Serving	
Calories	188
Fat	Fat-Free*
Cholesterol	1 milligram
Sodium	85 milligrams
Dietary Fiber	2.2 grams

*All foods contain some fat. Less than .5 gram of fat per serving is nutritionally insignificant and considered to be "Fat-Free."

creamy peach cheesecake

prep time: 15 minutes

cooking time: 50 minutes

chilling time: 7 hours

ingredients: 2 cups yogurt cheese (see page 139. Drain yogurt 24 hours in advance)

1 recipe Fat-Free Crust (see page 107) or
1 1/2 cups fat-free cookies, ground into fine crumbs

1 (16-ounce) can peach halves, packed in juice

2 tablespoons quick cooking tapioca

1/2 cup honey

1 teaspoon vanilla

1/2 teaspoon almond extract

1 1/2 tablespoons arrowroot

2 egg whites

directions:

1. Prepare crust for 8-inch nonstick springform pan, OR moisten fingers with water and press cookie crumbs over bottom and slightly up sides of 8-inch springform pan. Chill while preparing remaining ingredients.

2. Preheat oven to 325°F.

3. Drain peaches, reserving liquid. Combine liquid and tapioca in saucepan. Set aside for 5 minutes then cook over low heat until slightly thickened, about 3 minutes. Cool slightly.

4. For filling, in large bowl, with electric mixer on high, beat yogurt cheese, honey, vanilla and almond extracts, and arrowroot until thoroughly blended. Gradually add tapioca mixture, stirring until well blended.

5. In separate bowl, beat egg whites to soft peak stage. Fold egg whites into cheese mixture and beat until well blended. Pour half of filling into prepared nonstick springform pan.

6. Slice peaches thinly. Cover cheese filling with half of peaches. Pour remaining filling on top and smooth with spatula. Arrange remaining peach slices on top.

7. Bake at 325°F. for 50 minutes, or until done. Cheesecake is done when center appears set but jiggles slightly when shaken.

8. Remove cheesecake from oven and loosen edges with knife to prevent cracking. Cool on wire rack for 1 hour and then refrigerate for 6 hours or until chilled and set.

yield: 8 Servings

Cooking without Fat

YOU SAVE 186 CALORIES
This recipe contains 189 calories per serving
Typical recipe contains 375 calories per serving

carrot "cake"

Carrots find a place on the dinner table from appetizers to desserts. This carrot "cake" (actually a cheesecake) is sweet and spicy, yet is surprisingly light. It makes an excellent company or everyday dessert.

There's no need to feel guilty when you enjoy this cheesecake because it contributes to your daily need for fiber and beta carotene.

We developed this recipe using Health Valley Fat-Free Date Delight Cookies.

Nutrition Information Per Serving	
Calories	189
Fat	Fat-Free*
Cholesterol	1 milligram
Sodium	132 milligrams
Dietary Fiber	3.1 grams

All foods contain some fat. Less than .5 gram of fat per serving is nutritionally insignificant and considered to be "Fat-Free."

carrot "cake"

prep time: 20 minutes

cooking time: 55 minutes

chilling time: 7 hours

ingredients: 2 cups yogurt cheese (see page 139. Drain yogurt 24 hours in advance).

1 recipe Fat-Free Crust (see page 107) or
1½ cups fat-free cookies, ground into fine crumbs

2½ cups peeled, sliced carrots

½ cup honey

2 teaspoons vanilla

½ teaspoon orange extract

3 tablespoons arrowroot

2 teaspoons cinnamon

½ teaspoon ginger

¼ teaspoon allspice

5 egg whites

¼ cup fruit-juice-sweetened orange marmalade

directions:

1. Prepare crust for 8-inch nonstick springform pan, OR moisten fingers with water and press cookie crumbs over bottom and slightly up sides of 8-inch springform pan. Chill while preparing remaining ingredients.
2. Preheat oven to 325°F.
3. Steam carrots until tender, about 15 minutes and drain. Puree in food processor or food mill and set aside.
4. For filling, in large bowl, with electric mixer on high, beat yogurt cheese, honey, vanilla and orange extracts, arrowroot and spices until thoroughly blended. Fold in carrots.
5. In separate bowl, beat egg whites to soft peak stage. Fold egg whites into cheese mixture and mix until well blended. Pour filling into prepared nonstick springform pan.
6. Bake at 325°F. for 55 minutes, or until done. Cheesecake is done when center appears set but jiggles slightly when shaken.
7. Remove cheesecake from oven and loosen edges with knife to prevent cracking. Cool on wire rack for 1 hour and then refrigerate for 6 hours or until chilled and set.
8. Spread marmalade over top of cake and serve.

yield: 8 Servings

Cooking without Fat

YOU SAVE 70 CALORIES
This recipe contains 200 calories per serving
Typical recipe contains 270 calories per serving

old fashioned rice pudding

Rice pudding is an oldtime favorite dessert that consoles and nourishes the body. It is especially wholesome when brown rice is its base and nonfat milk and egg whites form the delicate structure that binds the pudding together. Compared with standard rice pudding recipes, which call for the entire egg and whole milk, ours is impressively lean. In fact, Old Fashioned Rice Pudding has only a trace of fat, while traditional rice pudding contains about 7 grams of fat per serving.

As you will discover, the absence of fat does not detract from the texture or taste.

Nutrition Information Per Serving	
Calories	200
Fat	.8 gram
Percentage of Calories from Fat	3%
Cholesterol	1 milligram
Sodium	59 milligrams
Dietary Fiber	2.8 grams

old fashioned rice pudding

prep time: 10 minutes

cooking time: 50 minutes

ingredients: 1 ½ cups nonfat milk
½ cup honey*
3 egg whites
2 teaspoons vanilla
½ teaspoon cinnamon
2 cups cooked brown rice (short grain preferred)
¼ cup raisins
¼ cup chopped dates
nutmeg

directions: 1. Preheat oven to 325°F.
2. In medium mixing bowl, combine milk, honey, egg whites, vanilla and cinnamon. Beat with rotary beater or hand mixer until smooth.
3. Stir in rice, raisins and dates. Spoon mixture into custard cups. Sprinkle lightly with nutmeg.
4. Place custard cups in a baking pan and surround with hot water to a depth of 1-inch. Bake at 325°F. for about 50 minutes, or until set in center and browned on top.
5. Remove from baking pan to cool. Serve warm or chill after pudding has cooled to room temperature.

yield: 6 Servings

note: *If a sweeter pudding is desired, you may increase honey to ⅔ cup.

Cooking without Fat

apple banana bread pudding

This variation of bread pudding reflects the delicious flavor of whole wheat bread combined with tender apples and bananas. It is truly indicative of how the guidelines of new nutrition can be merged with old fashioned taste appeal.

Apple Banana Bread Pudding is a nutritional powerhouse, chock full of vitamins, minerals, dietary fiber, high quality protein, and it's virtually fat-free.

Nutrition Information Per Serving	
Calories	247
Fat	1.5 gram
Percentage of Calories from Fat	5%
Cholesterol	2 milligram
Sodium	227 milligrams
Dietary Fiber	4 grams

apple banana bread pudding

prep time: 12 minutes

cooking time: 1 hour

ingredients: 8 slices fat-free whole wheat bread, cut into 1-inch cubes (approximately 3½ cups)

3 medium cooking apples (approximately 2½ cups)

3 bananas, sliced into ¼-inch slices (approximately 2 cups)

1 cup evaporated skimmed milk

3 egg whites, lightly beaten

½ cup frozen apple juice concentrate (defrosted)

1 teaspoon lemon juice

1¼ teaspoon cinnamon

¼ teaspoon ground nutmeg

⅓ cup pure maple syrup

1 teaspoon vanilla

½ cup raisins

directions: 1. Preheat oven to 325°F.

2. In large mixing bowl, combine bread cubes, apples, bananas, evaporated milk, egg whites, juice concentrate, lemon juice, cinnamon, nutmeg, maple syrup, vanilla and raisins. Mix well.

3. Pour mixture into 8x11x2-inch ovenproof glass baking dish and bake at 325°F. for 60-65 minutes, or until knife inserted in center comes out clean. Cool slightly.

4. Serve either warm or cold, plain or with a dollop of Non-fat Whipped Topping (see recipe in this section, page 135).

yield: 8 Servings

note: If you are lucky enough to have any leftovers, this pudding tastes delicious when it has been chilled for a day.

Cooking without Fat

YOU SAVE 120 CALORIES
This recipe contains 96 calories per serving
Typical recipe contains 216 calories per serving

jumbo lemon delight

This easy and satisfying dessert combines a rich creamy topping with our Health Valley Fat-Free Jumbo Cookies. In this recipe, the Apple Raisin Jumbo is my preferred choice. The tangy sweetness of the lemon flavored topping, which is made from nutritious homemade nonfat yogurt cheese, blends beautifully with these juice sweetened cookies.

If you are adventurous try experimenting with different flavor combinations; try orange extract and rind in place of lemon, or omit the rind and try almond extract using Raspberry Jumbos and fresh raspberries on top.

With a supply of nonfat yogurt cheese in your refrigerator and a box of Health Valley Fat-Free Jumbos in your pantry you can enjoy Jumbo Lemon Delights in minutes anytime.

We developed this recipe using Health Valley Fat-Free Apple Raisin Jumbo Cookies.

Nutrition Information Per Serving	
Calories	96
Fat	Fat-Free*
Cholesterol	.3 milligram
Sodium	40 milligrams
Dietary Fiber	3 grams

All foods contain some fat. Less than .5 gram of fat per serving is nutritionally insignificant and considered to be "Fat-Free."

jumbo lemon delight

prep time: 10 minutes

cooking time: 15 minutes

ingredients: ½ cup yogurt cheese (see page 139)
1/4 teaspoon lemon extract
2 tablespoons honey
2 teaspoons arrowroot
1/4 teaspoon finely grated lemon peel
1 egg white
8 fat-free cookies
fresh fruit for topping

directions:
1. Preheat oven to 325°F.
2. In medium size bowl, beat together yogurt cheese, lemon extract, honey, arrowroot and lemon peel.
3. In small bowl, beat egg white until stiff.
4. Fold egg white into lemon-yogurt mixture.
5. Spread a generous tablespoon of lemon-yogurt mixture over surface of each cookie. Place cookies on baking sheet and bake at 325°F. for 15 minutes.
6. Let cool for 5 minutes, then top each cookie with small pieces of sliced fruit of your choice – like kiwis, strawberries, drained mandarin orange segments – and serve.

yield: 8 Cookies/Servings

Cooking without Fat

YOU SAVE 61 CALORIES
This recipe contains 264 calories per serving
Typical recipe contains 325 calories per serving

poached pears with yogurt sauce

This fruit based dessert makes a grand finale to any meal. The yogurt sauce gives the pears an elegant touch while still keeping the fat and calorie levels to a minimum. Similar desserts range from 325 calories to Pears Helene at 677 calories.

About Pears

There are over 5,000 varieties of pears in existence today. Those commonly available in American markets all have a juicy white flesh with a complex sweet-acid flavor. Pears also have a distinctive, refreshing aroma. Bartlett pears, which are harvested in late summer and last in the market only through early winter, are bell shaped and yellow with a red blush when ripe; they are recommended for eating raw or poaching and are the most popular variety for canning. There is also a red variety of Bartlett. Light, yellow-green Anjou pears are a good eating pear that is available throughout the winter months and often into the early spring. The green Comice and ruddy Bosc, both winter varieties, are excellent choices for eating raw or cooking.

Pears break the rule that tree-ripened fruits are best. Pears are picked fully grown but still underripe and achieve their best flavor and texture off the tree. Pears should be ripened at room temperature until they yield to slight pressure. Try to eat them soon after, as their texture does not hold up well in the refrigerator. Avoid pears that are dull, shriveled or soft around the stem.

Nutrition Information Per Serving

Calories	264
Fat	.9 gram
Percentage of Calories from Fat	3%
Cholesterol	.8 milligram
Sodium	38 milligrams
Dietary Fiber	4.9 grams

poached pears with yogurt sauce

prep time: 15 minutes

cooking time: 30-45 minutes

ingredients: 4 firm, ripe pears
6 tablespoons honey
2 teaspoons lemon juice
dash ground ginger
dash ground cloves
1½ cups unsweetened apple juice

topping
½ teaspoon almond extract
1 tablespoon honey
½ cup yogurt cheese (see page 139)
fresh mint leaves for garnish (optional)

directions:
1. Core whole, unpeeled pears.
2. In a broad saucepan with tight-fitting lid, combine honey, lemon juice, ginger, cloves, and apple juice. Bring to boil over medium heat.
3. Place pears upright in boiling liquid. Cover, lower heat and simmer for 30-45 minutes, until pears are tender.
4. Remove pears carefully and transfer to serving dish. Spoon 1-2 tablespoons cooking syrup over each pear.

topping:
1. Beat almond extract and 1 tablespoon honey into yogurt cheese.
2. Serve pears hot or cold, with a dollop of topping.
3. Garnish each pear with fresh mint leaves at serving time.

yield: 4 Servings

Cooking without Fat

baked apples

These baked apples are as good as any old fashioned recipe. The pineapple, apple juice and raisins give the apples a delicious taste without the calories from more traditional ingredients such as butter, sugar and nuts.

About Apples

There are over 7,000 varieties of apples. Of these, less than two dozen are marketed throughout the entire United States. In some places the choice is reduced to only a few of the most common apples. Red Delicious remains the most popular worldwide, although most apple lovers agree it is not the best tasting apple. Other commonly available varieties include Golden Delicious, McIntosh, Rome Beauty and Granny Smith. The selection is greater in apple growing states. When they are in season, regional specialties like Macoun, Baldwin, Cortland, Stayman, Winesap, Jonathan, Northern Spy, Ida Red, Greening, Gravenstein and Newton Pippin make a brief appearance outside their local area.

Apples fall broadly into two groups: dessert apples ("eating" apples) and cooking apples. Some varieties are good for both. Those that are considered best for baking include Rome Beauty (the most popular baking apple), York Imperial, Jonathan, Ida Red, Cortland, Stayman, Winesap, Gravenstein, and Northern Spy.

Nutrition Information Per Serving	
Calories	154
Fat	.6 gram
Percentage of Calories from Fat	3%
Cholesterol	0 milligram
Sodium	4 milligrams
Dietary Fiber	4 grams

baked apples

prep time: 10 minutes

cooking time: 60 minutes

ingredients: 4 medium or large baking apples

1 tablespoon honey

⅓ cup canned unsweetened crushed pineapple, drained

2 tablespoons raisins

cinnamon

2-4 cups unsweetened apple juice

directions: 1. Preheat oven to 350°F.

2. Peel top third of each apple. Remove core but leave bottom intact so the hollow can be filled. Cut a thin slice from bottom, if necessary, so apple stands upright without toppling.

3. Combine honey, pineapple, raisins and ¼ teaspoon cinnamon. Spoon mixture equally into each apple hollow.

4. Place apples in a baking dish. Sprinkle additional cinnamon over peeled apple surfaces. Surround with apple juice to a depth of about ½ inch to prevent scorching.

5. Bake at 350°F. for about 1 hour. Baste with juice in pan several times during baking to keep moist. When done, apple will be tender, but not mushy. If not ready after 1 hour, continue to bake. Depending on size and variety, baking time can be as much as 15 minutes longer.

6. Serve warm, at room temperature or chilled if desired, garnish with lightly sweetened yogurt or Nonfat Whipped Topping (see recipe in this section, page 135) just before serving.

yield: 4 Servings

Cooking without Fat

YOU SAVE 51 CALORIES
This recipe contains 107 calories per serving
Typical recipe contains 158 calories per serving

raspberry-filled melon

This lovely dessert is a favorite of mine because it is so refreshing, easy to prepare and low in calories.

I know that raspberries can be hard to find because they have such a short season, being at their best in June and July. They're also expensive. If you prefer to use frozen berries for this recipe you will probably need the full measure of honey to balance the tartness and give this dessert maximum flavor. While you can substitute fresh strawberries or blackberries, they will not produce the same rich sauce texture and depth of flavor that you get with raspberries.

I recommend cantaloupe as the melon in this recipe. The color contrast is striking, plus cantaloupe is a superior source of potassium, vitamin C and beta carotene. Honeydew or casaba would also look pretty, but neither of these melons is as nutrient-rich.

If you really want to go all out when dessert time comes, place a scoop of our Frozen Fruit Creme (see recipe in this section, page 129) in the cavity of the melon before spooning on the sauce.

Nutrition Information Per Serving	
Calories	107
Fat	.7 gram
Percentage of Calories from Fat	5%
Cholesterol	0 milligram
Sodium	11 milligrams
Dietary Fiber	4.1 grams

raspberry-filled melon

prep time: 10 minutes

ingredients: 2 cups fresh or frozen raspberries
1-2 tablespoons honey to taste
1 tablespoon lemon juice
2 small or 1 medium-sized melon (cantaloupe, honeydew or casaba)
mint sprig for garnish

directions: 1. Wash fresh berries gently, and place on paper towel to dry. If frozen, defrost, drain off all juice and place on paper towel to dry.

2. Measure ½ cup berries into a small saucepan. Add honey, using 1 tablespoon if berries are fresh and sweet, full amount if tart or frozen. Add lemon juice. Simmer gently about 5 minutes, until berries are just soft. Press sauce through a strainer.

3. Cut melons into halves, or larger melon into quarters. Discard seeds.

4. Pour sauce over remaining 1½ cups uncooked berries. Spoon into melon cavities. Garnish with mint leaves. Serve at room temperature.

yield: 4 Servings

Cooking without Fat

YOU SAVE 131 CALORIES
This recipe contains 193 calories per serving
Typical recipe contains 324 calories per serving

frozen fruit creme

This smooth frozen fruit dessert compares favorably with commercial offerings in terms of taste, texture, and nutrition. It is more refreshing than fruit flavored ice cream and has far less calories and fat. If you don't already have one, this recipe should convince you that a food processor is an excellent investment.

I have made this recipe using raspberries, peaches, strawberries, and bananas, as well as a combination of the last two. Depending on the fruit itself and your taste buds, the amount of sweetening you need to add will vary. For myself I have discovered that this is a real ice cream treat if I don't skimp on the sweetening.

Preparing Fruit for Frozen Fruit Creme

A nice selection of unsweetened frozen fruit is available in most stores. Of these, strawberries, raspberries, blackberries and peaches are best suited to Frozen Fruit Creme. Because of their skins, blueberries and cherries do not puree as smoothly, however some people enjoy the flecks of peel and actually prefer these fruits.

Bananas are an excellent choice for Frozen Fruit Creme and while they are not sold frozen, this can be done at home by simply peeling the fruit, placing it in a plastic bag or freezer container, and sticking it in the freezer. The bananas will be ready to use in a few hours, or you can store them in the freezer for several months, ensuring a ready supply for last minute company or cravings.

Canned pineapple can also be drained and spread in a single layer on a cooking sheet, then placed in the freezer for several hours until hard. This, too, can be used at once, or transferred to a freezer container for the future. If you enjoy berry picking, you can preserve your harvest in the same way and have some on hand out of season for making frozen desserts.

Nutrition Information Per Serving

Calories	193
Fat	Fat-Free*
Cholesterol	2 milligrams
Sodium	91 milligrams
Dietary Fiber	2.4 grams

*All foods contain some fat. Less than .5 gram of fat per serving is nutritionally insignificant and considered to be "Fat-Free."

frozen fruit creme

prep time: 10 minutes

chilling time: 30 minutes

ingredients: 2 cups unsweetened frozen fruit of choice
$1/4$ cup honey
2 tablespoons + 1 tablespoon fruit juice sweetened preserves, choose flavor to correspond with frozen fruit
1 cup yogurt cheese (see page 139).
$1/3$ cup nonfat dry milk
$1/2$ teaspoon vanilla

directions: 1. Combine all ingredients except 1 tablespoon preserves in food processor and puree until smooth; stir in additional tablespoon of preserves.
2. Spoon into bowls and serve at once, or transfer to a freezer container and place in freezer for 30 minutes for a soft ice cream consistency.
3. Longer freezing will harden fruit creme. If made well in advance, let sit at room temperature for about 10 minutes before serving for best texture.

yield: 3 Cups or 6 Servings ($1/2$ cup)

YOU SAVE 239 CALORIES
This recipe contains 278 calories per serving
Typical recipe contains 517 calories per serving

banana split

What could be more enticing on a low fat diet than a cool, creamy banana split? Well there's no reason to deny yourself if you follow this recipe. In fact, this dessert is so nourishing that you could hardly call it an indulgence. Although it tastes rich it is actually fat free. Moreover, it is chock full of nutrients including vitamins A, C, B6, and folacin, the minerals calcium and potassium, and high quality protein.

We developed this recipe using Health Valley 98% Fat-Free Tropical Fruit Granola.

Nutrition Information Per Serving	
Calories	278
Fat	.8 gram
Percentage of Calories from Fat	2%
Cholesterol	2.1 milligrams
Sodium	104 milligrams
Dietary Fiber	4.3 grams

banana split

prep time: 10 minutes

ingredients: 1 scoop (¼ cup) frozen strawberry creme*
1 scoop (¼ cup) frozen peach creme*
1 small banana
2 tablespoons No Fat Added granola
2 tablespoons Nonfat Whipped Topping
(see recipe in this section, page 135)

directions: 1. Prepare frozen fruit cremes according to recipe directions and place in freezer for 15-30 minutes to set up.
2. Split banana in half lengthwise and place in serving bowl. Top with one scoop each frozen strawberry and peach creme.
3. Sprinkle cereal over all. Top with a dollop of whipped topping.
4. Serve at once.

yield: 1 Serving

note: *See previous page for recipe for "Frozen Fruit Creme"

Cooking without Fat

YOU SAVE 83 CALORIES
This recipe contains 28 calories per serving
Typical recipe contains 111 calories per serving

nonfat dessert topping

Those who have forsworn whipped cream in favor of the commercial reduced fat and nondairy whipped toppings should be happy to learn that there is now a choice that meets the same low fat criteria without relying on processed ingredients and chemical additives. This Nonfat Dessert Topping is another example of the versatility of nonfat yogurt cheese. If you enjoy rich desserts you should make a practice of keeping nonfat yogurt cheese in production in your refrigerator at all times.

Nutrition Information Per Serving

Calories	28
Fat	Fat-Free*
Cholesterol	.5 milligram
Sodium	22 milligrams
Dietary Fiber	0 gram

*All foods contain some fat. Less than .5 gram of fat per serving is nutritionally insignificant and considered to be "Fat-Free."

nonfat dessert topping

prep time: 5 minutes

ingredients: ½ cup yogurt cheese (see recipe page 139)
1½-2 tablespoons honey to taste
½ teaspoon vanilla

directions: 1. Whip all ingredients together with a fork until smooth. Use immediately or chill until needed.

yield: ½ Cup or 8 Servings (1 tablespoon each)

YOU SAVE 36 CALORIES
This recipe contains 14 calories per serving
Typical recipe contains 50 calories per serving

nonfat whipped topping

We present two choices of low calorie, low fat, whipped cream-style toppings to accent your favorite desserts. Nonfat Whipped Topping is similar to traditional whipped cream in flavor and texture; just be sure to use it within 20 minutes or it will begin to separate. Since you can prepare it quickly, make it just before serving.

Nutrition Information Per Serving	
Calories	14
Fat	Fat-Free*
Cholesterol	.7 milligram
Sodium	21 milligrams
Dietary Fiber	0 gram

*All foods contain some fat. Less than .5 gram of fat per serving is nutritionally insignificant and considered to be "Fat-Free."

nonfat whipped topping

prep time: 8 minutes

chilling time: 20 minutes

ingredients: ⅓ cup nonfat milk
⅓ cup instant nonfat dry milk solids
1-2 teaspoons honey to taste
¼ teaspoon vanilla

directions: 1. Pour nonfat milk into a small metal mixing bowl.
2. Set bowl in freezer until ice crystals begin to form, about 15-20 minutes. Chill beaters from mixer in freezer as well.
3. Using a hand held electric mixer, beat nonfat dry milk solids into nonfat milk.
4. Continue to beat on high until soft peaks form, about 2 minutes.
5. Add honey to taste and vanilla and beat until stiff peaks form, about 2 additional minutes. Use within 20 minutes to avoid cream separating.

yield: 1½ Cups Whipped Topping or 6 Servings (¼ cup each)

Cooking without Fat

YOU SAVE 46 CALORIES
This recipe contains 39 calories per serving
Typical recipe contains 85 calories per serving

fresh berry topping

This is a delicious topping that can be spooned over pies, plain cakes, or cheesecake. Try it as a healthy replacement for syrup on waffles or pancakes. Prepare with fresh berries in season, or frozen unsweetened berries throughout the year.

Nutrition Information Per Serving

Calories	39
Fat	Fat-Free*
Cholesterol	.3 milligram
Sodium	12 milligrams
Dietary Fiber	.5 gram

All foods contain some fat. Less than .5 gram of fat per serving is nutritionally insignificant and considered to be "Fat-Free."

fresh berry topping

prep time: 5 minutes

ingredients: 1 cup fresh or frozen unsweetened berries
(strawberries, blueberries, raspberries or
blackberries)
2½ tablespoons honey
½ cup plain nonfat yogurt

directions: 1. In medium bowl, crush berries and add honey. Mix well.
2. Combine berry mixture with yogurt.

yield: 1½ Cups or 8 Servings

YOU SAVE 33 CALORIES
This recipe contains 16 calories per tablespoon
Typical recipe contains 49 calories per tablespoon

nonfat yogurt cheese

Yogurt cheese is an excellent nonfat substitute for cream cheese, sour cream and mayonnaise. You can use it for making dips, as a sandwich spread, on baked potatoes, you can even use it for making cheesecake! In fact, you'll find *five* different, delicious recipes for *fat-free* cheesecake in this book!

The savings in calories and fat are tremendous. Just compare:

Per Tablespoon	Calories	Fat (grams)	Percent of Calories from Fat
Nonfat Yogurt Cheese	16	Fat-Free	0
Cream Cheese	49	5.0	90
Sour Cream	26	2.5	87
Mayonnaise	100	11.0	99

It's very easy to make nonfat yogurt cheese. All you have to do is drain off the whey from plain nonfat yogurt. It takes 4 to 24 hours, depending on the consistency you want. We use yogurt cheese in a variety of recipes ranging from salad dressings to desserts.

Important Note: Some brands of yogurt contain gelatin or guar gum which prevent the whey from draining as quickly. Read the label and avoid these brands.

Nutrition Information Per Serving

Calories	16
Fat	Fat-Free*
Cholesterol	.5 milligram
Sodium	22 milligrams
Dietary Fiber	0 gram

*All foods contain some fat. Less than .5 gram of fat per serving is nutritionally insignificant and considered to be "Fat-Free."

nonfat yogurt cheese

prep time: 5 minutes

chilling time: 4-24 hours depending on consistency desired

ingredients: 1 carton (32 ounces) plain nonfat yogurt

directions: 1. You may drain the yogurt using any one of several different methods: (a) Line a large strainer with either cheesecloth or coffee filters. Spoon in yogurt, refrigerate and let drain into a large bowl or jar. (b) You can use the same method with a drip coffee maker lined with double paper coffee filters. (c) A special yogurt cheese funnel designed for this specific purpose is now available in some health food and gourmet stores.

2. Drain for the desired time:
12 hours or longer for whipped cream cheese consistency and for dessert toppings in this section;
24 hours or longer for cream cheese consistency (appropriate for our cheesecake recipes).

yield: about 2 cups

note: For every cup of yogurt cheese desired, use two cups of yogurt. The liquid whey that drains off will be bright yellow in color. Discard liquid.

Yogurt cheese will keep in the refrigerator for up to five days.

A diagram of how to make yogurt cheese is on page 71.

Cooking without Fat POULTRY

We have included a wide variety of chicken and turkey recipes in this volume because these birds are so versatile and economical, in addition to being nutritious. Many of the recipes combine the poultry with vegetables and grains so the dish becomes practically a meal in itself.

You will find our poultry recipes are considerably lower in fat and calories than their traditional counterparts. The secrets of the Cooking Without Fat method used in this chapter include using skinless breast meat with all visible fat removed, sauteing in fat-free broth in place of oil, and utilizing a wide array of spices rather than depending on cream-laden sauces for flavor.

Health-conscious people are choosing chicken and turkey more often as an outstanding source of protein, which is low in total fat, cholesterol, and calories. Additionally the fat found in poultry is predominately polyunsaturated or monounsaturated, the same type of fat found in olive oil and considered to be highly beneficial in helping to maintain a healthy balance of lipids in the blood. Poultry is also inherently low in sodium.

Cooking without Fat

Fowl is an excellent source of several important vitamins and minerals including niacin, B6, phosphorus, magnesium, and iron. In addition, turkey is an excellent source of the mineral zinc, which is essential for growth and normal immune function, and one of the nutrients frequently deficient in people's diet.

Most of the fat in poultry is in or just under the skin, so it is easy to eliminate. You do not have this option with meat since even when you trim off all visible fat, the invisible, internal "marbling" results in a high fat content.

To minimize fat and calories, our chicken recipes use breast meat with the skin removed. In addition some recipes specify boneless chicken while others use chicken with the bone intact. For the recipes that call for skinless, boned chicken breast filets, you can buy chicken that has already had the skin and bone removed. When buying chicken breasts with skin and bones intact, look for split breasts weighing 6 ounces each (serves one) or whole breast with rib meat weighing about ¾ pound (serves two).

Turkey is being marketed in a variety of ways. The leanest cut is turkey breast, which is available as a split breast or as filets. Our recipes call for boned, skinless turkey breast meat; some recipes also specify that the breast meat be ground. We have chosen turkey breast meat due to its extreme leanness; only 5% of calories are from fat compared to 36% for turkey dark meat, 49% for ground beef labeled 10% fat by weight, and 66% for ground beef labeled 21% fat by weight.

POULTRY PREPARATION

While poultry preparation is not complicated, it does require special attention so that bacteria common in raw poultry are thoroughly destroyed and do not migrate into other foods. Before working with any other food, use *hot*, soapy water to wash countertop, cutting boards and utensils that have been used to prepare the raw poultry. Also be sure you wash your hands thoroughly before you handle other food or utensils.

To guarantee that all bacteria are killed, poultry must be thoroughly cooked. The most reliable measure is a meat thermometer. Insert to the center of a thick, fleshy area and be sure thermometer is not touching bone. Poultry with the bone in should reach 180°F., boneless poultry 170°F. For a visual assessment, when probed with a fork the juices should run clear and there should be no pink coloration in the meat. Not only is undercooked poultry unsafe to eat, it is not as tender as it takes this degree of heat to break down the protein so that it is no longer tough or rubbery. On the other hand, overcooking will reduce moisture and dry the meat out.

Cooking without Fat

YOU SAVE 198 CALORIES
This recipe contains 317 calories per serving
Typical recipe contains 515 calories per serving

peach baked chicken on bulgur

Peaches and chicken are a luscious combination. Team them up with sweet dates and a gently spiced peach barbecue sauce, for an exceptional dish. Add a green vegetable and a salad and the meal is complete.

We developed this recipe using Health Valley Fat-Free Chicken Broth. It has a full, rich flavor and only 30 calories per serving.

Nutrition Information Per Serving	
Calories	317
Fat	3.3 grams
Percentage of Calories from Fat	9%
Cholesterol	64 milligrams
Sodium	253 milligrams
Dietary Fiber	4.8 grams

peach baked chicken on bulgur

prep time: 30 minutes
cooking time: 20 minutes

ingredients: ¾ cup uncooked bulgur
⅓ cup + ⅓ cup chopped onion
¼ cup chopped dates
1¼ cups + ¼ cup fat-free chicken broth
1 can (16 ounces) sliced peaches in juice, undrained
¾ cup fruit juice sweetened peach preserves
3 tablespoons tomato paste
3 tablespoons apple cider vinegar
2 tablespoons lemon juice
2 cloves + 2 cloves garlic, chopped
pinch white pepper (optional)
1½ teaspoons prepared mustard, spicy or dijon
4 skinless, boned chicken breast filets (about 1 pound)

directions:
1. Preheat oven to 350°F.
2. In small saucepan, combine bulgur, ⅓ cup onion, dates and 1¼ cups broth. Bring to boil. Cover and cook for 20 minutes.
3. Drain peaches reserving 3 tablespoons juice. Dice 1 cup peaches, reserve the remaining peaches for later use. Remove bulgur mixture from heat and stir in diced peaches. Transfer mixture to shallow 2 quart baking dish.
4. In small saucepan, combine preserves, tomato paste, vinegar, lemon juice, peach juice, 2 cloves chopped garlic, pepper and mustard, and cook over medium heat for 10 minutes to blend flavors.
5. Cut filets in 2-inch cubes. Heat ¼ cup broth in medium-large skillet over medium-high heat. Stir-fry chicken, 2 cloves chopped garlic and onion for about 10 minutes, until chicken is no longer pink inside.
6. Place chicken pieces on bulgur and spoon preserve mixture over all. Bake at 350°F. for 15 minutes.
7. Arrange remaining peach slices around chicken. Bake uncovered 5 minutes longer, or until peaches are heated.

yield: 6 Servings

Cooking without Fat

YOU SAVE 182 CALORIES
This recipe contains 337 calories per serving
Typical recipe contains 519 calories per serving

bombay chicken

Chicken is part of almost every cuisine in the world. It is featured in such national favorites as Hungarian chicken paprika, Indian tandoori, Arabian couscous, Malayan satay, Florentine pollo alla diavola, Russian kunik and West Indian creole chicken. One thing that all these international recipes have in common is that they combine chicken with interesting vegetables and spices – very helpful when you are cooking without fat or salt.

In the Far East, they have cooked with curry, garlic and fruit for thousands of years. These ingredients bring wonderful flavors to chicken and they are very healthful, too.

I encourage you to cultivate your taste for herbs, spices and citrus, and use them freely to replace salt in cooking. This recipe for Bombay Chicken is a great delicacy that is worthy of being served to dinner guests.

We developed this recipe using Health Valley Fat-Free Chicken Broth. It has a full, rich flavor and only 30 calories per serving.

Nutrition Information Per Serving	
Calories	337
Fat	3.5 grams
Percentage of Calories from Fat	9%
Cholesterol	67 milligrams
Sodium	179 milligrams
Dietary Fiber	4 grams

bombay chicken

prep time: 30 minutes

cooking time: 30 minutes

ingredients: 4 skinless, boned chicken breast filets (about 1 pound)

1 tablespoon whole wheat flour

½ teaspoon +1 teaspoon curry powder

½ teaspoon paprika

1½ teaspoons Italian seasoning blend

2 tablespoons +2 tablespoons fat-free chicken broth

2 cloves garlic, chopped

1 cup finely chopped onion

2 cups peeled, cored and diced apples

1 tablespoon honey

1 cup raisins

1 tablespoon lemon juice

1 can (10½ ounces) unsweetened mandarin oranges in juice, undrained

2 cups brown rice, cooked in chicken broth

directions:

1. Cut filets in 2-inch cubes. In heavy bag, combine flour, ½ teaspoon curry powder, paprika, Italian seasoning and chicken pieces, tossing to coat chicken thoroughly.

2. In medium-large skillet over medium-high heat, stir-fry chicken in 2 tablespoons broth for about 10 minutes or until chicken is no longer pink inside. Remove from pan.

3. Preheat oven to 350°F.

4. Add garlic, onion and 2 tablespoons broth to skillet and cook, stirring often, 5 minutes or until the garlic and onion begin to color. Stir in apples, remaining 1 teaspoon curry, honey, raisins, lemon juice and oranges with juice. Cover and cook over medium heat for 10 minutes.

5. Remove skillet from heat. Set aside 1 cup of fruit mixture for topping; stir cooked rice into remaining mixture and spoon into 2 quart glass casserole. Place chicken pieces on top of rice mixture and top with remaining fruit mixture.

6. Bake uncovered at 350°F. for 20-30 minutes, until liquid is absorbed and casserole is golden brown.

yield: 6 Servings

Cooking without Fat

YOU SAVE 183 CALORIES
This recipe contains 279 calories per serving
Typical recipe contains 462 calories per serving

sweet and sour chicken

Sweet and sour is a classic concept, which I have found to be good for creating tempting dishes without salt or fat. It is a versatile recipe that can be adapted for meatless service by substituting tofu for the chicken and vegetable broth or water for the chicken broth. When served over a simple brown rice, the grain will absorb the sauce and provide a perfect balance to the seductive sweet and sour tang.

We developed this recipe using Health Valley Fat-Free Chicken Broth. It has a full, rich flavor and only 30 calories per serving.

Nutrition Information Per Serving	
Calories	279
Fat	3.5 grams
Percentage of Calories from Fat	11%
Cholesterol	72 milligrams
Sodium	105 milligrams
Dietary Fiber	3.7 grams

sweet and sour chicken

prep time: 15 minutes

cooking time: 20 minutes

ingredients: 1 cup pineapple chunks canned in juice
2 tablespoons arrowroot
3 tablespoons apple cider vinegar
3-4 tablespoons honey
1 teaspoon mustard, spicy or dijon
2 teaspoons no salt ketchup
dash cayenne pepper (optional)
¼ cup fat-free chicken broth
2 teaspoons minced fresh ginger
  or ¾ teaspoon powdered ginger
1 large onion, cut in crescents
2 cloves garlic, chopped
1 cup quartered mushrooms
1 green pepper, cut in 1½-inch strips
¾ pound boned, skinless, chicken breast meat,
  cut in 1-inch pieces
¼ pound snow peas, ends trimmed
1 tomato, cut in bite-sized pieces

directions: 1. Drain pineapple and reserve ½ cup juice. Mix juice with arrowroot, vinegar, honey, mustard, ketchup and cayenne and set aside.
2. Heat 2-4 tablespoons broth in wok or large skillet. Stir-fry ginger, onion, garlic, mushrooms, green pepper and chicken for about 10 minutes, until chicken is cooked. Pour off any accumulated liquid.
3. Stir juice mixture, and pour into pan along with pineapple chunks, snow peas and tomatoes. Stir over medium heat 3-5 minutes, until sauce thickens. Remove from heat and serve.

yield: 4 Servings

Cooking without Fat

YOU SAVE 135 CALORIES
This recipe contains 253 calories per serving
Typical recipe contains 388 calories per serving

orange honey baked chicken

In this recipe the subtle orange honey taste melds gently with the chicken, creating a dish that is not overpoweringly sweet, or fruity.

The orange slices used to garnish this dish are more than decorative. Squeeze some of their juice onto the chicken at serving time and you'll really enhance the flavor in the sauce.

Nutrition Information Per Serving

Calories	253
Fat	3 grams
Percentage of Calories from Fat	11%
Cholesterol	64 milligrams
Sodium	59 milligrams
Dietary Fiber	.6 gram

orange honey baked chicken

prep time: 10 minutes

cooking time: 26 minutes

ingredients: ¼ cup frozen orange juice concentrate

1 tablespoon lemon juice

2 tablespoons + 1 tablespoon honey

½ teaspoon finely grated orange peel

½ teaspoon ginger

4 skinless, boned chicken breast filets
(about 1 pound)

2 tablespoons fruit juice sweetened
orange marmalade

orange slices for garnish

directions:
1. Preheat oven to 400°F.
2. In baking dish, mix together orange juice concentrate, lemon juice, 2 tablespoons honey, orange peel and ginger. Add chicken pieces, turning to coat all sides. If time permits, let chicken marinate for 10 minutes.
3. Bake chicken uncovered at 400°F. for 8 minutes, baste with pan juices. Bake an additional 8 minutes, baste again. Glaze chicken with a mixture of marmalade and remaining 1 tablespoon honey; continue to bake 8-10 minutes or until done.
4. Transfer chicken to serving plate. Reduce pan juices until thickened and pour over chicken; garnish with orange slices.

yield: 4 Servings

Cooking without Fat

YOU SAVE 147 CALORIES
This recipe contains 246 calories per serving
Typical recipe contains 393 calories per serving

mexican chicken

Mexican seasonings create tempting dishes without salt or fat. This Mexican Chicken recipe can be adapted for meatless service by substituting tofu for the chicken and vegetable broth or water for the chicken broth.

This dish can be a meal in itself or you can choose to serve it over steaming brown rice accompanied with fresh salsa.

We developed this recipe using Health Valley Fat-Free Chicken Broth. It has a full, rich flavor and only 30 calories per serving. We also used Health Valley Fat-Free Mild Vegetarian Chili with 3 Beans. It's the only fat-free chili that contains 5,000 IU of beta carotene.

Nutrition Information Per Serving	
Calories	246
Fat	3.4 grams
Percentage of Calories from Fat	12%
Cholesterol	64 milligrams
Sodium	231 milligrams
Dietary Fiber	9.6 grams

mexican chicken

prep time: 15 minutes

cooking time: 18 minutes

ingredients: 4 tablespoons fat-free chicken broth
3 large cloves garlic, chopped
1½ cups chopped onion
1 cup diced red pepper
1 pound boned, skinless, chicken breast meat,
    cut into 1-inch pieces
1 can (15 ounces) no salt stewed tomatoes, drained
1 can (15 ounces) fat-free chili
¼ teaspoon chili powder
dash cayenne pepper (optional)
2 cups small broccoli florets, steamed
2 tablespoons chopped cilantro (optional)

directions:
1. Heat 4 tablespoons broth in large skillet over medium-high heat. Stir-fry garlic, onion, pepper and chicken for about 10 minutes, until chicken is cooked.
2. Stir in drained stewed tomatoes, chili, chili powder and cayenne pepper. Bring mixture to a boil. Cover, and reduce heat, simmer for about 8 minutes to allow the flavors to blend. Stir in steamed broccoli and simmer for an additional 2 minutes.
3. Remove from heat. Garnish with chopped cilantro if desired and serve.

yield: 6 Servings

Cooking without Fat

YOU SAVE 161 CALORIES
This recipe contains 226 calories per serving
Typical recipe contains 387 calories per serving

chicken cacciatore

Chicken cacciatore is a cherished Italian classic with as many versions as there are cooks. In our rendition, the generously seasoned sauce gets a lift at the end from the sweet balsamic vinegar.

Serve Chicken Cacciatore with a side of pasta and use the sauce from the chicken to flavor it. Round out the menu with a bountiful salad and take advantage of the variety of greens available in the market today. In addition to leaf lettuce, add such pungent offerings as chicory, escarole, endive, raddichio, watercress and arugula.

We developed this recipe using Health Valley Fat-Free Chicken Broth. It has a full, rich flavor and only 30 calories per serving.

Nutrition Information Per Serving	
Calories	226
Fat	3.4 grams
Percentage of Calories from Fat	14%
Cholesterol	65 milligrams
Sodium	144 milligrams
Dietary Fiber	2.7 grams

chicken cacciatore

prep time: 20 minutes

cooking time: 15 minutes

ingredients: 1 can (15 ounces) no salt tomatoes in juice, cut up
and thoroughly drained

1 cup no salt tomato sauce

1½ teaspoons crushed dried oregano

½ teaspoon crushed dried basil

1 tablespoon honey

¼ teaspoon white pepper (optional)

¼ cup fat-free chicken broth

3 cloves garlic, chopped

1 cup chopped onion

1 large green pepper, cut in 1-inch strips

¾ pound boned, skinless, chicken breast meat,
cut in 2-inch cubes

¾ cup frozen green peas

1 tablespoon balsamic vinegar

directions: 1. Place cut-up canned tomatoes that have been thoroughly
drained, tomato sauce, oregano, basil, honey and pepper
in 2-3 quart saucepan. Cover and simmer 15 minutes.

2. Heat 4 tablespoons broth in large skillet over medium-
high heat. Stir-fry garlic, onion, green pepper and
chicken for about 10 minutes, until chicken is no longer
pink inside.

3. Add chicken and green peppers to sauce and simmer,
partially covered, 10 minutes. Add peas and balsamic
vinegar, and cook uncovered an additional 5 minutes.

yield: 4 Servings

Cooking without Fat

chicken dijon

This dish gets its zesty flavor from the rich sauce it bakes in. The piquant blend of mustard, coriander, lime juice and a little honey penetrates the meat and also coats it, imparting the kind of full-bodied flavor you normally have to add oil, cream and salt to achieve.

The sauce is quite ample, so I serve the chicken breasts on a bed of lettuce and spoon the sauce over all, so as not to miss any of its goodness. If you want to add a garnish in addition to the lime wedges suggested in the recipe, sprinkle the finished dish with fresh chopped cilantro. Cilantro is the fresh form of the ground coriander; just a little has a dramatic effect.

Nutrition Information Per Serving

Calories	188
Fat	2.8 grams
Percentage of Calories from Fat	15%
Cholesterol	64 milligrams
Sodium	320 milligrams
Dietary Fiber	.8 gram

chicken dijon

prep time: 15 minutes

cooking time: 30 minutes

ingredients: ⅓ cup dijon mustard

2 tablespoons honey

2 tablespoons lime juice

1 tablespoon water

¾ teaspoon ground coriander (optional)

1½ teaspoons grated lime peel

4 skinless, boned chicken breast filets
(about 1 pound)

lettuce leaves

lime wedges

chopped fresh cilantro (optional)

directions: 1. Preheat oven to 350°F.

2. Whisk together mustard, honey, lime juice, water, coriander and lime peel.

3. Place chicken in shallow ovenproof casserole. Set aside ¼ cup mustard sauce, pour remaining sauce on chicken. Cover and bake 20 minutes. Uncover, spoon sauce from casserole on top and continue to bake, uncovered, for 10 minutes or until completely cooked.

4. Arrange chicken on lettuce leaves.

5. Add 2-4 tablespoons of remaining sauce from casserole to reserved sauce and heat through. Pour sauce over chicken and serve with lime wedges.

6. Sprinkle with fresh chopped cilantro.

yield: 4 Servings

YOU SAVE 184 CALORIES
This recipe contains 271 calories per serving
Typical recipe contains 455 calories per serving

chicken vegetable stew

Chicken Stew is a real comfort food. It will warm you on chilly days, yet seems refreshingly light when the sun shines. You will be surprised by the rich flavor of this stew despite the absence of added fat and salt.

We developed this recipe using Health Valley Fat-Free Chicken Broth. It has a full, rich flavor and only 30 calories per serving.

Nutrition Information Per Serving	
Calories	271
Fat	3.2 grams
Percentage of Calories from Fat	11%
Cholesterol	65 milligrams
Sodium	224 milligrams
Dietary Fiber	3.7 grams

chicken vegetable stew

prep time: 15 minutes

cooking time: 1 hour

ingredients: ¾ pound boned, skinless chicken breast meat,
cut in 2-inch cubes

¾ cup + ½ cup fat-free chicken broth

½ teaspoon Italian seasoning blend

1 teaspoon paprika

white pepper to taste (optional)

1 clove garlic, chopped

2 tablespoons chopped celery leaves

3 medium carrots, cut into ½-inch pieces

1 medium onion, cut into wedges

5 medium celery stalks, cut into ½-inch pieces

4 small potatoes, cut into 1-inch pieces

½ tablespoon lemon juice

2 tablespoons chopped parsley for garnish

directions: 1. Place chicken, ¾ cup broth, seasonings and garlic in large saucepan. Bring to boil, cover, reduce heat and simmer 10 minutes.

2. Add vegetables and remaining ½ cup chicken broth. Replace cover, and cook on low heat until chicken and vegetables are done, 45-50 minutes. Add lemon juice.

3. Serve in bowls. Garnish with chopped parsley.

yield: 4 Servings

Cooking without Fat

YOU SAVE 161 CALORIES
This recipe contains 162 calories per serving
Typical recipe contains 323 calories per serving

easy skillet chicken

This is a good basic chicken recipe, appealing in its simplicity. You will be amazed not only by how delectable the chicken is, but by the genuine flavor of the vegetables that is generated by slow, low-heat cooking. The mushrooms are a key ingredient in this recipe as they are a natural flavor enhancer.

We developed this recipe using Health Valley Fat-Free Chicken Broth. It has a full, rich flavor and only 30 calories per serving.

Nutrition Information Per Serving	
Calories	162
Fat	2.8 grams
Percentage of Calories from Fat	15%
Cholesterol	55 milligrams
Sodium	74 milligrams
Dietary Fiber	3.4 grams

easy skillet chicken

prep time: 15 minutes

cooking time: 25 minutes

ingredients: 2 tablespoons +2 tablespoons fat-free chicken broth
1 cup coarsely chopped onion
½ green pepper, cubed
½ red pepper, cubed
½ cup chopped celery
1 zucchini, cut in ½-inch thick rounds
2 carrots, cut in ¼-inch thick rounds
1 cup sliced mushrooms
½ teaspoon +½ teaspoon Italian seasoning blend
½ teaspoon +½ teaspoon paprika
4 skinless, boned chicken breast filets
  (about ¾ pound)
dash white pepper (optional)

directions: 1. Place 2 tablespoons chicken broth and onion in large skillet and cook over medium heat about 5 minutes or until onion softens. Add green pepper, red pepper, celery, zucchini, carrots, mushrooms and remaining broth and sprinkle with ½ teaspoon each Italian seasoning and paprika. Add chicken and cook slowly over low heat, uncovered, for 10 minutes.

2. Turn chicken. Add remaining Italian seasoning, paprika and pepper. Continue to cook for 10-15 minutes or until chicken and vegetables are tender.

yield: 4 Servings

Cooking without Fat

YOU SAVE 196 CALORIES
This recipe contains 253 calories per serving
Typical recipe contains 449 calories per serving

curried chicken

This recipe presents an excellent way to turn leftover cooked chicken into a delicious quick dish. You certainly won't have any leftovers.

I like to serve curried chicken with brown rice that has been mixed with chopped green onions and red pepper after cooking.

We developed this recipe using Health Valley Fat-Free 14 Garden Vegetable Soup. It has more vegetables than other vegetable soups and supplies one-third the recommended amount you need every day.

Nutrition Information Per Serving	
Calories	253
Fat	3.5 grams
Percentage of Calories from Fat	12%
Cholesterol	72 milligrams
Sodium	236 milligrams
Dietary Fiber	3.7 grams

curried chicken

prep time: 5 minutes

cooking time: 10 minutes

ingredients: 1 can (15 ounces) fat-free vegetable soup
1 tablespoon mild curry powder*
½ teaspoon onion powder
½ teaspoon garlic powder
¾ pound cooked, boned, skinless chicken breast meat, diced
2 teaspoons honey
¾ cup frozen peas
⅓ cup raisins

directions: 1. Combine soup with curry, onion and garlic powders; puree in blender or food processor.
2. Place soup in 1 quart saucepan and bring to boil. Add chicken and simmer 5 minutes. Add honey, peas and raisins and cook 5 minutes longer.
3. If desired, serve over brown rice or other cooked grain of choice.

yield: 4 Servings

note: *For a spicier curry use hot curry powder.

YOU SAVE 162 CALORIES

This recipe contains 274 calories per serving
Typical recipe contains 436 calories per serving

---

indian style turkey

Indian style curries are one of my favorite approaches to low-fat, no salt cooking because they offer so much flavor and such an imaginative mix of ingredients. Despite what many people think, curries do not have to be overly spicy; this mild, Indian-inspired turkey dish proves that. The sweetness of the yams and fruit creates a chutney-like taste.

Like most curried dishes, Indian Style Turkey is especially good with brown rice.

We developed this recipe using Health Valley Fat-Free Chicken Broth. It has a full, rich flavor and only 30 calories per serving.

Nutrition Information Per Serving	
Calories	274
Fat	1.1 grams
Percentage of Calories from Fat	4%
Cholesterol	79 milligrams
Sodium	188 milligrams
Dietary Fiber	2.6 grams

indian style turkey

prep time: 15 minutes

cooking time: 35 minutes

ingredients: 2 cups yams, peeled and cut in 1/4-inch cubes

1 cup chopped onion

1/2 cup chopped celery

2 cloves garlic, chopped

1 1/2 cups fat-free chicken broth

1 pound turkey breast meat, boned, skinned and cut in 1-inch cubes

1/4 teaspoon ground ginger

1/8 teaspoon ground thyme

1 tablespoon curry powder

2 tablespoons lemon juice

2 tablespoons fruit-juice-sweetened apricot preserves

1/3 cup raisins

1/3 cup diced dried apricots

3/4 cup frozen green peas, thawed

directions: 1. Steam yams for approximately 15 minutes and set aside.

2. In large skillet, combine onion, celery and garlic with 2 tablespoons chicken broth. Saute, stirring frequently, 3-5 minutes, until onions begin to color and liquid evaporates.

3. Add turkey and stir-fry 5 minutes or until turkey is no longer pink.

4. In medium bowl, mix ground ginger, ground thyme, curry powder, lemon juice, yams, preserves, raisins, apricots and remaining broth. Add to skillet and bring to simmer. Cover and reduce heat to low. Cook for 20 minutes.

5. Stir in peas. Cover and cook 5 minutes longer before serving.

yield: 6 Servings

YOU SAVE 138 CALORIES
This recipe contains 227 calories per serving
Typical recipe contains 365 calories per serving

italian meatballs

Compare the calorie and fat content of this dish, 227 calories and 1.3 grams of fat, to a typical Italian version made with ground beef, 365 calories and 19 grams of fat. Now compare the flavor. These juicy meatballs are not only healthy, they're tasty too.

While your first instinct may be to serve the turkey meatballs on pasta, you might want to try piling the meatballs on fat-free Italian bread or stuffing them into pita pockets for a hearty hero. I also think Italian Meatballs go well with rice, which has a texture that complements the ground meat and does an excellent job of carrying the thick, flavorful sauce. If you choose to serve the meatballs on pasta, you may want to double the sauce.

We developed this recipe using Health Valley Fat-Free Herb Crackers. They have three times as much fiber as similar crackers.

Nutrition Information Per Serving	
Calories	227
Fat	1.3 grams
Percentage of Calories from Fat	5%
Cholesterol	63 milligrams
Sodium	130 milligrams
Dietary Fiber	2.3 grams

italian meatballs

prep time: 15 minutes

cooking time: 30 minutes

ingredients: *sauce*
⅓ cup chopped onion
2 large cloves garlic, chopped
½ green pepper, cut in 1-inch strips
1 tablespoon water
1 can (15 ounces) no salt tomato sauce
3 tablespoons honey
1 teaspoon crushed dried oregano
1 teaspoon crushed dried basil

meat balls
1 pound ground turkey breast meat
⅓ cup chopped onion
¼ cup finely chopped celery
2 cloves garlic, chopped
½ teaspoon crushed dried oregano
¼ teaspoon crushed dried basil
½ cup fat-free crackers, processed to fine crumbs
¾ cup cooked brown rice
2 egg whites
dash white pepper (optional)

directions: 1. Combine sauce ingredients in large skillet, bring to a boil and simmer gently, uncovered, 5-10 minutes to blend flavors.

2. Combine meatball ingredients and shape into 1-inch balls. Place immediately into simmering sauce. Cover partially and simmer gently 15-20 minutes, until meat is no longer pink inside, turning meatballs during cooking until evenly browned.

yield: 6 Servings

YOU SAVE 232 CALORIES
This recipe contains 224 calories per serving
Typical recipe contains 456 calories per serving

glazed meatloaf

Our succulent turkey meatloaf disproves the myth that just because ground turkey breast is leaner than ground beef you end up with a dry product. Adding brown rice, fat-free cracker crumbs and tomato sauce to this recipe yields a loaf that is flavorful and juicy, and also nutritionally balanced. For an updated version of a traditional American dinner, serve the loaf with potatoes.

We developed this recipe using Health Valley Fat-Free Herb Crackers. They have three times as much fiber as similar crackers.

Nutrition Information Per Serving	
Calories	224
Fat	1.2 grams
Percentage of Calories from Fat	5%
Cholesterol	63 milligrams
Sodium	219 milligrams
Dietary Fiber	2.3 grams

glazed meatloaf

prep time: 10 minutes

cooking time: 45 minutes

ingredients: 1 pound ground turkey breast meat
$\frac{1}{2}$ cup fat-free crackers, processed to fine crumbs
  (or fat-free bread crumbs)
1 cup cooked brown rice
$\frac{1}{2}$ cup chopped onion
$\frac{1}{4}$ cup grated carrot
$\frac{1}{4}$ cup finely chopped celery
1$\frac{1}{2}$ teaspoons prepared mustard, spicy or dijon
1 teaspoon garlic powder
$\frac{1}{2}$ teaspoon ground thyme
$\frac{1}{2}$ teaspoon onion powder
$\frac{1}{8}$ teaspoon white pepper (optional)
$\frac{1}{4}$ cup no salt tomato sauce
2 egg whites
6 tablespoons no salt ketchup
2 tablespoons honey

directions: 1. Preheat oven to 350°F.
2. Combine all ingredients except ketchup and honey and mix well.
3. Turn mixture into a 7- or 8-inch loaf pan and bake at 350°F. for 40 minutes, until firm and brown on top.
4. Combine ketchup and honey. Spread evenly over top of loaf and bake 5 minutes longer.
5. If desired, serve with no salt ketchup.

yield: 6 Servings

note: For a moist, juicy meatloaf, be sure to use a loaf pan.

Cooking without Fat

YOU SAVE 86 CALORIES
This recipe contains 267 calories per serving
Typical recipe contains 353 calories per serving

sloppy joes

We have worked diligently at Health Valley to perfect our Fat-Free Chilis. Unlike other prepared canned chili products on the market, ours are uniquely low in fat and tastily seasoned without being overloaded with salt. We think they are delightful without any embellishment. Therefore you might wonder why we would suggest you do anything with them other than open the can and eat.

What we have discovered is that with just a little bit of creative energy, Health Valley Chilis take on an entirely different tenor. Therefore you can use chilis often without having to repeat the same menu.

For a wholesome version of Sloppy Joes, spoon this succulent turkey-bean combo over French bread, English muffins or hamburger buns.

We developed this recipe using Health Valley Fat-Free Mild Vegetarian Chili with 3 Beans. It's the only fat-free chili available that contains 5,000 IU of beta carotene.

Nutrition Information Per Serving	
Calories	267
Fat	1.6 grams
Percentage of Calories from Fat	5%
Cholesterol	47 milligrams
Sodium	302 milligrams
Dietary Fiber	10.2 grams

sloppy joes

prep time: 10 minutes

cooking time: 30 minutes

ingredients: ½ pound ground turkey breast meat
½ cup chopped onion
1 can (15 ounces) fat-free chili
¼ cup chopped celery
¼ cup chopped green pepper
½ cup corn kernels, fresh or frozen
½ cup no salt tomato sauce
1 teaspoon honey
⅛ teaspoon cayenne pepper (optional)
½ teaspoon paprika
½ teaspoon dry mustard
¾ teaspoon chili powder (optional)

directions: 1. In large heavy pan, cook ground turkey 3-5 minutes, until no longer pink. Add onion and saute 2-3 minutes longer, until softened.
2. Add chili, celery, green pepper, corn, tomato sauce, honey and seasonings to turkey. Cover and simmer 30 minutes, stirring occasionally.

yield: 4 Servings

Cooking without Fat

YOU SAVE 235 CALORIES
This recipe contains 116 calories per serving
Typical recipe contains 351 calories per serving

turkey vegetable burgers

These tasty burgers will save a lot of calories. As with all burgers, these are delicious on a whole wheat bun, English muffin or toast, heaped with onion, tomato, sprouts, lettuce, no salt ketchup, mustard, or your own favorite accoutrements.

We developed this recipe using Health Valley Fiber 7 Flakes® Cereal. It provides 5 grams of fiber in every serving from seven different whole grains.

Nutrition Information Per Serving	
Calories	116
Fat	.8 gram
Percentage of Calories from Fat	6%
Cholesterol	47 milligrams
Sodium	58 milligrams
Dietary Fiber	1.1 grams

turkey vegetable burgers

prep time: 15 minutes

cooking time: 20 minutes

ingredients: ½ cup finely chopped onion
2 large cloves garlic, chopped
1 tablespoon water
½ cup finely chopped celery
½ pound ground turkey breast meat
1 teaspoon onion powder
1½ teaspoons prepared mustard, spicy or dijon
¼ teaspoon white pepper (optional)
1 egg white
dash nutmeg
¾ cup fat-free cereal or fat-free crackers,
   processed into fine crumbs
2 tablespoons minced fresh parsley
   or 2 teaspoons dried

directions: 1. Preheat oven to 375°F.
2. Saute onion and garlic in 1 tablespoon water over medium-high heat for 3-5 minutes until water evaporates.
3. Add celery and saute, stirring, 3 minutes to soften. If vegetables begin to stick, add additional water as needed.
4. In large bowl, combine turkey meat, sauteed vegetables, onion powder, mustard, pepper, egg white, nutmeg, crumbs and parsley. Mix well.
5. Form turkey mixture into 4 patties and place on baking sheet or shallow pan. Bake at 375°F. for 20 minutes, or until firm and brown.

yield: 4 Servings

Cooking without Fat FISH

There are so many nutritional benefits from fish that authorities recommend you include it several times a week in your diet. Fish is a good source of vitamins and the minerals magnesium, iron, iodine, phosphorus, and copper. Fish provides the same high quality complete protein as red meat, yet contains only half the calories and a fraction of the saturated fat.

Most of the fat in fish is monounsaturated or polyunsaturated, and is considered to be beneficial in helping to maintain a healthy balance of blood lipids. Several varieties of fish, such as salmon and tuna, are very rich sources of omega-3 fatty acids. Studies of populations that consume diets high in these fatty acids show that cardiovascular heart disease is extremely low. Nutritional authorities recommend including fish rich in omega-3 fatty acids in your diet to help promote a healthy circulatory system.

Cooking without Fat

The fat content of fish varies with the species and can be classified into three categories:

Less than 10% of total calories from fat:
orange roughy, cod, haddock, scrod, pollack, whiting, pike, tuna

10-25% of total calories from fat:
bass, flounder, halibut, perch, rockfish, sole, snapper, turbot

Over 25% of total calories from fat and richest in omega-3 fatty acids:
bluefish, catfish, herring, mackerel, sardines, salmon, shad, swordfish, trout

TIPS ON BUYING FISH

Try to buy fresh, rather than frozen, fish whenever possible. Steaks and filets should look freshly cut, firm and moist, with no brown edges. If you choose frozen fish, avoid packages with a build-up of ice crystals, and dry or discolored fish – especially around the edges. When following a recipe, be sure fish is fully defrosted first or the results will be watery with diminished flavor.

TIPS ON COOKING FISH

Two things that will assure great fish dishes are freshness and proper cooking. With cooking, truly fresh fish generally turns to an opaque solid color within a matter of minutes. This is your signal that the fish is done. It should not have a "fishy" odor. If you can smell it, it's overcooked!

The best ways to cook fish are usually the simplest; bring out and enhance the natural delicate flavor of the fish, rather than disguising or overpowering it. Fish can be quickly poached, baked or broiled with nothing more than a few herbs or some fresh lemon. The general rule of cooking is 10 minutes per inch of thickness for *fresh* – not frozen – fish. For each ¼-inch above or below one inch, add or subtract 2 minutes. This rule applies no matter what method of cooking you select. Fish flakes readily with a fork when it is done. Avoid overcooking, which makes fish rubbery or mushy, depending on the species.

Of course, fish can be prepared in many imaginative ways that do not necessarily mean time-consuming preparation. We have included both simple and sophisticated recipes in this section so that it will be easy for you to make delicious, nourishing fish dishes a regular part of your healthy eating plan. Poached Fish Dinner with Mustard-Dill Sauce and Orange Roughy in Citrus Sauce are excellent choices for entertaining.

We are very fond of orange roughy for both nutrition and flavor reasons. This moist, flavorful white fish is exceptionally low in fat and calories, with only 69 calories per 3½ ounce serving. It is firmer than similar fish so it doesn't become mushy in recipes, and its delicate sweetness makes it particularly ideal for recipes with citrus sauce or breading. We recommend that you make orange roughy part of your healthy menus frequently.

Cooking without Fat

YOU SAVE 152 CALORIES
This recipe contains 278 calories per serving
Typical recipe contains 430 calories per serving

poached fish dinner with mustard-dill sauce

Poaching is one of the easiest methods of fish preparation, yet people seem to shy away from it, possibly fearing that this is something that can only be accomplished in a French restaurant by a trained chef. Nothing could be further from the truth. If you enjoy the delicate flavor and texture of fish, no cooking method is better.

Mustard-Dill Sauce gives the poached fish and steamed vegetables a flavorful and elegant touch, making this dish perfect for everyday meals, or for a special company dinner.

Nutrition Information Per Serving	
Calories	278
Fat	3.3 grams
Percentage of Calories from Fat	11%
Cholesterol	26 milligrams
Sodium	305 milligrams
Dietary Fiber	3.6 grams

poached fish dinner with mustard-dill sauce

prep time: 20 minutes

cooking time: 20 minutes

ingredients: 4 medium size thin-skinned boiling potatoes, cut in ¼-inch slices (about 3 cups)

2 medium carrots, cut into ¼-inch rounds (about 1 cup)

2 medium zucchini, cut into ¼-inch rounds (about 2 cups)

3 cups water

3 tablespoons lemon juice

1-inch strip lemon peel

2 slices onion

4 sprigs parsley

1 bay leaf

¾ pound halibut or salmon filets (1-inch thick)

1 cup Mustard-Dill Sauce (see recipe in Dressings & Sauces section, page 295)

directions: 1. Steam potatoes and carrots for 15 minutes; add zucchini and steam for additional 10 minutes or until desired texture is reached.

2. Bring poaching ingredients (water, lemon juice, lemon peel, onion, parsley, and bay leaf) to boil in a broad shallow pan or skillet. Simmer 5-10 minutes to extract flavor from seasoning.

3. Add fish. Simmer, partially covered, 10 minutes, or until fish flakes with a fork.

4. Remove fish with a slotted spatula and drain. Place on serving plate, surround with potatoes and vegetables.

5. Spoon Mustard-Dill Sauce over all, serve any remaining sauce on the side.

yield: 4 Servings

Cooking without Fat

YOU SAVE 142 CALORIES
This recipe contains 163 calories per serving
Typical recipe contains 305 calories per serving

orange roughy in citrus sauce

Orange roughy is a delicious, delicately flavored white fish that is very low in fat. It has become popular in recent years and is now widely available. It is important to use orange roughy and not a substitute like sole in this recipe to achieve the flavor and texture that makes this dish so remarkable.

This recipe maintains excellent taste without the additional calories and fat of a more traditional recipe calling for the fish to be marinated in oil and fried in butter. Orange Roughy in Citrus Sauce is an excellent choice for that special dinner when you wish to entertain with flair, confidence, and ease.

Nutrition Information Per Serving

Calories	163
Fat	1 gram
Percentage of Calories from Fat	5%
Cholesterol	23 milligrams
Sodium	99 milligrams
Dietary Fiber	.2 gram

orange roughy in citrus sauce

prep time: 10 minutes

marinating time: 45 minutes

cooking time: 15 minutes

ingredients: 1 pound orange roughy

¼ cup frozen orange juice concentrate

2 tablespoons lemon juice

1 teaspoon dried dill weed

1 teaspoon paprika

2 tablespoons minced fresh parsley
or 1 tablespoon dried

½ cup water

3 tablespoons + 3 tablespoons fruit juice sweetened
orange marmalade

1 teaspoon arrowroot

directions:
1. Place fish in shallow non-metal casserole.
2. Combine remaining ingredients except marmalade and arrowroot and mix to dissolve orange juice concentrate. Reserve ½ cup for sauce, pour remaining mixture over fish. Cover fish and marinate in refrigerator 45 minutes or longer, turning at least once.
3. Preheat broiler.
4. Remove fish from marinade and place on broiler pan. Add 3 tablespoons of marmalade to marinade and heat. Broil fish 4-inches from heat 10-15 minutes, until fish flakes, basting with marinade several times during cooking.
5. While fish is broiling, heat reserved orange sauce in small saucepan with arrowroot and remaining 3 table-spoons marmalade until sauce begins to thicken.
6. Transfer fish to serving dish. Pour sauce on fish or serve on side. If desired, decorate the plate with fresh orange slices and sprigs of parsley or dill.

yield: 4 Servings

Cooking without Fat

fish stew

After experimenting with several different vegetable combinations and a variety of fish and seafood in this recipe, we reached what we believe is the perfect balance of flavors. I strongly suggest you use more than one type of fish as variety is one of the true strengths of a stew. Although extremely flavorful with no embellishment, you may want to offer fresh lemon wedges or a touch of balsamic or red wine vinegar for individual seasoning at the table. To mimic the Spanish specialty paella, add some cooked brown rice.

A crusty whole grain bread and green salad are all it takes to make this simple stew a low-fat feast.

Nutrition Information Per Serving	
Calories	287
Fat	2 grams
Percentage of Calories from Fat	6%
Cholesterol	42 milligrams
Sodium	158 milligrams
Dietary Fiber	4 grams

fish stew

prep time: 15 minutes

cooking time: 1 hour

ingredients: 3 cloves garlic, chopped

¾ cup chopped onion

2 tablespoons water

1 medium green pepper, cut in 1-inch strips

2 medium carrots, cut in ½-inch rounds

3 stalks celery, cut in 1-inch pieces

2 cups potatoes, cut in 1-inch dice

1 can (15 ounces) no salt tomato sauce

1 can (15 ounces) no salt tomatoes in juice

1½ tablespoons honey

½ teaspoon ground thyme

⅛ teaspoon cayenne pepper (optional)

1 bay leaf

1 pound fish filets (two or more of the following: sea bass, red snapper, sole, halibut, salmon, or other fish of choice)

¼ cup chopped fresh parsley

directions: 1. Combine garlic, onion and 2 tablespoons water in soup pot. Cook 3-5 minutes over medium heat, until onion softens and liquid evaporates.

2. Add green pepper, carrots, celery, and potatoes. Add tomato sauce, canned tomatoes including juice, honey and seasonings. If tomatoes are whole, crush with back of spoon. Bring to boil. Cover and simmer 50 minutes or until potatoes are tender.

3. Cut fish into 1-inch pieces. Add to pot and cook, uncovered, 8 minutes or until fish is cooked.

4. Sprinkle liberally with fresh parsley before serving.

5. If desired offer fresh lemon wedges or balsamic vinegar or red wine vinegar for individual seasoning at the table.

yield: 4 Servings

YOU SAVE 160 CALORIES

This recipe contains 135 calories per serving
Typical recipe contains 295 calories per serving

islander fish filets

In this recipe the richness of the banana fosters a full-bodied sauce despite the absence of any fat. The delicious fruit flavors are just enough to enliven the fish, without overpowering it. Don't be alarmed by the unusual combination of ingredients – the results are sure to delight you.

Nutrition Information Per Serving

Calories	135
Fat	1 gram
Percentage of Calories from Fat	6%
Cholesterol	23 milligrams
Sodium	97 milligrams
Dietary Fiber	.5 gram

islander fish filets

prep time: 10 minutes

cooking time: 5-15 minutes

ingredients: 1 pound orange roughy filets or other mild white fish

½ cup plain nonfat yogurt

2 tablespoons frozen orange juice concentrate

1 tablespoon lemon juice

2 teaspoons fruit juice sweetened orange marmalade

⅓ cup mashed banana

⅛ teaspoon garlic powder

½ teaspoon ground ginger
or 1 teaspoon fresh grated

pinch white pepper (optional)

directions: 1. Preheat oven to 400°F.

2. Cut filets into 4 serving size pieces. Place side by side in baking pan large enough to hold fish in a single layer.

3. In a medium bowl, combine rest of ingredients; pour ½ cup of mixture evenly over fish.

4. Bake 5-15 minutes at 400°F. or until fish flakes. Timing will vary depending on thickness of filets.

5. Remove fish from pan, place on serving dish and serve with remaining sauce.

yield: 4 Servings

YOU SAVE 324 CALORIES
This recipe contains 166 calories per serving
Typical recipe contains 490 calories per serving

oven fried fish

This recipe is quick to fix and sure to please. For the final touch, try serving with no salt ketchup or Mustard-Dill Sauce (see recipe in Dressings & Sauces section, page 295).

We developed this recipe using Health Valley Fat-Free Herb Crackers. They have three times as much fiber as similar crackers.

Nutrition Information Per Serving

Calories	166
Fat	1.7 grams
Percentage of Calories from Fat	9%
Cholesterol	23 milligrams
Sodium	248 milligrams
Dietary Fiber	3.5 grams

oven fried fish

prep time: 5 minutes

cooking time: 15 minutes

ingredients: 2 cups fat-free crackers, processed to fine crumbs (or fat-free bread crumbs)

¼ teaspoon dry mustard powder

1 egg white

2 tablespoons nonfat milk

1 pound fish filets of choice (orange roughy, or other mild white fish)

lemon wedges (optional)

directions:
1. Preheat oven to 425°F.
2. Process crackers into fine crumbs using a food processor or blender. Stir dry mustard into crumbs.
3. Beat egg white with milk in a broad shallow bowl. Spread cracker crumbs on a plate.
4. Dip fish filets one at a time into egg white mixture, then place in cracker crumbs and turn to coat all surfaces.
5. Place on baking sheet and bake at 425°F. for about 15 minutes, until coating is crisp and fish flakes easily with a fork.
6. Serve with lemon wedges, if desired.

yield: 4 Servings

Cooking
without
Fat

YOU SAVE 130 CALORIES
This recipe contains 171 calories per serving
Typical recipe contains 301 calories per serving

fish cakes

Fish cakes are quick to fix and low in calories. By using such fat-free products as cereal and broth, and egg whites coupled with the oven-fry method, the calories are kept low and the flavor high. The Mustard-Dill Sauce blends well with the fish cakes adding an appealing tangy flavor while keeping this dish low in calories.

This recipe can be prepared with tuna or salmon depending on your taste and nutritional preferences. By choosing tuna you save 5 grams of fat per serving; however salmon is a richer source of beneficial omega-3 fatty acids and also lends itself to a moister fish cake.

A serving of this recipe prepared with salmon contains 198 calories with 29% of the calories coming from fat.

We developed this recipe using Health Valley Fiber 7 Flakes® Cereal. It provides 5 grams of fiber in every serving from seven different whole grains. We also used Health Valley Fat-Free Chicken Broth. It has a full, rich flavor and only 30 calories per serving.

Nutrition Information Per Serving

Calories	171
Fat	1.4 grams
Percentage of Calories from Fat	7%
Cholesterol	41 milligrams
Sodium	158 milligrams
Dietary Fiber	1.8 grams

fish cakes

prep time: 5 minutes

cooking time: 15 minutes

ingredients: 1 cup fat-free cereal

¼ cup fat-free chicken broth

1 can (6½ ounces) light tuna or pink salmon, packed in water, rinsed if salted and drained

dash white pepper (optional)

1 teaspoon onion powder

1 egg white

1 teaspoon prepared mustard, spicy or dijon

directions: 1. Preheat oven to 375°F. or preheat broiler if broiling is preferred.

2. Combine cereal and broth in small saucepan and cook for 3 minutes, stirring occasionally, until mixture thickens.

3. Remove cereal mixture from heat and add fish, pepper, onion powder, egg white, and mustard, mashing with a fork until well blended. When cool enough to handle, shape into 4 patties and place on a baking sheet.

4. To bake, place in 375°F. oven and bake 10 minutes; turn patties over and bake 5 minutes longer. *Or* if you prefer to broil, place about 5-inches beneath heat and broil 5 minutes on each side, until nicely browned.

yield: 2 Servings

note: Serve with no salt ketchup or Mustard-Dill Sauce (see recipe in Dressings & Sauces section, page 295) if desired. When using tuna you may wish to use an extra tablespoon of chicken broth.

Cooking without Fat PASTA AND GRAINS

When agriculture began around 7000 B.C., farmers planted mostly grains. Even today rice is a dietary staple for more than half the world's population. Where rice is not the principal grain, wheat, oats, corn, barley and millet can take its place.

We know that whole grains and pastas made from whole grains are among nature's most remarkable nutritional gifts. Grains are included as one of the basic food groups our bodies require every day to stay healthy. They are nature's richest source of dietary fiber. Count them, as well, as a storehouse of complex carbohydrates, protein, vitamin E, B vitamins and a variety of important minerals, including phosphorus, magnesium, iron and zinc. Although many people regard grains as "fattening," they actually furnish fewer calories than an equal weight of meat, dairy products and eggs. Besides, their fibrous nature creates a feeling of fullness that can keep us from overeating.

Cooking without Fat

In the last few decades, the American market has seen the emergence of many grains and an array of products made with them. Each year the selection expands. Such standards as rice, barley, oats, rye and wheat now have to compete with exotic offerings including buckwheat, millet, amaranth, quinoa, blue corn, wild rice, teff, kamut and spelt. Despite this array of choices, most people do not include enough of these nutritious foods in their daily menu.

Unfortunately, many experience pastas and grains only as spaghetti in a meat or heavy cream sauce, risottos laden with cheese and similar fare. Many people are confused by the vast array of pasta on the market these days. Keep in mind, all pastas aren't equal, nutritionally. The most common commercial pastas are made from semolina flour – durum wheat that has had the nutritious germ and bran removed.

In this section, we feature imaginative ways to prepare pasta and rice for low-fat entrees and side dishes. We have accomplished the seemingly impossible task of preparing a delicious Pasta Primavera and rich-tasting Lasagna without using any cheese or oil, as well as a zesty oil-free marinara sauce.

Additionally, we are pleased to note that fat-free pasta sauces are now becoming available.

Orange Honey Baked
Chicken
(See Poultry Section)

Chicken Dijon
(See Poultry Section)

Honey Mustard
Vegetables
(See Vegetable Section)

*Orange Roughy in
Citrus Sauce
(See Fish Section)*

Stuffed Peppers
(See Tofu Section)

Pasta Primavera
(See Pasta and Grain
Section)

Holiday Table
(See Special Holiday Section)

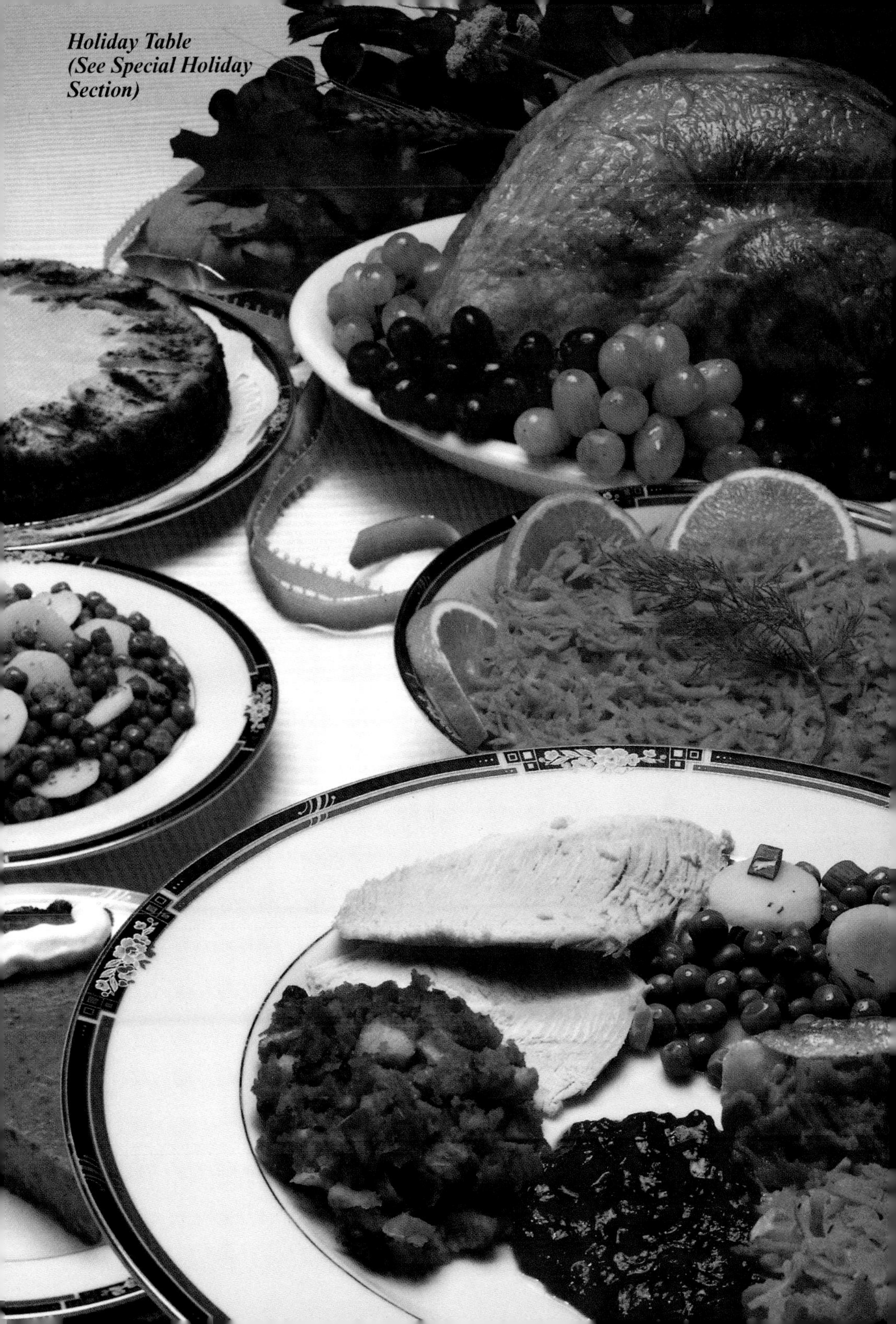

Carrot "Cake"
(See Dessert Section)

basic grain cooking guidelines

There are several approaches to grain cookery as you will discover when you look through our recipes. To get you started, here are basic instructions for preparing most of the common grains. Since cooked grains will keep for about a week in the refrigerator, smart cooks plan for leftovers. This way you already have something available for last minute situations.

1. Rinse grains in colander and drain.

2. Bring recommended quantity of water to boil.

3. Add grains and reduce heat so water is barely simmering.

4. Cover pot and simmer for recommended amount of time. Do not stir during cooking unless otherwise directed. Stirring loosens starch from the surface and makes grains gummy.

When fully cooked, lift lid, fluff grains with a fork, replace cover, and let grains rest for 5 to 10 minutes.

Timetable for Cooking Grains

1 Cup Grain	Cups of Water	Minutes
Barley	3	30
Buckwheat	2	20
Bulgur	2	20
Cornmeal	4	20 to 25
Millet	2	30
Oats	2	10
Rice, Brown	2	45
Rice, Wild	3½	60
Wheat or Rye Berries	2½	60

Note: Cooking times may vary somewhat with the freshness of the grain and the size of the flame. One cup of raw grain almost triples in volume. As an accompaniment to the entree a cup of uncooked grain will provide 4-6 modest servings.

Cooking without Fat

YOU SAVE 270 CALORIES
This recipe contains 314 calories per serving
Typical recipe contains 584 calories per serving

mushroom-marinara sauce on pasta

Both tomato sauce and pasta by themselves are low in calories and practically fat-free. It's what goes on top of them that can run a pasta recipe up to 1000 calories or more per serving. This dish makes for hearty eating without the addition of cheese, oil, butter, cream or eggs.

This recipe works well with any type of whole grain pasta. Serve this easy to make dish as an accompaniment or with a salad and whole grain rolls as an entree. It is fast and easy to prepare, making it a perfect choice for unexpected company.

Contrary to old myths, you don't need to add oil or salt to the cooking water. To prevent pasta from sticking, stir to separate after adding it to the boiling water. To prevent the water from boiling over, make sure you use a pot large enough to allow the water to boil; do not cover. Be sure to have the sauce ready before the pasta is finished cooking, to avoid overcooked and gluey pasta; then toss with sauce and serve immediately.

We developed this recipe using Health Valley Fat-Free Chicken Broth. It has a full, rich flavor and only 30 calories per serving.

Nutrition Information Per Serving	
Calories	314
Fat	1.9 grams
Percentage of Calories from Fat	5%
Cholesterol	0 milligram
Sodium	53 milligrams
Dietary Fiber	10.3 grams

mushroom-marinara sauce on pasta

prep time: 10 minutes

cooking time: 25 minutes

ingredients: ⅔ cup chopped onion
4 cloves garlic, chopped
1 cup sliced mushrooms
2-3 tablespoons fat-free chicken broth
2 cans (15 ounces each) no salt tomato sauce
3 tablespoons honey
2 teaspoons crushed dried oregano
2 teaspoons crushed dried basil
pinch white pepper (optional)
1 tablespoon balsamic vinegar
12 ounces whole grain pasta, cooked
2 tablespoons chopped green onion (optional)

directions: 1. In medium saucepan, cook onion, garlic and mushrooms in broth 5-7 minutes or until softened, over medium high heat.
2. Add tomato sauce, honey, oregano, basil and white pepper. Bring to a boil, reduce heat and simmer gently for 20 minutes.
3. Add balsamic vinegar and simmer for additional 5 minutes.
4. Pour the sauce over cooked pasta and toss thoroughly. Sprinkle green onion over top and serve immediately.

yield: 6 Servings

Cooking without Fat

YOU SAVE 190 CALORIES
This recipe contains 285 calories per serving
Typical recipe contains 475 calories per serving

pasta primavera

Despite the Italian sounding name, Pasta Primavera is an American creation. The traditional dish is laden with butter, parmesan cheese, and often ham and nuts. I think our version stands out among all the other recipes for this popular dish. It is remarkably light and fresh tasting, with a colorful array of vegetables that receive a unique flavor lift from balsamic vinegar.

If you have not used balsamic vinegar previously be sure you don't overlook it here. Balsamic vinegar is available in most markets. While it may seem a bit costly compared to other vinegars, just a few spoonfuls transform this dish from ordinary to exceptional.

On days when time is of the essence, you might want to try a quick version of this recipe using a frozen blend of vegetables and one of the new ready made fat-free marinara sauces.

We developed this recipe using Health Valley Fat-Free Chicken Broth. It has a full, rich flavor and only 30 calories per serving.

Nutrition Information Per Serving	
Calories	285
Fat	1.7 grams
Percentage of Calories from Fat	5%
Cholesterol	0 milligram
Sodium	75 milligrams
Dietary Fiber	10.8 grams

pasta primavera

prep time: 25 minutes

cooking time: 20 minutes

ingredients: 1 cup chopped onion

4 cloves garlic, chopped

2 tablespoons + 2 tablespoons fat-free chicken broth

2 cans (15 ounces each) no salt tomato sauce

4 tablespoons honey

2 teaspoons crushed dried oregano

2 teaspoons crushed dried basil

pinch white pepper (optional)

1 large red pepper, cut in 1-inch strips

1½ cups sliced mushrooms

1½ cups yellow summer squash or zucchini,
cut in thin sticks 1½-inches long

1½ cups carrot cut in very thin sticks 1½-inches long

1½ cups small broccoli florets

2 tablespoons + 1 tablespoon balsamic vinegar

¾ cup peas

10 ounces whole grain pasta, cooked

¼ cup chopped green onion

2 tablespoons chopped fresh parsley

directions:

1. In medium saucepan, cook onion and garlic in 2 tablespoons broth 5-7 minutes or until softened, over medium high heat. Add tomato sauce, honey, oregano, basil and white pepper. Bring to a boil, reduce heat and simmer gently for 20 minutes.

2. In skillet or wok, combine red pepper, mushrooms, squash, carrots, broccoli and 2 tablespoons each balsamic vinegar and broth. Stir-fry over high heat until crisp tender, about 10 minutes; add peas and stir-fry an additional 2 minutes. Set aside.

3. Add 1 tablespoon balsamic vinegar to sauce and cook for 5 minutes.

4. Reserve 1 cup sauce to serve at the table; pour remaining sauce over cooked pasta and toss thoroughly. Add stir-fried vegetables and toss again thoroughly. Sprinkle green onion and parsley over top and serve immediately.

yield: 6 Servings

Cooking without Fat

YOU SAVE 316 CALORIES
This recipe contains 226 calories per serving
Typical recipe contains 542 calories per serving

spinach mushroom lasagna

It is difficult to imagine forgoing forever the pleasures of lasagna, but the traditional recipe, with its characteristic ground beef and thick layers of melted cheese, make this Italian specialty a disaster area for low-fat (and low-salt) cuisine. The creamy vegetable renditions are not an improvement either.

Happily, we have managed to pare down the fat without losing the dense, chewy, rich taste. The generously seasoned sauce compensates for the missing fat and salt; meaty mushrooms impart a substantive texture and robust flavor; chopped spinach enriches the filling.

As an added bonus, our simplified technique makes the preparation of Spinach Mushroom Lasagna an easy two-step operation. As you will notice when you read through the directions, the lasagna noodles are layered *uncooked* in the pan along with the other ingredients. This cuts out the laborious task of precooking the pasta, a job that is time-consuming and requires careful attention and handling to avoid overcooking or tearing the pasta. In our alternate approach, the uncooked pasta is tenderized during baking by absorbing liquid from the sauce that is trapped inside the covered pan. Remember, covering the pan is essential to the cooking of the pasta. This recipe can be doubled and baked in a larger pan.

We developed this recipe using Health Valley Fat-Free Chicken Broth. It has a full, rich flavor and only 30 calories per serving.

Nutrition Information Per Serving	
Calories	226
Fat	1.4 grams
Percentage of Calories from Fat	6%
Cholesterol	3 milligrams
Sodium	298 milligrams
Dietary Fiber	5 grams

spinach mushroom lasagna

prep time: 25 minutes   **cooking time:** 1-1/2 hours

ingredients: ⅔ cup chopped onion

4 cloves garlic, chopped

2-3 tablespoons fat-free chicken broth

2 cups sliced mushrooms

2 cans (15 ounces each) no salt tomato sauce

3 tablespoons honey

2 teaspoons crushed dried oregano

1 teaspoon crushed dried basil

pinch white pepper (optional)

1 10-ounce package frozen chopped spinach, thawed and well drained

2 cups nonfat cottage cheese

4 egg whites, lightly beaten

1½ teaspoons Italian seasoning blend

9 whole wheat lasagna noodles, uncooked

directions:

1. In medium saucepan, cook onion and garlic in broth for 3 minutes, until softened and beginning to color, over medium high heat. Add mushrooms and cook, stirring constantly, until they soften and release their juices.

2. To above mixture add tomato sauce, honey, oregano, basil and white pepper. Bring to a boil and simmer gently 5-10 minutes to blend flavors.

3. Preheat oven to 350°F.

4. Press as much moisture as possible from thawed frozen spinach. Combine with cottage cheese, egg whites and Italian seasoning blend.

5. Spread ½ cup sauce over bottom of an 8-inch baking pan. Cover with one third of the noodles (break noodles to fit 8-inch pan), 1¼ cups sauce and half the cottage cheese mixture.

6. Repeat this layering with noodles, 1¼ cups sauce and remaining cottage cheese.

7. Top with remaining noodles. Spread remaining sauce (about 1 cup) over top of lasagna.

8. Cover pan and bake at 350°F. 1 hour. Remove cover and bake 15-30 minutes longer, until pasta is tender.

yield: 6 Servings

Cooking without Fat

YOU SAVE 23 CALORIES
This recipe contains 123 calories per serving
Typical recipe contains 146 calories per serving

basic rice recipe

Rice is one of the oldest food crops known and is considered one of the two most important foods in the world (the other is wheat). Chinese records of rice cultivation go back 4,000 years. Rice was first introduced to the American colonies in the mid 17th century and has been a staple crop since then.

In the West, rice is generally a side dish – average annual consumption is only about 6 to 10 pounds per person. But in the East it is cherished for its simple nourishment and the per capita yearly intake is 200 to 400 pounds. The people of Japan, China, Thailand and the Philippines do not consider a meal to be complete without rice.

Rice is primarily carbohydrate, but also provides enough protein, thiamine (B1), niacin, phosphorus and potassium to be of significance. It is important to use brown rice – not white rice – in your diet. White rice, like white flour, has had the nutritious bran and germ removed, leaving mostly starch. Frequently rice is cooked with oil – we find this unnecessary in our recipes.

We developed this recipe using Health Valley Fat-Free Chicken Broth. It has a full, rich flavor and only 30 calories per serving.

Nutrition Information Per Serving

Calories	123
Fat	.6 gram
Percentage of Calories from Fat	4%
Cholesterol	0 milligram
Sodium	106 milligrams
Dietary Fiber	2.2 grams

basic rice recipe

prep time: 3 minutes

cooking time: 50 minutes

ingredients: 1 cup uncooked brown rice, rinsed and drained
1¾ cups fat-free chicken broth, vegetable stock
or water

directions for basic method:
1. Bring liquid of choice to a boil over high heat in a heavy saucepan.
2. Add rice, cover, and reduce heat to low setting so rice bubbles gently. Cook for 50 minutes or until rice is tender and liquid is absorbed.
3. If desired, uncover and let rice dry out 3-5 minutes before serving. Fluff with a fork.

directions for oven method:
1. Preheat oven to 350°F.
2. Heat liquid of choice to boiling point.
3. In medium casserole, combine rice and hot liquid. Cover and bake at 350°F. for 50-60 minutes, until rice is tender and liquid is absorbed.

yield: 6 Servings

quick ways to dress up rice

BEFORE RICE IS COOKED:

Almond-Flavored Rice–Instead of using plain water to cook rice, boil 2 cups water, add 2 almond tea bags and let steep 10 minutes. Remove tea bags and proceed as for basic rice.

AFTER RICE IS COOKED:

Tomato–Add 1 cup finely chopped tomatoes. Mix well.

Confetti–Add ½ cup chopped green pepper and ½ cup chopped red pepper. Mix well.

Parsley–Add ½ cup finely chopped parsley. Mix well.

Green Onion–Add ½ cup chopped green onion or chives.

YOU SAVE 54 CALORIES
This recipe contains 156 calories per serving
Typical recipe contains 210 calories per serving

greek rice

There are over 2,500 different varieties of rice, some of which are red, blue and even purple. What we call brown rice is simply the whole grain with its nutritious bran intact. It is actually cream colored and unlike white rice, which is flavorless, has a rich nutty taste.

Rice comes in three sizes: long grain, medium grain and short grain. Long grain rice is four to five times longer than it is wide. When cooked the grains are separate and fluffy. Short and medium grain rice have plumper grains that tend to be more tender and moist and cling together after cooking. Personal preference can be used to determine choice. Long grain rice is most popular for rice salads, stews, and chicken and fish dishes. Indian cooks generally like a dry rice and so choose long grain for pilafs; the Japanese and Chinese prefer short grain rice, which can be shaped by the fingers and easily handled with chopsticks.

Just about every nation has its rice specialty. This tasty dish originated in Greece.

We developed this recipe using Health Valley Fat-Free Chicken Broth. It has a full, rich flavor and only 30 calories per serving.

Nutrition Information Per Serving	
Calories	156
Fat	.8 gram
Percentage of Calories from Fat	5%
Cholesterol	0 milligram
Sodium	171 milligrams
Dietary Fiber	3.5 grams

greek rice

prep time: 10 minutes

cooking time: 55 minutes

ingredients: 1 cup long grain brown rice
⅓ cup chopped green onions
3 cloves garlic, minced
1 can (15 ounces) fat-free chicken broth
2 tablespoons chopped fresh parsley or
  1 tablespoon dried
2 tablespoons chopped fresh dill or
  1 tablespoon dried
1 package (10 ounces) frozen chopped spinach,
  thawed
1½ tablespoons lemon juice
2 tablespoons honey
lemon wedges

directions: 1. For moistness, wash rice. Combine with green onions and garlic in medium saucepan. Cook over medium high heat until rice dries and becomes aromatic, about 5 minutes.

2. Add chicken broth and bring to boil. Add parsley and dill. Cover and adjust heat to simmer. Cook for about 55 minutes, or until rice is tender.

3. Squeeze spinach gently to remove excess liquid. Stir into rice and cook for 5 minutes, or until heated through. Stir in lemon juice and honey.

4. Serve with lemon wedges for additional seasoning at the table.

yield: 6 Servings

YOU SAVE 166 CALORIES
This recipe contains 159 calories per serving
Typical recipe contains 325 calories per serving

spanish rice

Rice is said to be the staple food for about 6 out of every 10 people in the world. Not all of these people are Asian. Central and South Americans, too, find their meals are lacking without the customary rice and beans.

This highly acclaimed version of Spanish Rice is one of many. You will find it rich in flavor without the added calories of oil and cheese found in traditional recipes. It is the perfect accompaniment to chicken or fish. In fact, if you wish you can add leftover diced chicken or seafood and serve this as an entree. For a tasty paella, add some of each, along with a cup of cooked peas.

We developed this recipe using Health Valley Fat-Free Chicken Broth. It has a full, rich flavor and only 30 calories per serving.

Nutrition Information Per Serving	
Calories	159
Fat	1 gram
Percentage of Calories from Fat	6%
Cholesterol	0 milligram
Sodium	120 milligrams
Dietary Fiber	3.3 grams

spanish rice

prep time: 15 minutes

cooking time: 55 minutes

ingredients: 1¾ cups fat-free chicken broth
1 cup long grain brown rice
3 cloves garlic, chopped
¾ cup finely chopped onion
½ cup finely chopped green pepper
⅓ cup chopped celery
1 can (15 ounces) no salt tomatoes, undrained
1 teaspoon chili powder
½ teaspoon crushed dried oregano
½ teaspoon crushed dried basil
½ teaspoon paprika
2 teaspoons honey

directions: 1. In medium saucepan bring broth to a boil, over high heat. Add rice, cover and reduce heat to low setting, so rice bubbles gently. Cook for 50 minutes or until rice is tender and liquid is absorbed.

2. While rice is cooking, combine garlic, onion, green pepper, celery and 3-4 tablespoons juice from tomatoes in a large skillet. Saute over medium high heat 5-7 minutes or until softened.

3. Add tomatoes with remaining juice; coarsely cut up tomatoes. Stir in seasonings and honey, and bring to a boil; cover and reduce heat to simmer. Cook for 10 minutes or longer.

4. When rice is tender, stir into tomato mixture. Heat until rice mixture is hot and at desired consistency, approximately 5 minutes. Be careful not to overcook! Remove from heat and serve.

yield: 6 Servings

206

Cooking without Fat

YOU SAVE 98 CALORIES
This recipe contains 180 calories per serving
Typical recipe contains 278 calories per serving

hawaiian rice

This rice recipe is Hawaiian in style, rich in flavor, yet without the calorie-laden oil and nuts found in traditional recipes.

The mechanical milling and polishing of rice reduces spoilage, but it also depletes some of the protein and vitamins. In the late 19th century, Asia was stricken with beriberi, a disease that can inflame and degenerate the nerves, digestive system and heart. Scientific investigation identified the lack of the vitamin thiamine (B1) as the nutrient deficiency causing beriberi. By feeding rice bran to the sick, the disease could be reversed. Today, milled rice is commonly "enriched" with three of the B vitamins.

We developed this recipe using Health Valley Fat-Free Chicken Broth. It has a full, rich flavor and only 30 calories per serving.

Nutrition Information Per Serving	
Calories	180
Fat	1.0 gram
Percentage of Calories from Fat	5%
Cholesterol	0 milligram
Sodium	152 milligrams
Dietary Fiber	2.7 grams

hawaiian rice

prep time: 15 minutes

cooking time: 1 hour

ingredients: 1½ cups +2 tablespoons fat-free chicken broth
¾ cup long grain brown rice
½ cup chopped green pepper
¼ cup chopped celery
⅓ cup canned pineapple tidbits, packed in juice, drained
1 tablespoon honey
1 tablespoon apple cider vinegar
dash white pepper (optional)
½ cup finely chopped green onions

directions: 1. In medium saucepan, bring 1½ cups broth to a boil over high heat. Add rice, cover and reduce heat to low setting, so rice bubbles gently. Cook for 50 minutes or until rice is tender and liquid is absorbed.

2. When rice is almost done, saute green pepper and celery in 2 tablespoons broth in small skillet for 5-7 minutes or until softened, over medium high heat.

3. Add sauteed green pepper and celery, drained pineapple, honey, vinegar and white pepper to rice and mix well. Heat 2-3 minutes over medium high heat. Remove from heat, stir in green onions and serve.

yield: 4 Servings

Cooking without Fat

YOU SAVE 161 CALORIES
This recipe contains 127 calories per serving
Typical recipe contains 288 calories per serving

risi e bisi

Carbohydrates are far from boring with such classic dishes as this one. Risi e Bisi is a type of "risotti" or soft rice mixture. Risotto is to the north of Italy what pasta is to the south.

This fast and easy recipe uses tomatoes and a seasoning blend for added flavor rather than butter and cheese, making this dish 161 calories lighter than its traditional counterpart. Try Risi e Bisi as an excellent accompaniment to poultry and fish entrees.

We developed this recipe using Health Valley Fat-Free Chicken Broth. It has a full, rich flavor and only 30 calories per serving.

Nutrition Information Per Serving

Calories	127
Fat	.7 gram
Percentage of Calories from Fat	5%
Cholesterol	0 milligram
Sodium	128 milligrams
Dietary Fiber	3 grams

risi e bisi

prep time: 10 minutes

cooking time: 55 minutes

ingredients: 1¾ cups fat-free chicken broth
1 cup long grain brown rice
8 ounces canned no salt tomatoes in juice*
3 cloves garlic, finely chopped
1 cup peas, fresh or frozen
1 teaspoon Italian seasoning blend
dash white pepper (optional)
½ cup finely chopped green onion

directions: 1. In medium saucepan bring broth to a boil, over high heat. Add rice, cover and reduce heat to low setting, so rice bubbles gently. Cook for 50 minutes or until rice is tender and liquid is absorbed.
2. While rice is cooking, cut up canned tomatoes, reserve ¼ cup juice. Combine cut up tomatoes, ¼ cup juice, garlic, peas and seasonings in a large skillet. Saute over medium high heat 5-7 minutes or until garlic and peas are at desired doneness.
3. When rice is tender, stir into skillet. Heat until rice mixture is hot, approximately 5 minutes. Remove from heat, sprinkle with green onion and serve.

yield: 6 Servings

note: *Canned tomatoes are usually sold in 15-ounce cans. If you can't find an 8-ounce can, use half of the larger can.

YOU SAVE 104 CALORIES
This recipe contains 171 calories per serving
Typical recipe contains 275 calories per serving

barley pilaf

Barley is native to Mesopotamia, where it was ground to make bread and fermented to make beer. It is an easily digested grain and the flour milled from it is now being used in many wheat-free cookies. In the British Isles, barley water is an ancient remedy for an upset stomach.

We developed this recipe using Health Valley Fat-Free Chicken Broth. It has a full, rich flavor and only 30 calories per serving.

Nutrition Information Per Serving	
Calories	171
Fat	.6 gram
Percentage of Calories from Fat	3%
Cholesterol	0 milligram
Sodium	103 milligrams
Dietary Fiber	4.9 grams

barley pilaf

prep time: 15 minutes

cooking time: 1 hour

ingredients: 1¾ cups fat-free chicken broth
water
¾ cup barley
½ cup chopped onion
¼ cup finely chopped celery
1 cup chopped mushrooms
1 cup diced apple
⅓ cup raisins
dash of white pepper (optional)
2-3 teaspoons honey
1 tablespoon lemon juice
2 tablespoons fresh chopped parsley
1 red apple (optional)

directions: 1. In medium saucepan, bring broth and 6 ounces water to a boil over high heat. Add barley and reduce heat to low setting, so barley bubbles gently. Cook for 45 minutes or until barley is tender and liquid is absorbed.

2. In large skillet, saute onions and celery in 2 tablespoons water for about 2 minutes over medium high heat, add mushrooms and continue to saute for 3 minutes to release juices. Add ¼ cup water, diced apple, raisins and pepper; simmer, until apples are soft about 20 minutes.

3. Stir barley into apple mixture and simmer for 3 minutes to blend flavors.

4. Remove from heat. Stir in honey and lemon juice, fluff with a fork, replace cover, and let stand until serving.

5. Just before serving, sprinkle pilaf with fresh parsley, and if desired garnish with freshly cut red apple wedges.

yield: 6 Servings

Cooking without Fat BEANS

One of the best ways to benefit from a low-fat diet is to select more bean dishes at meal time. Not only are most beans practically fat-free, current studies show them to be rich in the kind of fiber that is most active in reducing blood cholesterol levels, particularly the low-density lipoproteins (LDL's) associated with increased risk of heart disease. An abundance of complex carbohydrates also makes beans beneficial in regulating blood sugar and bowel function.

Many people are surprised by the large amount of protein that beans contain. They are also an excellent source of B vitamins, especially thiamine, riboflavin and niacin, and the minerals phosphorus, iron, magnesium, zinc and potassium.

In addition to being so nutritious, beans make excellent eating. If they didn't we doubt they would play such an important part in so many cuisines. All the way from Latin America to Eastern Europe, bean spe-

Cooking without Fat

cialties abound. We present several examples in this chapter. While designed as the focal point of the meal, these dishes can also be served as a vegetable accompaniment alongside a simple fish or poultry entree.

Bean dishes are easy to prepare and can even be quick if you plan ahead. Since beans require lengthy cooking from the dried state, cook up a pot full at a time and keep them refrigerated for use over the course of a week. Alternately, most beans can be pressure cooked for more immediate use. In fact, pressure cooking times range from a mere 5 minutes for soaked limas to less than 50 minutes for the longest cooking varieties without soaking. To guide you, we have outlined all the steps of bean cookery, including a table of cooking times for different methods.

If you still cannot find the time to incorporate bean preparation into your lifestyle, a no-work option remains – canned beans. Although the texture of canned beans is softer and the taste more muted, they are still brimming with bean nutrition. A one-pound can of beans measures about 1-1/2 cups beans. When buying canned beans read the label carefully. Give preference to organic and no salt offerings. Avoid those with added sweeteners and starches. Finding an unsalted brand can be a challenge. If they are not available, you can reduce the sodium significantly by placing the beans in a colander or strainer and running cold water over them for two minutes. When using canned beans in a recipe cook gently for the minimum amount of time specified or just long enough to heat them through. Overcooking renders canned beans mushy.

At Health Valley we believe so strongly in the value of beans in the diet that we manufacture several canned products to make your hectic days easier. You can eat our fat-free chilis as they come, or use them to turn out some of the reduced-work vegetarian entrees in this chapter.

Basic Bean Cookery

1. Rinse dried beans

2. Soak using one of the following methods:

All-Day or Overnight Soak
Submerge beans in three times their volume of water (for 1 cup beans use 3 cups water). Cover and let soak 8 hours or longer. If beans will not be cooked within about 15 hours, place in the refrigerator to prevent sprouting. Soak at night to cook in the morning, soak all day for evening preparation.

Quick Soak Method
Submerge beans in three times their volume of water in a large pot. Bring to boil. Boil 2 minutes. Remove from heat, cover and let beans stand in soak water for at least 1 hour.

Note: Lentils, split peas and baby lima beans do not need soaking. Beans that will be pressure cooked can be soaked or not, determined by what is most suited to your time schedule.

3. Cook the soaked beans. For maximum vitamin retention cook in the soaking liquid. If you are plagued by bean gas, however, you may prefer to discard this liquid and start with fresh water. Some of the indigestible carbohydrates that contribute to bean gas dissolve in the soak water and many people claim they are less reactive to beans if they get rid of this water. You need only add as much water as you discard. (Much of the original soaking liquid is absorbed by the beans; measure what you pour off and replenish by this amount.)

Bring beans and water to a boil. Reduce heat as low as possible so liquid is just simmering. Cover and cook until beans are tender.

For pressure cooking, bring beans and water to boil, skim any scum from the surface and cover the pressure cooker. Bring pressure up over medium high heat. Reduce heat to just maintain pressure and cook for the time indicated. When cooking is complete, reduce pressure either by letting the pot cool down on its own, waiting 5 minutes and running under cold water, or slowly turning the quick steam release valve on newer cookers, allowing the gas to escape gradually. Do not open the valve all at once.

4. On average, 1 cup dry beans yields 2½ to 3 cups cooked beans.

Bean Cooking Chart

Beans (soaked)	In saucepan	In pressure cooker
Black beans	1 to 1½ hours	6 minutes
Black-eyed peas	1 to 1½ hours	5 minutes
Garbanzos	2 to 3 hours	18 minutes
Great Northern	1 to 1½ hours	7 minutes
Kidney beans	1½ to 2 hours	8 to 10 minutes
Lima beans (large)	1 hour	5 minutes
Navy beans	1 to 1½ hours	7 minutes
Pintos	1½ to 2 hours	7 to 8 minutes
Soy beans	3 hours	16 to 18 minutes

Beans (unsoaked)	In saucepan	In pressure cooker
Black beans	not recommended	25 minutes
Black-eyed peas	not recommended	15 minutes
Garbanzos	not recommended	48 minutes
Great Northern	not recommended	35 minutes
Kidney beans	not recommended	35 to 40 minutes
Lentils*	45 minutes	10 minutes
Lima beans (large)	not recommended	15 minutes
Lima beans (small)	45 to 60 minutes	not recommended
Navy beans	not recommended	30 minutes
Pintos	not recommended	35 minutes
Soy beans	not recommended	45 minutes
Split peas*	45 minutes	10 minutes

*Some authorities advise not to cook these beans in the pressure cooker as they can clog the steam hole.

Cooking without Fat

YOU SAVE 205 CALORIES
This recipe contains 192 calories per serving
Typical recipe contains 397 calories per serving

sweet and sour cabbage and beans

Nutritionists rank cabbage, a member of the cruciferous family along with broccoli, cauliflower and Brussels sprouts, among the most important vegetables to include in our diet.

Rather than taking the time to stuff cabbage rolls, why not combine all the delicious components in a simple low fat stew. By serving these sweet and sour vegetables on rice you realize all the taste sensations of the more laborious, calorie-laden traditional stuffed cabbage.

Nutrition Information Per Serving	
Calories	192
Fat	.7 gram
Percentage of Calories from Fat	3%
Cholesterol	0 milligram
Sodium	54 milligrams
Dietary Fiber	7.2 grams

sweet and sour cabbage and beans

prep time: 10 minutes

cooking time: 15 minutes

ingredients: ¾ pound cabbage cut in strips ½-inch wide (6 cups)
1 cup no salt tomato sauce
1 tablespoon lemon juice
1 teaspoon apple cider vinegar
1 tablespoon apple juice concentrate
2 tablespoons honey
1 teaspoon dijon mustard
¼ cup raisins
1 large clove garlic, chopped
¼ teaspoon celery seed
1 teaspoon onion powder
dash white pepper (optional)
1½ cups cooked great northern beans, drained

directions: 1. In large saucepan, combine all ingredients except beans. Bring cabbage mixture to a boil while stirring. Cover and simmer 10 minutes.

2. Add beans to cabbage and cook 5 minutes to heat through.

yield: 4 Servings

note: This dish serves 4 as a main entree and 6 as an accompaniment.

Cooking without Fat

YOU SAVE 60 CALORIES
This recipe contains 170 calories per serving
Typical recipe contains 230 calories per serving

southwestern garbanzo beans

Garbanzos, derived from the Spanish, is another name for chickpeas. In fact, this bean goes by a variety of nomenclatures depending upon where you are in the world. The Italian word for chickpeas is *ceci*. When the French occupied Sicily in the Middle Ages, the Sicilians would determine if a person was French or Sicilian by asking him to pronounce ceci (the correct pronunciation is 'tchay-tchee'). If the person failed to pronounce the word correctly, he was put to death. On the basis of this, we'd have to say that good elocution is as important to your health as good nutrition.

As in many Southwestern dishes, lime, coriander (and its fresh counterpart, cilantro), cumin, and hot pepper are integral seasonings. The dates in this dish add a touch of sweetness to offset the gentle bite of the spices.

Southwestern Garbanzos can be served warm or at room temperature. Dishes like this one that do not require immediate service help to make cooking a more relaxed experience. They are especially compatible with buffet service or for entertaining when the cook wants to socialize with the company rather than work in the kitchen.

Nutrition Information Per Serving

Calories	170
Fat	2.2 grams
Percentage of Calories from Fat	12%
Cholesterol	0 milligram
Sodium	255 milligrams
Dietary Fiber	7.1 grams

southwestern garbanzo beans

prep time: 15 minutes

cooking time: 20 minutes

ingredients: 1 cup chopped onion
1 large clove garlic, chopped
1 tablespoon finely chopped fresh ginger
1 cup chopped ripe tomato
2 tablespoons + ⅔ cup water
1½ teaspoons ground cumin
1 teaspoon ground coriander
⅛ teaspoon cayenne pepper (optional)
2 cups cooked garbanzo beans, drained
1 tablespoon honey
¼ cup chopped dates
1 tablespoon lime juice
½ lime, cut in wedges, for garnish (optional)
1 tablespoon chopped fresh cilantro, for garnish (optional)

directions: 1. In a medium skillet, combine onion, garlic, ginger, tomato and 2 tablespoons water. Saute over medium high heat until tomato and onion soften and all liquid has cooked off, about 5-8 minutes.

2. Add seasonings. Cook briefly to blend flavors.

3. Add beans, ⅔ cup water, honey and dates. Bring to boil, cover, reduce heat and simmer 10-15 minutes.

4. Stir in lime juice.

5. To serve, place in serving bowl. Garnish with lime wedges and cilantro, if desired.

yield: 4 Servings

note: This dish serves 4 as a main entree and 6 as an accompaniment.

Cooking without Fat

YOU SAVE 205 CALORIES
This recipe contains 261 calories per serving
Typical recipe contains 466 calories per serving

spanish garden chili

Combining Health Valley Fat-Free Vegetarian Chili with Black Beans with grains and vegetables consolidates all the essential components of the meal in one pot. This outstanding rendition won everyone's praise. It is easy to prepare and satisfies the heartiest of appetites. Serve with warm tortillas.

We developed this recipe using Health Valley Fat-Free Mild Vegetarian Chili with Black Beans. It's the only fat-free chili available that contains 5,000 IU of beta carotene.

Nutrition Information Per Serving	
Calories	261
Fat	1.1 grams
Percentage of Calories from Fat	4%
Cholesterol	.1 milligram
Sodium	287 milligrams
Dietary Fiber	13.7 grams

spanish garden chili

prep time: 10 minutes

cooking time: 30 minutes

ingredients: ½ cup chopped onion
½ cup diced green pepper
1 can (5 ounces) diced green chiles
2 tablespoons chicken or vegetable broth
½ cup uncooked bulgur
1 can (15 ounces) no salt tomato sauce
1 can (15 ounces) fat-free chili (mild or spicy according to taste)
1 cup corn kernels, fresh or frozen

topping
plain nonfat yogurt
chopped fresh cilantro
chopped jalapeno pepper (optional)
chopped green onion

directions: 1. In medium saucepan, combine onion, green pepper, chiles and broth. Cook over medium high heat about 5 minutes, until vegetables begin to soften.
2. Add bulgur and cook 1 minute longer, stirring constantly. Add tomato sauce and bring to boil.
3. Lower heat, cover, and simmer 15 minutes, until bulgur is just tender.
4. Add chili and corn. Cook uncovered 10 minutes, stirring occasionally, to heat through.
5. Serve in bowls topped with yogurt, cilantro, jalapeno peppers and green onion to taste.

yield: 4 Servings

224

YOU SAVE 180 CALORIES
This recipe contains 279 calories per serving
Typical recipe contains 459 calories per serving

chili pie

Chili Pie is a quickly assembled entree, thanks once again to our convenient and nourishing fat-free canned chili. In this recipe the chili is topped with a savory, corn-studded, cornbread cover. Here is proof that cornbread can be made successfully not only without bacon drippings, but without adding fat at all.

We developed this recipe using Health Valley Fat-Free Mild Vegetarian Chili with Black Beans. It's the only fat-free chili available that contains 5,000 IU of beta carotene.

Nutrition Information Per Serving

Calories	279
Fat	1.1 grams
Percentage of Calories from Fat	3%
Cholesterol	1.1 milligrams
Sodium	366 milligrams
Dietary Fiber	12.6 grams

chili pie

prep time: 15 minutes

cooking time: 40 minutes

ingredients: 2 cans (15 ounces each) fat-free chili (mild or spicy according to taste)

2 cups cooked black beans, drained

¾ cup corn kernels, fresh or frozen

½ cup chopped onion

2 tablespoons whole wheat flour

½ teaspoon chili powder (optional)

topping

¾ cup corn meal

⅓ cup whole wheat flour

1 teaspoon baking soda

¾ cup buttermilk (low fat if available)

2 egg whites

¼ cup honey

directions: 1. Preheat oven to 375°F.

2. Mash black beans with fork in medium saucepan.

3. Stir in chili, corn, chopped onion, flour and chili powder if desired. Cook on medium high heat for 10 minutes, stirring frequently. Transfer mixture to a 8" x 11" glass rectangular baking dish.

4. In a small bowl, mix topping ingredients together with a fork until well blended, and spread on top of chili mixture.

5. Bake in the center of the oven at 375°F. for 20-25 minutes or until topping is set and nicely browned.

yield: 8 Servings

Cooking without Fat

tex mex tortillas

When choosing the tortillas, look for a brand that contains nothing more than corn, lime and water. Reject those that have any added shortening. There are a number of offerings free of preservatives and other chemical additives and these are worth seeking out. Since tortillas store well in the freezer, when you find a brand you like, stock up.

We developed this recipe using Health Valley Fat-Free Mild Vegetarian Chili with Black Beans. It's the only fat-free chili available that contains 5,000 IU of beta carotene.

Nutrition Information Per Serving

Calories	281
Fat	1.3 grams
Percentage of Calories from Fat	4%
Cholesterol	.5 milligram
Sodium	341 milligrams
Dietary Fiber	10.6 grams

tex mex tortillas

prep time: 15 minutes

cooking time: 10 minutes

ingredients: 1 can (15 ounces) fat-free chili (mild or spicy according to taste)

1½ tablespoons no salt tomato paste

8 corn tortillas

1 cup chopped tomato

½ cup chopped green pepper

½ cup chopped onion

½ cup plain nonfat yogurt

salsa

chopped fresh cilantro (optional)

directions: 1. Preheat oven to 350°F.

2. Combine chili and tomato paste in medium saucepan. Bring to boil and simmer uncovered over low heat 5-10 minutes, until thickened.

3. Place tortillas in covered baking dish and bake at 350°F. for 10 minutes or until warmed through.

4. To serve, place ⅓ cup chili in a strip down center of each tortilla. Cover with 2 tablespoons chopped tomato, 1 tablespoon chopped green pepper, 1 tablespoon chopped onion and 1 tablespoon yogurt. Add salsa to taste, fold tortilla over filling and serve.

5. Garnish with chopped fresh cilantro.

yield: 4 Servings

Cooking
without
Fat

YOU SAVE 178 CALORIES
This recipe contains 312 calories per serving
Typical recipe contains 490 calories per serving

black bean chili bake

This recipe is great when you need a quick meal. It takes only five minutes to prepare and 15 minutes to cook. What's more, the ingredients are easy to keep on hand.

We developed this recipe using Health Valley Fat-Free Mild Vegetarian Chili with Black Beans. It's the only fat-free chili available that contains 5,000 IU of beta carotene. We also used Health Valley Blue Corn Flakes.

Nutrition Information Per Serving

Calories	312
Fat	.8 gram
Percentage of Calories from Fat	2%
Cholesterol	.5 milligram
Sodium	460 milligrams
Dietary Fiber	19.3 grams

black bean chili bake

prep time: 5 minutes

cooking time: 15 minutes

ingredients: 1 can (15 ounces) fat-free chili (mild or spicy according to taste)

½ cup frozen corn kernels

¼ teaspoon onion powder

¼ teaspoon garlic powder

¼ teaspoon ground cumin

1 cup corn flakes, crushed

plain nonfat yogurt for garnish (optional)

directions: 1. Preheat oven to 375°F.

2. Combine chili, corn and seasonings in a shallow 1 quart baking dish. Sprinkle crushed corn flakes over entire perimeter, leaving an open area in center.

3. Bake in a 375°F. oven for 15 minutes, until hot and bubbly.

4. Remove from oven and if desired, spoon yogurt onto exposed chili in center.

yield: 2 Servings

Cooking without Fat

YOU SAVE 322 CALORIES
This recipe contains 228 calories per serving
Typical recipe contains 550 calories per serving

moroccan eggplant and garbanzo beans

Eggplant is a member of the nightshade family, which includes tomatoes, red and green peppers, and potatoes. While this vegetable is quite popular in many parts of the world it has been largely ignored in the United States. Most peoples' exposure is limited to greasy eggplant parmesan.

One possible reason eggplant is not more popular is the involved steps many cookbooks outline for its use. It's an old wives' tale that eggplant has to be peeled, sliced, salted and weighted for a couple of hours to squeeze out the juice. Just slice and use it – it really doesn't even have to be peeled unless the skin has been waxed or is quite tough.

If you have worked with eggplant before you know it is like a sponge when it comes to absorbing oil. Although frying is the most well known approach, by steaming the eggplant, as we do here, you dramatically reduce the fat content of the finished dish, while retaining the soft, egglike texture.

In India, the Mideast, and North Africa, eggplant is frequently teamed with garbanzo beans (more commonly known as chickpeas in those areas of the world) on the menu. When you taste this appealing combination you will recognize why. The creaminess of well-cooked eggplant contrasts perfectly with the firm, crunchy bean.

Raisins, while not essential to success, add an interesting dimension to this North African inspired rendition. If you omit the raisins, chutney would make a nice accompaniment.

This dish serves 4 as a main entree and 6-8 as an accompaniment.

Nutrition Information Per Serving

Calories	228
Fat	2.4 grams
Percentage of Calories from Fat	9%
Cholesterol	.1 milligram
Sodium	314 milligrams
Dietary Fiber	10.4 grams

moroccan eggplant and garbanzo beans

prep time: 15 minutes

cooking time: 15 minutes

ingredients: 1 medium eggplant

1 large onion, cut in thin crescents

1 large clove garlic, chopped

1 medium green pepper, cut in 1-inch pieces

1/8 teaspoon crushed red pepper flakes (optional)

1 cup water

1 teaspoon curry powder

1 tablespoon lemon juice

2 teaspoons honey

3 tablespoons no salt ketchup

2 cups cooked garbanzo beans, drained

1/2 cup raisins (optional)

garnish 1 cup chopped tomato

1 orange cut in wedges

plain nonfat yogurt

directions:
1. To prepare eggplant, peel and cut into 1-inch pieces (about 4 cups). Place on vegetable steamer, set over boiling water, cover and cook for 12 minutes, until tender but not mushy.

2. In saucepan or skillet, combine onion, garlic, green pepper, red pepper flakes, and 2 tablespoons water. Cover, place over low heat for 10 minutes, or until green pepper softens.

3. Add curry powder and cook briefly to combine with vegetables. Then add lemon juice, honey, ketchup and remaining water and bring to boil.

4. Stir in garbanzos, eggplant, and raisins, and simmer uncovered for 5 minutes.

5. Garnish with tomato, orange and yogurt.

yield: 4 Servings

Cooking without Fat TOFU

Tofu is made by cooking soybeans with purified water and pureeing this into a creamy soy milk. A precipitant is then added to the milk to separate it into protein-rich curds and liquid whey (quite similar to the steps taken to produce cheese curds from animal milk). In the process, the protein in the soybean is concentrated to make tofu comparable to meat, fish, poultry, eggs and dairy products. That's why in Asia tofu is sometimes referred to as "the meat of the fields" or "soy cheese."

The assets of tofu are many, including not only its remarkable culinary capacity, but also its commendable nutritional profile and its convenience.

There are several styles of tofu on the market, usually designated on the label as soft, firm and extra firm tofu. It is the differences between these forms that make them more appropriate to certain recipes and methods of preparation. The distinction from soft to extra firm is determined by water content; the more water, the softer the texture. Soft tofu is well suited for creamy dressings, dips and dessert recipes such as pudding or pie filling; firm tofu is best for recipes that call for slicing or dicing and subsequent cooking.

Freshness is an important attribute to look for when buying tofu. Tofu is sold in sealed packages or tubs with a freshness code date on the wrapper. Be sure to check the code date, just as you do with dairy products. Once you get tofu home, keep it in the refrigerator. If you open the package and use only part of the contents, the remainder should be transferred to a deep bowl or container and covered with cold water. Replace the water with fresh water daily. Use tofu within a week of opening the package.

Tofu can be sliced into individual portions, wrapped in freezer paper, and frozen. This changes the texture and makes the tofu more like cooked chicken or ground beef. Many people like to use defrosted frozen tofu as a replacement for these ingredients in a recipe and you may occasionally come across cookbooks calling for frozen tofu as an ingredient.

Tofu is a nutritionally valuable food, especially for strict vegetarians. We use light tofu in all of our recipes because one serving contains 28% of calories from fat, much less than regular tofu. All of the recipes in this section meet our strict criteria of less than 15% of calories from fat so they are suitable for even the lowest fat diets.

3 kinds of tofu
soft, firm, extra firm

available in several styles of packaging, tofu can come dry-packed or packed in water—it's easy to drain and use

blend tofu with honey for a thick puree

mash tofu with baked potato for a great stuffing

crumble tofu and sauté with onions and garlic

slice tofu in cubes and use in place of meat for a protein-rich meatless dish

YOU SAVE 182 CALORIES
This recipe contains 266 calories per serving
Typical recipe contains 448 calories per serving

stuffed peppers

Stuffed peppers are extremely popular in Greek and Slavic cuisines and if you glance through cookbooks you will discover many delicious variations of this dish. Most of the recipes, however, are based on fatty ground lamb or beef, or simply omit the meat in favor of an all-grain filling. While these meat-free versions are lower in fat and often extremely tasty, they rarely take protein into account.

By including crumbled tofu in the filling we have added back the protein. Now you can enjoy low-fat stuffed peppers without missing out on any essential nutrition.

About Green & Red Peppers
Red peppers are simply green peppers that have been left on the vine until mature. When choosing either kind, look for bright color, firm and thick fleshed body and glossy skin. Avoid pale peppers or those that are shrivelled or bruised. They'll keep for about a week in the crisper of your refrigerator. Green bell peppers are an outstanding source of vitamin C, and red bell peppers are even better – plus being a fabulous source of vitamin A.

When choosing peppers for stuffing, try to pick ones that stand upright on their own. If you cannot find a properly sized pepper, you can cut a thin slice from the bottom to make an even base.

Nutrition Information Per Serving	
Calories	266
Fat	1.8 grams
Percentage of Calories from Fat	6%
Cholesterol	0 milligram
Sodium	74 milligrams
Dietary Fiber	5.8 grams

stuffed peppers

prep time: 20 minutes

cooking time: 40 minutes

ingredients:
4 small to medium green peppers
4 sun-dried tomatoes
6 ounces firm light tofu, drained
½ cup chopped onion
4 cloves garlic, chopped
1 teaspoon crushed dried oregano
1 teaspoon crushed dried basil
2 cups cooked brown rice
¼ cup raisins
1 cup + ¼ cup no salt tomato sauce
1 tablespoon + 2 teaspoons honey
pinch cayenne pepper (optional)

directions:
1. Preheat oven to 350°F.
2. Cut tops from peppers, remove seeds and tough inner ribs and steam 4 minutes to soften slightly. Remove peppers from steamer and invert to drain. Place tomatoes in boiling water in steamer base and blanch 2 minutes. Drain and chop.
3. Crumble tofu and combine in a skillet with onion and garlic. Saute over medium high heat until tofu is dry. Remove from heat and add sundried tomatoes, oregano, basil, brown rice, raisins, 1 cup tomato sauce and 1 tablespoon honey. Mix well.
4. Fill peppers with tofu-rice mixture and stand upright in a baking pan. Mix remaining ¼ cup tomato sauce with remaining 2 teaspoons honey and a pinch of cayenne. Spoon sauce on top of each pepper.
5. Pour hot water around peppers to a depth of about 1 inch and bake in a 350°F. oven for 40 minutes, or until peppers are tender and sauce on top is thick.

yield: 4 Servings

Cooking without Fat

YOU SAVE 234 CALORIES
This recipe contains 117 calories per serving
Typical recipe contains 351 calories per serving

southwestern frittata

For this frittata, we take the classic food of the east, tofu, and prepare it southwestern-style with onions, pepper, potatoes and salsa. This easy-to-prepare recipe is a good choice for breakfast, lunch or dinner. For a larger frittata, double the ingredients and prepare in a larger pan.

You will find this tofu dish high on taste; all that is lacking are the high calories, cholesterol and sodium found in the traditional version made with whole eggs, oil, salt and cheese.

We developed this recipe using Health Valley Fat-Free Chicken Broth. It has a full, rich flavor and only 30 calories per serving.

Nutrition Information Per Serving	
Calories	117
Fat	1 gram
Percentage of Calories from Fat	8%
Cholesterol	0 milligram
Sodium	174 milligrams
Dietary Fiber	2.6 grams

southwestern frittata

prep time: 20 minutes

cooking time: 15 minutes

ingredients: 2-4 tablespoons fat-free chicken broth
1 cup thin skinned boiling potatoes, diced
½ cup chopped onion
⅓ cup chopped green pepper
½ teaspoon +½ teaspoon chili powder
5 ounces firm light tofu, drained
5 egg whites
1 teaspoon honey
pinch cayenne pepper
½ teaspoon cumin
6 tablespoon drained salsa
paprika

directions: 1. Steam or boil diced potatoes for 15 minutes or until almost soft.
2. In 10-inch non-stick frying pan, saute potato, onion and green pepper in chicken broth for 10 minutes or until all vegetables are soft. Stir in ½ teaspoon chili powder.
3. Puree tofu with egg whites and honey in blender or food processor. Mix in remaining ½ teaspoon chili powder, cayenne and cumin. Spread vegetables around in skillet evenly and pour tofu mixture uniformly over vegetables, cover and cook over low heat about 10 minutes. Add 6 tablespoons drained salsa to center and cook for an additional 5 minutes or until firm and puffed.
4. Garnish with paprika; cut into wedges and serve immediately.

yield: 3 Servings

note: Serving Suggestion–serve with no salt ketchup or additional salsa.

Cooking without Fat

YOU SAVE 243 CALORIES
This recipe contains 98 calories per serving
Typical recipe contains 341 calories per serving

italian frittata

This Italian seasoned frittata makes a delightful main dish or side serving for any time of day. It puffs up exceptionally well and the rice gives it a satisfying texture.

You will find this dish is not only delicious, it has no cholesterol, is low in fat and high in nutrition. It is an excellent source of protein, potassium, iron, vitamin C, thiamine, riboflavin, niacin, calcium, phosphorus and dietary fiber. Be sure to make this nutritional powerhouse often.

Nutrition Information Per Serving	
Calories	98
Fat	1 gram
Percentage of Calories from Fat	9%
Cholesterol	0 milligram
Sodium	72 milligrams
Dietary Fiber	1.7 grams

italian frittata

prep time: 20 minutes

cooking time: 15 minutes

ingredients: ½ cup chopped onion
2 cloves garlic, minced
¾ cup zucchini, chopped
⅓ cup green pepper, chopped
⅓ cup celery, chopped
2 tablespoons red wine vinegar
4 ounces firm light tofu, drained
5 egg whites
½ teaspoon honey
⅛ teaspoon white pepper (optional)
1 teaspoon Italian seasoning
¼ teaspoon tumeric
¾ cup cooked brown rice
paprika

directions:
1. In 10-inch non-stick frying pan, saute onion, garlic, zucchini, green pepper and celery in red wine vinegar for 10-15 minutes, or until all vegetables are soft.
2. Puree tofu with egg whites, honey, pepper, Italian seasoning and tumeric in blender or food processor. Spread vegetables evenly in skillet and pour tofu mixture uniformly over them. Cover and cook over low heat 1-2 minutes until partially set. Stir in cooked brown rice, cover and cook until mixture is completely firm and nicely puffed, about 12 minutes.
3. Garnish with paprika; cut into wedges and serve immediately.

yield: 3 Servings

note: Serving Suggestion – serve with no salt ketchup.

Cooking without Fat

YOU SAVE 166 CALORIES
This recipe contains 254 calories per serving
Typical recipe contains 420 calories per serving

tofu mushroom stuffed baked potatoes

Stuffed baked potatoes are admired in restaurants and imitated at home by many cooks. Unfortunately, typical recipes call for lots of butter, salt, and cheese and the formerly innocent potato has disastrous repercussions on your diet when you compute the fat, sodium and calories. Most menus also ignore the potential of this vegetable dish to provide main dish protein, in addition to all the other important nutrients we derive from potatoes.

For potato-lovers, Tofu Mushroom Stuffed Potatoes offer the best of all situations. They are lean when it comes to fat, but ample in protein. The savory mushroom and onion filling, agreeably seasoned with tangy mustard and a touch of honey to arouse the flavor, holds its own without salt.

For the creamiest texture, soft tofu is preferred. Unless you are skilled in the techniques of food processing, we suggest you whip the filling by hand. If you are careful, you can blend them in a food processor; however, just a few seconds too long in this powerful machine makes cooked potatoes gluey.

A generous salad and whole grain breadstuff is all you need to complete the menu. If you prefer to serve Tofu Mushroom Stuffed Baked Potatoes as a side dish, figure one-half potato per person rather than a whole.

About Potatoes

The potato is nearly nutritionally perfect. An average size tuber, weighing in at 3-1/3 to 4 ounces, packs seven of the eight essential amino acids and a commendable supply of vitamin C, B vitamins, iron, potassium, and magnesium into a mere 88 to 110 calories. This fat- and salt-free vegetable is also extremely versatile. With these assets, potatoes should appear on your table often.

Nutrition Information Per Serving	
Calories	254
Fat	1.1 grams
Percentage of Calories from Fat	4%
Cholesterol	0 milligram
Sodium	215 milligrams
Dietary Fiber	3 grams

tofu mushroom stuffed baked potatoes

prep time: 20 minutes

cooking time: 60-80 minutes

ingredients: 4 medium to large baking potatoes
1⅓ cups chopped onion
1⅓ cups chopped mushrooms
½ teaspoon sage
dash white pepper (optional)
8 ounces firm light tofu, drained and mashed (1½ cups)
3 tablespoons finely chopped parsley
1 tablespoon prepared mustard, spicy or dijon
½ teaspoon honey
paprika

directions: 1. Bake potatoes in preheated 425°F. oven for 40-60 minutes. In the meantime, you can begin to prepare filling.

2. Combine onion, mushrooms and sage in skillet. Cover and saute 5 minutes over medium heat, until mushrooms become tender and release their juices. Season with white pepper.

3. Cut baked potatoes in half lengthwise and scoop out insides, leaving a shell that is about ¼-inch thick.

4. Combine scooped out potato with tofu, parsley, mustard and honey. Mash together making the mixture as smooth as possible. Stir in mushroom-onion mixture.

5. Fill potato skins with tofu-potato mixture, mounding the filling above the shell. Sprinkle potatoes generously with paprika. Place on baking sheet and bake at 375°F. for 20 minutes.

yield: 4 Servings

Cooking without Fat SOUPS

While the notion of "comfort food" is a recent one, its reality is probably age old. Simply put, comfort foods are those that give emotional succor – they make us feel safe and secure. For the most part, comfort foods are unique to the individual. Some people are nurtured by the foods of their heritage, some by the foods of their childhood. While chocolate is a common comfort food for many, for others pasta is just as likely to do the trick. Unfortunately, the same foods that nourish our spirit do not necessarily nourish our bodies.

Soup, however, fills all the criteria for a truly nurturing food. It makes us feel good both physically and emotionally. Perhaps this is due to the fact that soup is as basic a food as bread and has been the cornerstone of most cuisines in the world since antiquity.

Try to include a bowl of soup daily as part of your healthy way of eating. We say this because soup provides a variety of benefits: (1) Properly prepared soup can be a source of significant nutrition, especially when the ingredients include fresh vegetables, whole grains, and legumes. (2) Starting your meal with soup gets your digestive system going and wakes up

Cooking without Fat

your taste buds so you can really enjoy the meal and digest it properly.
(3) Soup takes the edge off your appetite so you won't overeat. (4) Soup
makes people feel good.

A recent study showed when people started their meals with soup, they
consumed about 20% fewer calories than they normally ate. This explains
why researchers have found that people who eat soup regularly have an
easier time maintaining their ideal weight. Of course, this excludes
creamed soups which are usually high in calories and sodium and may
derive over 50% of their calories from fat.

Typical Creamed Soups	Calories	Fat gm	Sodium mg	% Calories Fat
Cream of Mushroom Soup	203	13.6	1076	60
Cream of Chicken Soup	191	11.5	1046	54
Cream of Celery Soup	165	9.7	1010	52
Cheese Soup	230	14.6	1020	57

Eating soup helps make it easy for you to fulfill the dietary guidelines
for healthier eating. By including fresh vegetables in our recipes, such as
Garden Vegetable Soup and Hot Borscht, most are superior sources of
vitamins A and C.

Keep in mind that soup recipes are really only guidelines. No food is as
amenable as soup is to change. Feel free to be creative by using whatever
vegetables and herbs are at their freshest and in season.

A Healthy Alternative for Extra Convenience

Although soup is such a valuable food, with today's hectic schedules people often lack the time or inclination to make it from scratch. This is why Health Valley offers a complete line of your favorite soups, each prepared with the same wholesome ingredients you would use for home-made soup. So when you want a delicious bowl of soup made the healthy way – without added fat and low in salt – and you also want the convenience of 5 minute preparation time, open a lead-free can of Health Valley Fat-Free Soup.

Cooking without Fat

YOU SAVE 10 CALORIES
This recipe contains 36 calories per 1 cup serving
Typical recipe contains 46 calories per 1 cup serving

chicken broth

Chicken broth is a valuable commodity in the low fat kitchen because it substitutes so well for fat in sauteing and adds savor to fat- and salt-free dishes. Of course, its use can only be justified if it is made with wholesome ingredients and to low fat, low salt specifications. At Health Valley we make our canned Fat-Free Chicken Broth extra rich by using high grade seasonings and cooking the chicken slowly to draw out all the flavor. As a result, our broth works especially well in recipes.

In evaluating a commercial broth for purchase you will want to look for (and avoid) the following ingredients: salt, hydrogenated vegetable fat, hydrolyzed vegetable protein, monosodium glutamate, disodium guanylate and disodium inosinate. We have included a recipe for chicken broth if you choose to make one from scratch. Although few people take the time to make homemade stock any more, it is not difficult to do.

The long slow simmering called for in this recipe maximizes the flavor extracted from the chicken and the vegetables. Thus, despite the absence of added salt, this broth is very flavorful. Be sure to keep the heat as low as possible; too vigorous cooking will cause the liquid to evaporate and reduce the volume of broth in the end.

When the Chicken Broth is done, skin and bone the chicken pieces and reserve them for salad or your favorite cooked chicken recipe. If you have cooked the chicken gently, the meat will be surprisingly tender and will not have the flat, spent taste of a bird that has been devitalized by stock.

Nutrition Information Per Serving	
Calories	36
Fat	Fat-Free*
Cholesterol	0 milligram
Sodium	309 milligrams
Dietary Fiber	0 gram

*All foods contain some fat. Less than .5 gram of fat per serving is nutritionally insignificant and considered to be "Fat-Free."

chicken broth

prep time: 5 minutes

cooking time: 2 hours

ingredients: 1 3-pound chicken, cut into serving pieces
6 cups water
1 medium onion, halved and stuck with 2 cloves
1 carrot, halved
1 stalk celery including leaves, halved
2 bay leaves
3 sprigs parsley
½ teaspoon crushed dried basil, sage or thyme

directions:
1. Place chicken pieces and water in a large soup pot. Bring to boil, reduce heat, and skim off particles that rise to the surface.
2. Add remaining ingredients and simmer gently for 2 hours leaving the pot uncovered.
3. Strain broth through a fine sieve. Discard vegetables. Use chicken at once or reserve in the refrigerator.
4. Let broth stand at room temperature until lukewarm, then refrigerate for several hours or overnight. Before using, skim off all the fat that has risen to the surface.

yield: About 3 cups

Cooking without Fat

YOU SAVE 96 CALORIES
This recipe contains 164 calories per 1 cup serving
Typical recipe contains 260 calories per 1 cup serving

---

zesty mexican chicken soup

The first time I tasted this soup was in Mexico, during a trip I made there searching for Amaranth, the lost grain of the ancient Aztecs. It was a particularly rewarding trip because I not only discovered Amaranth and brought it back, I also brought back this recipe.

One reason I like it so much is because of the interesting variety of herbs and spices, including oregano, chili powder, basil, tarragon, cumin and cilantro. Usually, soup recipes that are based on chicken need salt to taste good, but with this blend of seasonings this soup is flavorful and lives up to its name as "zesty" without any added salt.

In addition to the protein from the chicken, the tomatoes, green onions and red peppers make it an outstanding source of vitamin C and vitamin A. The corn and mushrooms are rich in B vitamins and phosphorus.

This soup is practically a meal in itself. The addition of a green salad and whole grain bread is a nice complement.

We developed this recipe using Health Valley Fat-Free Chicken Broth. It has a full, rich flavor and only 30 calories per serving.

Nutrition Information Per Serving

Calories	164
Fat	2.4 grams
Percentage of Calories from Fat	13%
Cholesterol	48 milligrams
Sodium	263 milligrams
Dietary Fiber	2.1 grams

zesty mexican chicken soup

prep time: 20 minutes

cooking time: 20 minutes

ingredients: ¾ pound chicken breast, skinned, boned, cubed
4 cups fat-free chicken broth
1 cup sliced mushrooms
½ cup thinly sliced celery
½ cup diced tomatoes
1 cup chopped onion
¼ cup diced red or green pepper
2 cloves garlic, minced
½ teaspoon crushed dried oregano
½ teaspoon chili powder
½ teaspoon crushed dried basil
½ teaspoon crushed dried tarragon
¼ teaspoon ground cumin
pinch cayenne pepper (optional)
½ tablespoon finely chopped fresh cilantro
1 cup fresh or frozen whole kernel corn
1 teaspoon lemon juice

directions: 1. In soup pot, combine chicken, chicken broth, and all vegetables and seasonings except corn and lemon juice.
2. Bring to boil. Cover, reduce heat and simmer 20 minutes.
3. Add corn, cover and cook about 2 minutes, until heated through.
4. Stir in lemon juice and serve.

yield: 4-6 Servings

Cooking without Fat

YOU SAVE 67 CALORIES
This recipe contains 77 calories per 1 cup serving
Typical recipe contains 144 calories per 1 cup serving

golden squash soup

Crookneck squash is a member of the summer squash family that also includes zucchini and pattypan. Like these other soft skinned squashes, crookneck does not have to be peeled, and in this case the vibrant golden shell endows this delicate soup with a rich, appetizing hue. This soup is a good source of vitamins A and C, and calcium.

We developed this recipe using Health Valley Fat-Free Chicken Broth. It has a full, rich flavor and only 30 calories per serving.

Nutrition Information Per Serving	
Calories	77
Fat	.7 gram
Percentage of Calories from Fat	8%
Cholesterol	1.2 milligrams
Sodium	156 milligrams
Dietary Fiber	2.5 grams

golden squash soup

prep time: 15 minutes

cooking time: 20 minutes

ingredients: ¾ cup chopped onion
½ cup chopped tomato
1½ cups + 2 tablespoons fat-free chicken broth
2 cups thinly sliced yellow crookneck squash
  (about ¾ pound)
¾ teaspoon crushed dried basil
¼ teaspoon garlic powder
¼ teaspoon crushed dried oregano
¼ teaspoon white pepper (optional)
½ cup buttermilk, low fat if available
1 tablespoon honey
½ teaspoon lemon juice

garnish
4 fresh basil leaves
4 thin tomato slices
plain nonfat yogurt

directions: 1. In soup pot, combine onion and tomato, and saute in 2 tablespoons chicken broth 5 minutes to soften vegetables.
2. Add remaining chicken broth, squash, and spices. Bring to boil. Cover and simmer 15 minutes or until squash is tender. Remove from heat.
3. Puree soup in blender with buttermilk.
4. Return soup to pot and stir in honey and lemon juice. Cover and set over low heat just to warm through.
5. Garnish each serving with a basil leaf, a thin slice of tomato and a dollop of nonfat yogurt.

yield: 4 Servings

Cooking without Fat

YOU SAVE 80 CALORIES
This recipe contains 75 calories per 1 cup serving
Typical recipe contains 155 calories per 1 cup serving

garden vegetable soup

I think our Health Valley Fat-Free 14 Garden Vegetable Soup is hard to beat when it comes to taste and nutrition. However when time permits and you want the warm and nurturing atmosphere generated by a pot of homemade soup simmering on the stove, I suggest Garden Vegetable Soup. Each of the chosen vegetables is welcome for its distinct flavor, texture, and nutritional contribution. The mellow leek tempers the bite of the onion; the sweetness of the carrot, along with the natural sodium in the celery, makes salt expendable. The earthy taste of the greens and crunchy texture produced by cooking them just long enough to wilt adds an unusual dimension.

Another good thing about Garden Vegetable Soup is how accommodating it is. Browse through your vegetable bin and see what else you have on hand; the soup pot will welcome it heartily. If you would like a more substantial soup, throw in some cooked barley or brown rice and a cup of cooked beans. If you have used up your refrigerated supply of cooked grains, substitute 1/2 cup of uncooked whole grain elbows, small shells, or spaghetti broken into 1-inch lengths. If you add the pasta about 10 minutes before you add the greens it will cook to perfection. Let season and availability guide your creativity.

Nutrition Information Per Serving

Calories	75
Fat	Fat-Free*
Cholesterol	0 milligram
Sodium	186 milligrams
Dietary Fiber	3.1 grams

*All foods contain some fat. Less than .5 gram of fat per serving is nutritionally insignificant and considered to be "Fat-Free."

garden vegetable soup

prep time: 15 minutes

cooking time: 45 minutes

ingredients: 1 cup chopped leek, white portion only, thoroughly washed

2 celery stalks with leaves, chopped

¾ cup chopped onion

1 cup diced carrots

2 cloves garlic, chopped

¼ cup water + 3 cups water (or vegetable stock)

1¼ cups tomato juice (no salt if available)

1 cup diced potato

1 cup cauliflower florets

¼ cup chopped fresh parsley or 2 tablespoons dried

1 teaspoon crushed dried basil

1 teaspoon Italian seasoning blend

⅛ teaspoon white pepper (optional)

1½ teaspoons honey

1 cup chopped greens (romaine lettuce, escarole, bok choy, beet greens, or other)

fresh lemon wedges

directions: 1. Combine leek, celery, onion, carrots, garlic and ¼ cup water in soup pot. Cover and cook over medium heat 5 minutes stirring occasionally.

2. Add 3 cups of water, tomato juice, potato, cauliflower, parsley, and herbs. Bring to boil, cover, reduce heat and simmer 30 minutes, or until vegetables are tender.

3. Add honey and greens. Cover and cook 5 minutes longer, or until greens are wilted.

4. Serve with lemon wedges perched on the rim of each bowl so the fresh juice can be squeezed in to taste at the table.

yield: 6 Servings

Cooking without Fat

YOU SAVE 133 CALORIES
This recipe contains 192 calories per 1 cup serving
Typical recipe contains 325 calories per 1 cup serving

cream of corn-potato soup

Most health conscious people shy away from any recipe that contains the word "cream" in the title and for good reason. Creamed soups are generally laden with fat and calories. The dictionary, however, offers as one definition of cream: "the best part of anything," as in "cream of the crop."

That is precisely how I think of this rich soup. The velvety texture of a smooth puree is offset by the presence of fine nuggets of potato and corn.

Added to the intricate texture is the fresh taste of the vegetables that is magnified by the perky seasoning ingredients. As a result, salt is completely unnecessary–quite unusual for potato soup.

Nutrition Information Per Serving	
Calories	192
Fat	.5 gram
Percentage of Calories from Fat	2%
Cholesterol	2.6 milligrams
Sodium	211 milligrams
Dietary Fiber	2.9 grams

cream of corn-potato soup

prep time: 10 minutes

cooking time: 25 minutes

ingredients: 1 cup peeled and diced potatoes
1 can (12 ounces) evaporated skimmed milk
3 cups frozen corn kernels, defrosted
½ cup diced onion
½ cup diced celery
2 tablespoons Dijon mustard
2 cloves garlic, minced
2 teaspoons honey
¼ teaspoon celery seed
⅛ teaspoon white pepper
⅛ teaspoon cayenne pepper
1 cup nonfat milk

directions:
1. Boil diced potatoes until tender, about 15 minutes.
2. In saucepan, combine evaporated skimmed milk, corn kernels, onion, celery, mustard, garlic, honey, celery seed, white and cayenne peppers and bring to low simmer for 15 minutes.
3. Put half boiled potatoes into blender and add half of soup mixture. Blend until smooth. Return mixture to saucepan and add remaining potatoes.
4. Add nonfat milk and gently reheat without boiling and serve.

yield: 6 Servings

note: If you wish to make this soup dairy-free, substitute Health Valley Fat-Free Soy Moo® for the nonfat milk.

Cooking without Fat

YOU SAVE 79 CALORIES
This recipe contains 78 calories per 1 cup serving
Typical recipe contains 157 calories per 1 cup serving

hot borscht

When most people hear the word borscht they envision the crimson red, cold beet soup associated with Jewish dairy tradition. That is one form of borscht, but so is the hot Russian version, handed down through generations, that is made with hearty root vegetables and cabbage, the winter staples of Eastern Europe.

If human characteristics can be used to describe food, I would declare Hot Borscht to be one of the most compassionate soups. I attribute this to its down-to-earth ingredients, its gentle sweet and sour undertones. Unlike other high fat versions of borscht that call for egg yolks or fatty meats and sour cream topping, this borscht is low in fat. This is a soup that is unpretentious, yet in its simplicity, delicious.

With the aid of a food processor the preparation of borscht is greatly accelerated. Lacking this tool, the vegetables can be chopped small and the final pureeing done in a blender or hand food mill. As this is a soup of peasant origins, precision is not essential. In fact, you may prefer to give it more body by increasing the puree, or you can leave the soup thin and skip this step altogether, although I find the latter less satisfying.

Nutrition Information Per Serving

Calories	78
Fat	Fat-Free*
Cholesterol	.1 milligram
Sodium	177 milligrams
Dietary Fiber	2.8 grams

*All foods contain some fat. Less than .5 gram of fat per serving is nutritionally insignificant and considered to be "Fat-Free."

hot borscht

prep time: 20 minutes

cooking time: 35 minutes

ingredients: 3 cups water

1 cup tomato juice (no salt if available)

¾ cup chopped onion

1 cup shredded carrots

1 cup peeled shredded beets

1 cup shredded potatoes

2 cups shredded cabbage

1½ tablespoons honey

1½ tablespoons lemon juice

plain nonfat yogurt for garnish

directions: 1. In soup pot, combine water and tomato juice and bring to boil. Add vegetables, cover and simmer 30 minutes, until tender.

2. Remove 2 cups soup from the pot and puree in blender or food processor.

3. Return pureed soup to pot and stir in honey and lemon juice. Cover and simmer 5 minutes.

4. Serve with yogurt for garnish.

yield: 6 Servings

Cooking without Fat

gazpacho

I am glad to see that cold soups are becoming more fashionable as this chilled Gazpacho has long been a favorite of mine. It is especially refreshing in the summer as a light lunch, although I tend to serve it all year long as a first course preceding fish, chicken or grain entrees.

The first time I tasted gazpacho was in Spain, where they have wonderful tomatoes that are plump and full of flavor. Since sweet, juicy tomatoes have a limited season, I have taken the liberty of using high quality tomato sauce to intensify the taste. Our recipe avoids the common practice of adding oil to this soup. We don't think it's necessary and it certainly holds down the calories and fat.

Nutrition Information Per Serving	
Calories	42
Fat	.5 gram
Percentage of Calories from Fat	11%
Cholesterol	0 milligram
Sodium	24 milligrams
Dietary Fiber	1.2 grams

gazpacho

prep time: 15 minutes

chilling time: 2 hours or longer

ingredients: 1 ½ cups no salt tomato sauce
¼ cup water
1 cup chopped tomato
1 large clove garlic, chopped
½ teaspoon ground cumin
2 tablespoons red wine vinegar
1 tablespoon lemon juice
½ cup peeled, chopped cucumber
½ cup chopped green pepper
2 green onions including tops, chopped
dash hot pepper sauce to taste (optional)
chopped fresh parsley or chopped fresh cilantro
for garnish

directions: 1. Combine all ingredients except parsley or cilantro in medium bowl.
2. Cover bowl, chill several hours or overnight to allow flavors to blend.
3. Serve very cold, garnished with parsley or cilantro to taste sprinkled on top.

yield: 4 Servings

Cooking without Fat VEGETABLES

Most of the attention we give to meal preparation goes to the entree. But much of the life-enhancing nutrition and a great deal of the taste and textural variety can be supplied by the side dishes served along with the entree.

Vegetable side dishes are extremely important because they are the foods that provide the foundation for a healthy diet. The vegetable side dishes in this book can elevate the quality of your diet with many essential nutrients, including vitamins A, C, B_6, thiamine, riboflavin, niacin, and folacin and the minerals magnesium, iron, phosphorus, zinc, and potassium, along with dietary fiber.

Just look at the appetizing names of the recipes in this section: Dijon Carrots and Zucchini, Creamy Skillet Cabbage, Glazed Curried Carrots and Raisins, Mexican Corn...and many more. Every dish lives up to its name by combining garden fresh vegetables with interesting seasonings and sauces that complement their flavors. They transform everyday vegetables into flavorful foods that make healthier eating a culinary pleasure. All of this is accomplished without oil, butter, sour cream or cheese found in so many traditional vegetable recipes. As a result our recipes are high in flavor and nutrition, but low in calories, fat and sodium.

YOU SAVE 80 CALORIES
This recipe contains 56 calories per serving
Typical recipe contains 136 calories per serving

honey mustard mixed vegetables

The three vegetables highlighted in this dish – broccoli, cauliflower and carrots are a powerful triumvirate. Broccoli and cauliflower are cruciferous vegetables. Scientific studies show that people who regularly eat cruciferous vegetables may have a lower risk of developing cancers of the digestive and respiratory systems. Other cruciferous vegetables include cabbage, Brussels sprouts, rutabaga, kale, and turnips.

Broccoli, cauliflower and carrots are also excellent sources of fiber, beta carotene and vitamin C. Fiber plays an important role in maintaining a healthy digestive system, beta carotene is converted as needed to vitamin A which may also help protect you against cancers of the digestive and respiratory systems. Vitamin C may be a protective factor against several forms of cancer as well. All in all Honey Mustard Mixed Vegetables are filled with potential protective factors and great taste. Try to include this easy to prepare recipe in your menus frequently.

Nutrition Information Per Serving

Calories	56
Fat	Fat-Free*
Cholesterol	0 milligram
Sodium	111 milligrams
Dietary Fiber	1.5 grams

*All foods contain some fat. Less than .5 gram of fat per serving is nutritionally insignificant and considered to be "Fat-Free."

honey mustard mixed vegetables

prep time: 10 minutes

cooking time: 18 minutes

ingredients: ½ cup carrots, cut in thin 2-inch sticks
1½ cups florets of cauliflower and broccoli
2 tablespoons dijon mustard
2 tablespoons honey
½ teaspoon dried dill weed

directions: 1. Steam carrots for 10 minutes. Add cauliflower and broccoli and steam until barely tender, approximately 8 additional minutes.
2. Combine mustard with honey and dill to make a smooth sauce.
3. Mix sauce with hot cooked vegetables and stir gently until sauce is evenly distributed.

yield: 4 Servings

Cooking without Fat

YOU SAVE 85 CALORIES
This recipe contains 113 calories per serving
Typical recipe contains 198 calories per serving

glazed curried carrots and raisins

Carrots were known to the ancient Greeks and Romans, although the earliest varieties were red, purple and black. It was much later in the 17th century that the familiar orange carrot, rich in carotene (the precursor of vitamin A), was developed.

I like to think of this dish as a curry recipe even for people who don't normally enjoy curry. The curry doesn't overpower the carrots as it so often does in Indian cooking.

Curry is often misunderstood. It isn't really a spice, but a blend of spices. There are hundreds of variations, but the most popular curry powders contain ginger, coriander, cardamom, cayenne, turmeric and cumin seed. As exemplified by this vegetable dish, curries are not necessarily palate-searing. In fact, a properly made curry should animate the taste buds, not destroy them.

Nutrition Information Per Serving

Calories	113
Fat	Fat-Free*
Cholesterol	0 milligram
Sodium	58 milligrams
Dietary Fiber	4.3 grams

*All foods contain some fat. Less than .5 gram of fat per serving is nutritionally insignificant and considered to be "Fat-Free."

glazed curried carrots and raisins

prep time: 15 minutes

cooking time: 12 minutes

ingredients: 1 pound carrots, sliced diagonally into ¼-inch pieces
⅓ cup raisins
2-3 tablespoons water
1½ tablespoons honey
1 teaspoon prepared mustard, spicy or dijon
½ teaspoon curry powder
1 tablespoon lemon juice

directions: 1. Combine carrots, raisins and 2 tablespoons water in heavy skillet. Bring to boil. Cover and cook 8-10 minutes, until barely tender. Add more water if necessary to keep from burning.
2. Add remaining ingredients. Cook, stirring constantly, about 2 minutes, until carrots are glazed.

yield: 4 Servings

Cooking without Fat

YOU SAVE 60 CALORIES
This recipe contains 45 calories per serving
Typical recipe contains 105 calories per serving

dijon carrots and zucchini

A native to North America, zucchini is a member of the squash family. The European settlers were first introduced to the large variety of squashes by the American Indians.

Squash can be classified as either "summer" (soft-skinned) or "winter" (hard-skinned). Zucchini, along with pattypan and yellow crookneck or straightneck squash, is a summer squash. All three are tender skinned and delicately flavored. Zucchini and yellow squash can frequently be interchanged with one another.

The blend of mustard and carrots gives the zucchini a sweet and spicy taste in this recipe.

We developed this recipe using Health Valley Fat-Free Chicken Broth. It has a full, rich flavor and only 30 calories per serving.

Nutrition Information Per Serving	
Calories	45
Fat	Fat-Free*
Cholesterol	0 milligram
Sodium	75 milligrams
Dietary Fiber	3 grams

*All foods contain some fat. Less than .5 gram of fat per serving is nutritionally insignificant and considered to be "Fat-Free."

dijon carrots and zucchini

prep time: 10 minutes

cooking time: 17 minutes

ingredients: 1½ cups carrots cut in thin 2-inch sticks
2 tablespoons fat-free chicken broth
1½ cups zucchini cut in thin 2-inch sticks
1 teaspoon apple cider vinegar
1 teaspoon honey
1½ teaspoons dijon mustard

directions: 1. Combine carrots and broth in saucepan. Cover and cook over medium heat 10 minutes. Add zucchini and cook an additional 5 minutes or until vegetables are just tender. Add more broth, if necessary, to keep from burning.
2. Stir vinegar, honey and mustard into vegetables. Cook for a few minutes over medium heat until liquid cooks off.

yield: 4 Servings

*Cooking
without
Fat*

YOU SAVE 80 CALORIES
This recipe contains 72 calories per serving
Typical recipe contains 152 calories per serving

orange glazed carrots

Ginger is grown in the tropics and widely used in Chinese and Indian cooking. Along with cinnamon, it is a very useful spice when you are trying to cut down on fat, salt and sugar. Its hot, clean spiciness adds intense flavor without calories.

Ginger is also considered to be an excellent digestif. It has been used to calm gastric rumblings for centuries. Master chef and ginger aficionado Bruce Cost describes it as the "Alka-Seltzer of the Roman Empire."

One reason I like this dish so much is that it enhances the sweetness of carrots with exciting flavor accents, without drowning them in the usual butter sauce.

Nutrition Information Per Serving

Calories	72
Fat	Fat-Free*
Cholesterol	0 milligram
Sodium	44 milligrams
Dietary Fiber	3.4 grams

*All foods contain some fat. Less than .5 gram of fat per serving is nutritionally insignificant and considered to be "Fat-Free."

orange glazed carrots

prep time: 10 minutes

cooking time: 20 minutes

ingredients: 1 pound carrots, cut in ½-inch rounds
1 teaspoon arrowroot
¼ teaspoon ginger
½ cup orange juice
1 tablespoon honey
1 tablespoon finely chopped fresh parsley or
    1½ teaspoons dried parsley

directions: 1. Steam carrots 15-20 minutes, leaving them slightly crunchy. Set carrots aside.
2. In saucepan, combine arrowroot and ginger. Gradually add orange juice, stirring to dissolve arrowroot.
3. Set pan over medium heat, stir in honey and cook, stirring constantly, until thickened to consistency of light syrup.
4. Add carrots and parsley and warm through.

yield: 4 Servings

YOU SAVE 73 CALORIES
This recipe contains 80 calories per serving
Typical recipe contains 153 calories per serving

mexican corn

The pre-Columbian diet relied on corn, beans and the grain called amaranth, along with a wide variety of herbs and spices, especially chili peppers. This ancient model of using a few flavorful seasonings along with freshly squeezed lime is still one of the most sound approaches to healthful cooking.

Cilantro is another name for the leaves of the coriander plant. Some describe its flavor as a combination of parsley and citrus, but it is really much more complex than that. Many people first encounter cilantro in Mexican food, although it is a signature of Indian and Thai cooking as well.

During corn season, it is worth cutting the kernels off a cob of sweet corn for this dish. At other times you may need to add a little honey to enhance the natural sweetness.

Nutrition Information Per Serving

Calories	80
Fat	Fat-Free*
Cholesterol	.1 milligram
Sodium	18 milligrams
Dietary Fiber	2.4 grams

*All foods contain some fat. Less than .5 gram of fat per serving is nutritionally insignificant and considered to be "Fat-Free."

mexican corn

prep time: 10 minutes

cooking time: 10 minutes

ingredients: 2 tablespoons chopped green onions

⅓ cup chopped green pepper

⅓ cup chopped red pepper

½ cup chopped fresh tomato

1 tablespoon apple cider vinegar

1-2 tablespoons water

1 teaspoon chili powder

pinch cayenne pepper (optional)

1 10-ounce package frozen corn, thawed, or 2 cups fresh corn kernels

1 teaspoon honey (optional)

2 tablespoons chopped fresh cilantro and/or fresh parsley

1 wedge lime

plain nonfat yogurt for garnish (optional)

directions: 1. In large skillet over medium heat, cook green onions, peppers and tomato in vinegar and water for 5 minutes.

2. Add chili powder and cayenne, and cook briefly.

3. Add corn, sweeten with honey if desired. Cook, stirring occasionally, for 5 minutes.

4. Sprinkle with cilantro and/or parsley and squeeze lime over all.

5. Garnish with a dollop of yogurt.

yield: 4 Servings

YOU SAVE 115 CALORIES
This recipe contains 177 calories per serving
Typical recipe contains 292 calories per serving

stuffed baked winter squash

Acorn squash belongs to the hard-skinned variety of the squash family. Other members include hubbard, butternut, buttercup, golden nugget and spaghetti squash. They are generally harvested in autumn and have come to be known as winter squash.

If you are trying to convince someone to eat more vegetables, there is no better way to do it than with this recipe. I think it is possibly my favorite squash dish. The combination of sweet and crunchy ingredients that comprise the filling meld together into a rich and satisfying stuffing.

Orange fleshed winter squash, like most similarly colored fruits and vegetables, are extremely rich in vitamin A. Their potassium content is equally impressive. Winter squashes are also a good source of dietary fiber.

We developed this recipe using Health Valley Fat-Free Date Delight Cookies.

Nutrition Information Per Serving

Calories	177
Fat	Fat-Free*
Cholesterol	0 milligram
Sodium	37 milligrams
Dietary Fiber	6.3 grams

All foods contain some fat. Less than .5 gram of fat per serving is nutritionally insignificant and considered to be "Fat-Free."

stuffed baked winter squash

prep time: 10 minutes

cooking time: 1 hour

ingredients: 2 medium acorn squash

⅓ cup chopped onion

¼ cup chopped celery

1 cup chopped apple

⅔ cup canned crushed pineapple packed in juice, drained

½ cup crumbled fat-free cookies

cinnamon

directions: 1. Preheat oven to 375°F.

2. Cut each squash in half through the stem and scoop out seeds. In medium bowl, combine remaining ingredients except cinnamon and pack into squash shells, mounding if necessary.

3. Place squash in a deep casserole, surround with ½ inch hot water, cover, and bake at 375°F. for 45 minutes, or until almost tender.

4. Uncover, sprinkle with cinnamon, and return to oven uncovered 10-15 minutes longer, until squash is fork tender.

yield: 4 Servings

Cooking without Fat

YOU SAVE 61 CALORIES
This recipe contains 114 calories per serving
Typical recipe contains 175 calories per serving

baked orange beets

Beets are native to Europe, and records of cultivation date back to the Romans. When you shop for beets, look for solid, smooth, globe-shaped ones with firm roots. Avoid those that are flabby, scaly or have soft spots.

Two of the most popular American beet preparations take their names from prominent universities. Beets served in a sweet and sour sauce are known as Harvard beets. Served in an orange sauce they are called Yale beets. This recipe makes the grade by combining great taste with excellent nutrition.

Beets are a good source of potassium and selenium. If you buy young beets, be sure to use the beet greens, too, because they are an excellent source of vitamin A and iron.

Nutrition Information Per Serving

Calories	114
Fat	Fat-Free*
Cholesterol	0 milligram
Sodium	66 milligrams
Dietary Fiber	3.2 grams

*All foods contain some fat. Less than .5 gram of fat per serving is nutritionally insignificant and considered to be "Fat-Free."

baked orange beets

prep time: 15 minutes

cooking time: 1 hour

ingredients: 1 pound beets, washed, trimmed, peeled and thinly sliced

$\frac{1}{2}$ cup chopped onion

1 tablespoon water

2 tablespoons honey

1 tablespoon frozen orange juice concentrate

$\frac{1}{4}$ teaspoon nutmeg

$\frac{1}{4}$ cup orange juice

1 tablespoon lemon juice

2 tablespoons fruit juice sweetened orange marmalade

orange slices for garnish

directions: 1. Steam or boil beets until they are tender. This will vary from 30 to 45 minutes depending on the size and age of the beets.

2. In small skillet, cook onion in 1 tablespoon water until onion softens.

3. Preheat oven to 350°F.

4. Layer beets in shallow baking dish. Scatter onion on top.

5. In small bowl, combine honey, orange juice concentrate, nutmeg, orange juice, lemon juice and orange marmalade. Stir to dissolve honey and orange juice concentrate. Pour evenly over beets.

6. Cover and bake at 350°F. for 15 minutes.

7. Decorate with a few slices fresh orange and serve.

yield: 4 Servings

note: To save time, you may substitute canned beets that have been rinsed and drained.

Cooking without Fat

YOU SAVE 117 CALORIES
This recipe contains 73 calories per serving
Typical recipe contains 190 calories per serving

honey glazed beets

Beets take a long time to cook, but the results are worth it. The natural sugar content of beets can be as high as 8%, which is what makes them taste so good. Most beet dishes capitalize on their sweetness, as in this reconceptualization of Harvard beets with its sweet and sour glaze. The creamy texture and mild tartness of yogurt add a soothing touch.

Nutrition Information Per Serving

Calories	73
Fat	Fat-Free*
Cholesterol	.1 milligram
Sodium	60 milligrams
Dietary Fiber	2.4 grams

*All foods contain some fat. Less than .5 gram of fat per serving is nutritionally insignificant and considered to be "Fat-Free."

honey glazed beets

prep time: 10 minutes

cooking time: 50 minutes

ingredients: 1 pound beets
2 tablespoons honey
2 tablespoons apple cider vinegar
1 teaspoon arrowroot
plain nonfat yogurt

directions: 1. Scrub beets and remove tops and long roots. Cut beets into quarters. Steam or boil beets until they can be pierced easily with a fork. This will vary from 30 to 45 minutes depending on the size and age of the beets.

2. When beets are cool enough to handle, slip off skins. Cut into bite size pieces.

3. In small saucepan, combine honey, vinegar, arrowroot and beets. Cook over medium heat 3-5 minutes, stirring constantly, until beets are coated with glaze and warmed through.

4. Serve with yogurt.

yield: 4 Servings

note: To save time, you may substitute canned beets that have been rinsed and drained.

Cooking without Fat

creamy skillet cabbage

Cabbage is so good for you that nutritionists recommend you serve it (and other members of the Brassica family) several times a week. But finding fat-free recipes for cabbage is not so easy.

One thing that makes this cabbage dish so admirable is brief cooking. A history of overcooking has given cabbage an unfair reputation as a smelly, sharp vegetable. Moreover, while many cooks rely on oil or butter to moderate the assertive flavors brought out by cooking, we find cider vinegar a much more effective medium. Cider vinegar not only assuages cabbage's strong taste, it mitigates the cooking odors. Cider vinegar also enhances the absorption of the nutrients and adds additional potassium of its own.

Nutrition Information Per Serving	
Calories	110
Fat	1.8 grams
Percentage of Calories from Fat	14%
Cholesterol	.4 milligram
Sodium	100 milligrams
Dietary Fiber	2.3 grams

creamy skillet cabbage

prep time: 10 minutes

cooking time: 8 minutes

ingredients: 6 cups coarsely chopped green cabbage

2 medium carrots, shredded

4 scallions, chopped

¼ cup fat-free chicken broth

1½ tablespoons honey

2-3 teaspoons prepared mustard, spicy or Dijon

⅓ cup plain nonfat yogurt

directions: 1. In large pot or skillet, combine cabbage, carrots, scallions and broth and cook, covered, over medium heat for 8 minutes, or until cabbage is softened but still has some crunch. Remove from heat.

2. Combine honey, mustard and yogurt. Stir into warm cabbage mixture just before serving.

yield: 4 Servings

YOU SAVE 58 CALORIES
This recipe contains 60 calories per serving
Typical recipe contains 118 calories per serving

braised red cabbage

Braised Red Cabbage offers an uncommon gathering of tastes and textures. It is important to cook the cabbage sufficiently so that it is soft and distinct from the crunchy water chestnuts. Each of these elements blend delightfully with the cool yogurt spooned on top at the table.

Nutrition Information Per Serving

Calories	60
Fat	Fat-Free*
Cholesterol	.2 milligram
Sodium	75 milligrams
Dietary Fiber	2.3 grams

*All foods contain some fat. Less than .5 gram of fat per serving is nutritionally insignificant and considered to be "Fat-Free."

braised red cabbage

prep time: 10 minutes

cooking time: 15 minutes

ingredients: 1 ½ tablespoons no salt tomato paste
¼ cup water
1 tablespoon honey
4 cups coarsely chopped red cabbage
½ cup chopped onion
1 tablespoon lemon juice
2 tablespoons plain nonfat yogurt
4 tablespoons diced canned water chestnuts, drained
additional yogurt for garnish

directions: 1. In large pot, combine tomato paste with water and honey. Bring to boil.

2. Add cabbage and onion. Cover and cook over low heat, stirring occasionally, about 15 minutes, or until cabbage is tender.

3. Remove from heat and stir in lemon juice. Then stir in yogurt and water chestnuts.

4. Garnish with additional yogurt to taste at the table.

yield: 4 Servings

Cooking without Fat DRESSINGS AND SAUCES

Sometimes the smallest changes we make in our lives have the greatest effect. When it comes to diet, the simple switch from standard salad dressings, gravies and toppings to lower-fat alternatives can add up dramatically. It doesn't seem possible that a little salad dressing or sauce could be so devastating to your health, but when you look at typical recipes and commercial offerings, the problem becomes apparent.

Dressing	Calories	Fat	Sodium	% Calories From Fat
Italian (1 tablespoon)	83	9 gm	318 mg	98
Russian (1 tablespoon)	74	7.6 gm	130 mg	92
Tartar Sauce (1 tablespoon)	75	8 gm	98 mg	96

Dressings, dips and toppings are among the highest calorie-fat-sodium laden foods in existence. Even light and reduced calorie dressings contain 3 to 4 grams of fat per tablespoon and range from 100 to 180 mg. sodium. And how many people do you know who use only one tablespoon of salad dressing?

In the following pages you will find recipes for light and lively salad dressings and condiments. All of the yogurt-based dressing recipes can be used for dips; for a thicker dip you can substitute yogurt cheese or blended fat-free cottage cheese for all or part of the yogurt. Of all the recipes in this book, these were the most challenging to create. But we feel confident that we have come up with an exceptional selection that will enhance your food with flavor interest and added nutritional value. While they are low in total fat, saturated fat, cholesterol, sodium, and calories, these add-ons are rich in key minerals like calcium, magnesium, phosphorus, iron, and zinc, and important vitamins like A, C, and the B complex.

If you're unaccustomed to making your own dressings, you'll be surprised by how simple they are to prepare. To inspire you, take a look and see how significantly lower our dressings are in calories, fat and sodium.

Dressing	Calories	Fat	Sodium	% Calories From Fat
Italian (1 tablespoon)	13	Fat-Free	6 mg	0
Mock Russian (1 tablespoon)	10	Fat-Free	24 mg	0
Mustard Dill Sauce (1 tablespoon)	12	Fat-Free	57 mg	0

With these dressings there's no need to deprive yourself. In fact, you needn't be concerned if you happen to use a little extra. Here's what you'll save:

Dressing (calories per tablespoon)	Calories Typical Dressing	Calories Cooking Without Fat	Calories You Save
Mock Russian Dressing	74	10	64
Creamy French Dressing	65	14	51
Southwest Dressing	59	10	49
Honey Mustard Dressing	125	17	108
Buttermilk Yogurt Dressing	65	11	54
Creamy Tomato Curry Dressing	76	9	67
Italian Dressing	83	13	70
Mustard-Dill Sauce	75	12	63
Salsa	15	5	10

mock russian dressing

prep time: 5 minutes

chilling time: 15 minutes

ingredients: ½ cup plain nonfat yogurt
2 tablespoons no salt ketchup
1 teaspoon honey
2 tablespoons finely chopped green pepper
dash hot pepper sauce

directions: 1. Combine all ingredients in a wide mouth jar or small bowl. Mix vigorously with a fork or wire whisk until yogurt, ketchup and honey are evenly blended.
2. Chill 15 minutes before serving.
3. Store any remaining dressing in covered container in refrigerator.

yield: ¾ Cup

The key to many of our dressings is that they have a base of nonfat yogurt instead of mayonnaise or oil. Tablespoon per tablespoon, nonfat yogurt contains only 8 calories as compared to mayonnaise at 100 calories and oil at 120 calories per tablespoon. Nonetheless, taste is uncompromised while calories are spared. You will find the following dressings provide a rich and zesty flavor to all kinds of vegetable salads.

Where ketchup is used as a principal flavoring ingredient, keep in mind that the sweetness can vary from brand to brand. Therefore, you may need to slightly increase or decrease to taste the honey called for in these recipes. Be sure to choose a no salt added ketchup.

Nutrition Information Per Serving

Calories	10
Fat	Fat-Free*
Cholesterol	.17 milligram
Sodium	24 milligrams
Dietary Fiber	.01 gram

*All foods contain some fat. Less than .5 gram of fat per serving is nutritionally insignificant and considered to be "Fat-Free."

creamy french dressing

prep time: 5 minutes

chilling time: 15 minutes

ingredients: ½ cup plain nonfat yogurt

2 tablespoons no salt ketchup

2 teaspoons honey

1 teaspoon prepared mustard, spicy or dijon

2 sundried tomatoes, chopped and blanched (optional)

directions: 1. Combine all ingredients in blender or food processor. Process using a pulsing motion in order to blend all ingredients, yet retain some tomato texture.

2. Chill 15 minutes before serving.

3. Store any remaining dressing in covered container in refrigerator.

yield: ¾ Cup

Sundried tomatoes add a special touch to recipes with their deeply concentrated tomato flavor and meaty texture. Brief blanching of 1 minute in boiling water is recommended to plump them up.

Nutrition Information Per Serving

Calories	14
Fat	Fat-Free*
Cholesterol	.17 milligram
Sodium	29 milligrams
Dietary Fiber	.13 gram

*All foods contain some fat. Less than .5 gram of fat per serving is nutritionally insignificant and considered to be "Fat-Free."

southwest dressing

prep time: 5 minutes

chilling time: 15 minutes

ingredients: ½ cup plain nonfat yogurt
2 tablespoons no salt ketchup
1 teaspoon honey
½ teaspoon chili powder
dash hot pepper sauce
2 tablespoons chopped fresh cilantro
¼ cup chopped tomato

directions: 1. Combine all ingredients in blender or food processor. Process for a few seconds at a time using a pulsing motion in order to blend all ingredients yet retain some tomato texture.
2. Chill 15 minutes before serving.
3. Store any remaining dressing in covered container in refrigerator.

yield: ¾ Cup

Nutrition Information Per Serving

Calories	10
Fat	Fat-Free*
Cholesterol	.17 milligram
Sodium	24 milligrams
Dietary Fiber	.09 gram

All foods contain some fat. Less than .5 gram of fat per serving is nutritionally insignificant and considered to be "Fat-Free."

honey mustard dressing

prep time: 5 minutes

chilling time: 15 minutes

ingredients: ½ cup plain nonfat yogurt
1 tablespoon honey
1-2 teaspoons prepared mustard, spicy or dijon

directions: 1. Combine all ingredients in wide mouth jar or small bowl, mixing to a smooth dressing.
2. Chill 15 minutes before serving.
3. Store any remaining dressing in covered container in refrigerator.

yield: ½ Cup

Nutrition Information Per Serving

Calories	17
Fat	Fat-Free*
Cholesterol	.25 milligram
Sodium	19 milligrams
Dietary Fiber	0 gram

*All foods contain some fat. Less than .5 gram of fat per serving is nutritionally insignificant and considered to be "Fat-Free."

buttermilk yogurt dressing

prep time: 5 minutes

chilling time: 15 minutes

ingredients: ¼ cup buttermilk, low fat if available
½ cup plain nonfat yogurt
2 tablespoons lemon juice
1 teaspoon honey
1 teaspoon chopped garlic
2 tablespoons chopped green onion
pinch white pepper (optional)
½ teaspoon celery seed

directions: 1. Combine all ingredients in wide mouth jar or small bowl. Mix well until uniformly blended.
2. Chill 15 minutes before serving.
3. Store any remaining dressing in covered container in refrigerator.

yield: ⅔ Cup

Buttermilk contributes a pleasant tang to salad dressings. Commercial dressings like this one, often called "Ranch" dressings, typically furnish 65 calories and 6 grams of fat per tablespoon. Even "reduced calorie" versions contain 3 grams of fat per tablespoon. By contrast, homemade Buttermilk Yogurt Dressing boasts only 11 calories and less than ¹⁄₁₀ gram of fat per tablespoon.

Nutrition Information Per Serving	
Calories	14
Fat	Fat-Free*
Cholesterol	.3 milligram
Sodium	14 milligrams
Dietary Fiber	.04 grams

*All foods contain some fat. Less than .5 gram of fat per serving is nutritionally insignificant and considered to be "Fat-Free."

creamy tomato curry dressing

prep time: 5 minutes

chilling time: 15 minutes

ingredients: 1/3 cup tomato juice (no salt if available)
1/3 cup nonfat cottage cheese
1 tablespoon lemon juice
1 teaspoon honey
1/2 to 1 teaspoon curry powder*
1/4 cup chopped tomato

directions: 1. Combine tomato juice, cottage cheese, lemon juice, honey and curry powder in blender or food processor. Puree until smooth (about 45 seconds).

2. Add tomato and process briefly so small pieces remain.

3. Chill 15 minutes before serving.

4. Store any remaining dressing in covered container in refrigerator.

yield: 3/4 Cup

note: *Use lesser amount of curry for mild dressing, larger amount for spicier dressing.

With the addition of a little liquid, cottage cheese can be pureed quite successfully in the blender or food processor for creamy dressings like this one, or for use as a sour cream substitute.

Nutrition Information Per Serving

Calories	9
Fat	Fat-Free*
Cholesterol	.28 milligram
Sodium	50 milligrams
Dietary Fiber	1.2 grams

*All foods contain some fat. Less than .5 gram of fat per serving is nutritionally insignificant and considered to be "Fat-Free."

italian dressing

prep time: 5 minutes

chilling time: 15 minutes

ingredients: 2 tablespoons apple cider vinegar
1 tablespoon chopped onion
¼ cup water
2 tablespoons frozen apple juice concentrate
1 clove garlic, cut in half
1 teaspoon honey
½ teaspoon crushed dried basil
½ teaspoon crushed dried oregano
pinch white pepper (optional)
1 can (7 ounces) artichoke hearts, packed in water,
rinsed and drained

directions: 1. Combine all ingredients in blender or food processor
and puree until smooth.
2. Chill 15 minutes before serving.
3. Store any remaining dressing in covered container in
refrigerator.

yield: 1 Cup

We are especially proud of this dressing. Unlike the commercial "diet dressings," which rely on synthetic thickeners for texture and are appallingly sweet, this one is rich and flavorful using only the finest natural ingredients.

Nutrition Information Per Serving	
Calories	13
Fat	Fat-Free*
Cholesterol	0 milligram
Sodium	6 milligrams
Dietary Fiber	.3 gram

*All foods contain some fat. Less than .5 gram of fat per serving is nutritionally insignificant and considered to be "Fat-Free."

mustard-dill sauce

prep time: 5 minutes

ingredients: ¾ cup plain nonfat yogurt
¼ cup prepared mustard, spicy or dijon
1 teaspoon dried dill weed
½ teaspoon onion powder
½ teaspoon honey

directions: 1. Mix ingredients thoroughly in a small bowl.
2. Serve on vegetables or fish.
3. Store any remaining sauce in covered container in refrigerator.

yield: 1 Cup

Mustard-Dill Sauce can be used when you want to add more appeal to a simple vegetable side dish or dress up poached or broiled fish. A much healthier choice than tartar sauce.

Nutrition Information Per Serving

Calories	12
Fat	Fat-Free*
Cholesterol	.19 milligram
Sodium	57 milligrams
Dietary Fiber	0 gram

*All foods contain some fat. Less than .5 gram of fat per serving is nutritionally insignificant and considered to be "Fat-Free."

Cooking without Fat

YOU SAVE 10 CALORIES
This recipe contains 5 calories per tablespoon
Typical recipe contains 15 calories per tablespoon

salsa

Mexican cooks use as many as 100 varieties of chilies and each has its well-defined role. North of the border, most of us have a hard time telling one hot pepper from another. If you're not an experienced chili-user, proceed with restraint until you've had a chance to judge their potency. After working with hot pepper, be sure to scrub all traces from your hands. Take care not to accidentally touch your eyes or mouth; the smallest iota of their fiery essence is enough to irritate sensitive membranes. Should this occur, flush immediately with lots of cold water.

Mexican salsa is nothing more than a well seasoned blend of tomato and herbs. It is one of the easiest condiments to prepare at home, with many variations ranging from hot to fire fighter intensity. This version is quite benign without the fresh hot pepper; one small jalapeno turns it into a medium-hot salsa. If your salsa turns out to be too hot for your liking, you can always redeem it by adding more of the other ingredients.

A food processor is most convenient for salsa making. A blender can do the job, too, but you might have to start and stop it several times to push the ingredients into the vortex. The most important rule is not to over-grind. Little flecks of herbs and vegetables are a desirable part of its texture; a little too long in the processor makes salsa thin and watery. If you don't mind the work, a perfectly good salsa can be created with just a cutting board, sharp knife and willing hand.

Salsa needn't be reserved for Mexican dishes. It can be used for spicing up a bean dish, tofu, grains, vegetables, or as a last-minute sauce for broiled chicken or fish. Salsa is best used the day it is prepared. To keep for more than a day or two, follow the directions in the recipe.

Nutrition Information Per Serving

Calories	5
Fat	Fat-Free*
Cholesterol	0 milligram
Sodium	2 milligrams
Dietary Fiber	.32 gram

All foods contain some fat. Less than .5 gram of fat per serving is nutritionally insignificant and considered to be "Fat-Free."

salsa

prep time: 20 minutes

chilling time: 15 minutes

ingredients: 2 medium tomatoes
½ medium onion
½ medium green pepper
1 small fresh jalapeno pepper (optional)
¼ cup fresh cilantro leaves
1 tablespoon lime or lemon juice
1 tablespoon apple cider vinegar
1 clove garlic, split
¼ teaspoon chili powder
¼ teaspoon cumin

directions: 1. Cut vegetables into pieces of about equal size, ½ inch or smaller pieces.
2. Combine all ingredients. Put aside ½ cup mixture. Put remaining mixture in food processor or blender. Using a pulsing (on-off) motion, process to desired texture. The optimum salsa has an uneven coarse consistency, rather than a paste or puree. If you do not have a food processor and wish to make this by hand, chop vegetables as fine as possible and combine with remaining ingredients.
3. Add ½ cup mixture back into blended salsa and stir. This will provide chunkier texture.
4. Transfer to shallow serving dish. Chill for 15 minutes before serving.
5. To keep for more than a day or two, bring salsa to boil, then transfer to covered container and chill. Salsa should be used up within a week.

yield: About 1¼ Cups

Cooking without Fat SALADS

Many people still think of a salad as a bowl of iceberg lettuce (the least nutritious variety) accompanied by a few slices of pale, hot-house tomato. Such a salad provides little nutritional benefit. But the real trap in salad eating is to add too much dressing. One small ladle of dressing can break your calorie budget with 300 or more calories and about 35 grams of fat, ruining what might otherwise have been a low-calorie, fat-controlled meal.

We have designed our salad recipes with balanced nutrition in mind. They are high in fiber, vitamins A and C, and several also boast a high level of protein. At the same time we have kept down the calories, fat, cholesterol and sodium.

In crafting your own salads, give attention to the balance of textures, colors and flavors. Mild greens such as leaf lettuce should be set off by more assertive ingredients such as sweet seasonal tomatoes, tangy watercress or crunchy red cabbage. Firm vegetables such as celery, radish, sweet red and green peppers, and carrots are well complemented by softer ingredients such as plump, meaty cucumbers, tender raw mushrooms, and favorite cooked vegetables including beets, potatoes, green beans, and broccoli.

Cooking without Fat

Mix several greens for maximum variety and nutrition. To reduce the need for dressing, toss in some "wilder" tasting leafy vegetables including arugula, raddichio, spinach, endive, chicory and escarole, along with fresh herbs such as dill, mint and basil. Red onion and scallions, also called green onions, contribute genuine flavor where salt and fat are minimized.

Be daring about including new ingredients in your salads. Consider sweet edible pea pods, succulent jicama, snappy fresh green beans or asparagus, crisp slices of zucchini, thinly sliced raw beets or artichoke hearts, and fresh wedges cut from the bulb of licorice-flavored fennel. Fruit, too, can uplift a simple salad – apple wedges, orange segments, a few dried dates or a handful of raisins. Most of all, don't forget sprouts, one of the few foods we eat that are still growing and replete with life-promoting nutrients.

To make salads suitable for main dish service add protein. Tuna, cooked garbanzos, leftover poultry or fish can fill the bill.

Tips For Handling Greens
It is essential to wash greens well to remove dirt and insects. It is also important to dry the greens thoroughly or you will end up with soggy salad and diluted dressing. A salad spinner is an excellent investment for drying produce quickly and easily. You can clean a whole head or more at one time and refrigerate the greens for several day's worth of salad.

Ready-to-eat greens keep for several days. In fact, with proper handling refrigerated washed greens make salads extra crisp and cool. The secret to keeping the greens in good condition is to store them in a sealed container or "crisper" and to line it with a linen napkin or paper towels. This serves a dual purpose. First, any moisture still clinging to the leaves will drip onto the cloth, reducing the potential for the greens to become water logged and begin to decay. Second, the now moist cloth provides humidity and keeps the leaves from drying out.

A final tip for handling greens: Tear lettuce instead of cutting it. Cut edges are more susceptible to browning.

salad spinner

spinner lid
with crank

crank is turned
clockwise

basket holds salad
wet from washing

inner
basket spins

water
removed
from salad

container
that will collect
excess water

excess water is collected

Cooking
without
Fat

YOU SAVE 252 CALORIES
This recipe contains 108 calories per serving
Typical recipe contains 360 calories per serving

honey mustard potato salad

It's really a shame the way we treat potatoes. A simple potato, boiled or baked in its skin, is a model of good nutrition – low in fat, high in fiber and well endowed with vitamins and minerals. But typical potato preparations sabotage all these virtues. Potato salad is a perfect example. If you follow a popular cookbook recipe calling for French dressing, you receive upwards of 12 grams of fat per serving; when made based on mayonnaise, the fat count leaps above 20 grams. It is not unusual to find 650 mg. sodium in a half cup of a typical deli or fast food offering.

A fat-free, low-sodium potato salad may break with tradition but I don't think it's one you'll regret. The creamy dressing that coats the potato slices in our Honey Mustard Potato Salad is lively enough to wake up even salt-jaded taste buds. The crunchy bits of sweet pepper and red onion make each mouthful a treat.

The nutritional rewards are as gratifying as the taste. Each serving of Honey Mustard Potato Salad offers 440 mg. potassium and 17 mg. vitamin C.

Nutrition Information Per Serving

Calories	108
Fat	Fat-Free*
Cholesterol	.5 milligram
Sodium	59 milligrams
Dietary Fiber	1.2 grams

*All foods contain some fat. Less than .5 gram of fat per serving is nutritionally insignificant and considered to be "Fat-Free."

honey mustard potato salad

prep time: 10 minutes

chilling time: 15 minutes

ingredients: ¾ cup plain nonfat yogurt or ¾ cup yogurt cheese*
1 tablespoon prepared mustard, spicy or dijon
2 teaspoons honey
1 tablespoon lemon juice
2 tablespoons chopped fresh parsley
2 tablespoons chopped red or green pepper
¼ cup chopped red onion
3 cups cooked, sliced potatoes

directions: 1. In serving bowl, combine yogurt, mustard, honey, lemon juice, parsley, sweet pepper, and onion.
2. Gently stir in potato slices to coat.
3. Cover and chill for a minimum of 15 minutes. Toss again before serving and drain liquid, if desired. Use a slotted spoon to serve.

yield: 6 Servings

note: *Use a firm yogurt or yogurt cheese (see page 139) if a thicker dressing is desired.

YOU SAVE 164 CALORIES
This recipe contains 61 calories per serving
Typical recipe contains 225 calories per serving

healthy coleslaw

Coleslaw is a great American favorite. Most recipes include large amounts of mayonnaise or oil, as well as sugar and salt. Our lean yogurt dressing trims all this fat and sodium. We think you'll find this coleslaw as good as any you've eaten, and it's a good deal healthier.

How to Choose Cabbage

Look for firm heads that are heavy for their size, with fresh, crisp leaves. Store in the crisper of your refrigerator, where they will last for 1 to 2 weeks. All types of cabbage are good sources of vitamin C and potassium. Scientific data also indicates that cabbage may be helpful in reducing the risk of certain types of cancer.

Nutrition Information Per Serving

Calories	61
Fat	Fat-Free*
Cholesterol	.3 milligram
Sodium	28 milligrams
Dietary Fiber	1.4 grams

*All foods contain some fat. Less than .5 gram of fat per serving is nutritionally insignificant and considered to be "Fat-Free."

healthy coleslaw

prep time: 10 minutes

chilling time: 15 minutes

ingredients: ⅓ cup plain nonfat yogurt or ⅓ cup yogurt cheese*
1 tablespoon apple cider vinegar
2 tablespoons honey
2 cups coarsely chopped cabbage
½ cup shredded carrots
¼ cup chopped green pepper
¼ cup finely chopped celery

directions: 1. Combine yogurt, vinegar and honey in bowl large enough to hold coleslaw. Stir until smooth and well blended.

2. Add vegetables and mix well.

3. Cover and chill for a minimum of 15 minutes. Toss again before serving and drain liquid, if desired. Use a slotted spoon to serve.

yield: 4 Servings

note: *Use a firm yogurt or yogurt cheese (see page 139) if a thicker dressing is desired.

Cooking without Fat

YOU SAVE 68 CALORIES
This recipe contains 64 calories per serving
Typical recipe contains 132 calories per serving

mediterranean salad

Most food lovers who travel to Greece, Turkey or the Middle East marvel at the delicious produce and tangy yogurt. In these temperate climates tomatoes enjoy a long growing season and they appear in stores seasonally. Similarly, the yogurt is likely to be made from freshly milked animals, including sheep and goats more often than cows.

This thick creamy blend of tomatoes and cucumber in garlic- and mint-seasoned yogurt represents one of the most popular regional dishes. This recipe will be at its best, if you give careful attention to select, ripe full bodied tomatoes.

Because most commercial-scale yogurt production does not turn out as distinctive a culture as homemade versions, we have added honey to the recipe to temper its flavor. With ripe summer tomatoes and a lively fresh yogurt, you may be able to reduce the honey.

Nutrition Information Per Serving

Calories	64
Fat	Fat-Free*
Cholesterol	.8 milligram
Sodium	40 milligrams
Dietary Fiber	1.9 grams

*All foods contain some fat. Less than .5 gram of fat per serving is nutritionally insignificant and considered to be "Fat-Free."

mediterranean salad

prep time: 15 minutes

chilling time: 15 minutes

ingredients: 1½ cups chopped tomatoes
1½ cups peeled, chopped cucumber
¼ cup finely chopped onion
1 clove garlic, chopped
½ cup plain nonfat yogurt or ½ cup yogurt cheese*
1-2 tablespoons honey
2 teaspoons dried mint

directions: 1. Combine tomatoes, cucumber and onion in serving bowl. Cover and chill for 15 minutes.

2. Combine garlic, yogurt and honey for dressing.

3. Just before serving, drain vegetables of any liquid that has accumulated and combine with yogurt dressing. Scatter mint on top. Use a slotted spoon to serve.

yield: 4 Servings

note: *Use a firm yogurt or yogurt cheese (see page 139) if a thicker dressing is desired.

Cooking without Fat

YOU SAVE 122 CALORIES
This recipe contains 93 calories per serving
Typical recipe contains 215 calories per serving

super carrot raisin salad

Super Carrot Raisin Salad is a filling and sprightly salad with a delicate nature. The sweetness of the carrots, raisins and pineapple is highlighted by the touch of cinnamon in the dressing.

A food processor can speed preparation of this dish. Use the coarse shredding blade for the best texture. This salad benefits from chilling, even if you can only give it 15 minutes, and it keeps well for several days in the refrigerator.

Carrots are an abundant source of beta carotene, which your body uses to make vitamin A. This vitamin is a potent antioxidant that current research suggests plays a role in cancer prevention, keeping your skin healthy, and probably protecting your coronary system, as well.

Another plus for this recipe is that it derives only 2% of its calories from fat. This is especially noteworthy when you consider that a typical creamy carrot salad, made with sour cream or mayonnaise, can be over 60% fat.

Choosing and Using Carrots

Young tender carrots are best for eating raw, as in salads. Choose firm, straight, bright orange carrots with no green or yellow areas at the top. If you purchase carrots that still have their foliage, remove before storing since the tops drain the moisture from the root. Carrots will keep well if you store them in a bag in the refrigerator. Unless they are old and have a noticeably thick skin, carrots should not be peeled because important nutrients are just under the skin. A good scrubbing will suffice.

Nutrition Information Per Serving

Calories	93
Fat	Fat-Free*
Cholesterol	.3 milligram
Sodium	29 milligrams
Dietary Fiber	2.6 grams

*All foods contain some fat. Less than .5 gram of fat per serving is nutritionally insignificant and considered to be "Fat-Free."

super carrot raisin salad

prep time: 10 minutes

chilling time: 15 minutes

ingredients: ½ cup plain nonfat yogurt
1½ tablespoons honey
1 tablespoon lemon juice
¼ teaspoon cinnamon
2 cups shredded carrots
½ cup raisins
¼ cup canned unsweetened crushed pineapple,
   drained

directions: 1. In serving bowl, combine yogurt, honey, lemon juice and cinnamon into a smooth dressing.
2. Add carrots, raisins and pineapple to dressing and stir gently, but thoroughly, until salad is uniform.
3. Cover and chill for a minimum of 15 minutes. Toss again before serving and drain liquid, if desired. Use a slotted spoon to serve.

yield: 6 Servings

Cooking without Fat

YOU SAVE 219 CALORIES
This recipe contains 118 calories per serving
Typical recipe contains 337 calories per serving

waldorf salad

Waldorf Salad deserves its reputation as a classic salad recipe. It's a deliciously sweet and crunchy combination of apples, fruit, and celery in a smooth and creamy dressing.

The only trouble with the traditional recipe is its reliance on mayonnaise and nuts. One reason this Health Valley version of Waldorf Salad is such a favorite of mine is that we've successfully replaced all of the high fat mayonnaise and nuts and without compromising taste or texture.

I like to mix two types of apples together–one red variety and one green–for a subtle air of sophistication.

Nutrition Information Per Serving	
Calories	118
Fat	Fat-Free*
Cholesterol	.3 milligram
Sodium	30 milligrams
Dietary Fiber	2.9 grams

*All foods contain some fat. Less than .5 gram of fat per serving is nutritionally insignificant and considered to be "Fat-Free."

waldorf salad

prep time: 15 minutes

chilling time: 30 minutes

ingredients: 2 medium apples, cored & chopped (1 green, 1 red preferred)
1 tablespoon + 3 tablespoons orange juice
1 tablespoon lemon juice
¾ cup chopped celery
⅓ cup chopped dates
⅓ cup raisins
½ cup plain nonfat yogurt or ½ cup yogurt cheese*
2 tablespoons honey

directions: 1. Toss apples with 1 tablespoon only of the orange juice and 1 tablespoon lemon juice and mix well to preserve color. Add celery, dates and raisins.
2. Mix together yogurt, honey and remaining orange juice to make a smooth dressing. Pour over fruit mixture and stir until evenly blended.
3. Cover and chill 30 minutes before serving to give flavors a chance to mingle. Toss again before serving. Use a slotted spoon to serve.

yield: 6 Servings

note: *Use a firm yogurt or yogurt cheese (see page 139) if a thicker dressing is desired.

Cooking without Fat

YOU SAVE 73 CALORIES
This recipe contains 70 calories per serving
Typical recipe contains 143 calories per serving

red cabbage and apples

This is really a delicious salad and the rich purple tones of the cabbage make it a very pretty dish as well.

More than 7,000 varieties of apples have been recorded in the United States alone. The brilliant Red Delicious is the most popular of the eating apples, but we find that the mellow, honeyed flavor of the Golden Delicious is more harmonious with the other ingredients in this recipe.

When buying apples, look for mature, firm, crisp specimens with the stems attached. They should have good color for the variety, and no soft spots, brownish bruises or shriveling.

A food processor can speed preparation of this dish. Use the coarse shredding blade for best texture.

Nutrition Information Per Serving	
Calories	70
Fat	Fat-Free*
Cholesterol	.3 milligram
Sodium	16 milligrams
Dietary Fiber	2.4 grams

*All foods contain some fat. Less than .5 gram of fat per serving is nutritionally insignificant and considered to be "Fat-Free."

red cabbage and apples

prep time: 10 minutes

chilling time: 15 minutes

ingredients: ½ cup plain nonfat yogurt
2-3 tablespoons honey to taste
1 tablespoon apple cider vinegar
1 medium golden delicious apple, cored and chopped
2½ cups coarsely shredded red cabbage
2 tablespoons dark raisins

directions: 1. In large serving bowl, combine yogurt, honey and vinegar and stir until smooth.
2. Add apples, cabbage and raisins and mix well.
3. Cover and chill for a minimum of 15 minutes. Toss again before serving and drain liquid, if desired. Use a slotted spoon to serve.

yield: 4 Servings

Cooking without Fat

YOU SAVE 117 CALORIES
This recipe contains 178 calories per serving
Typical recipe contains 295 calories per serving

three bean salad

This buffet classic (without the usual oil and salt) is one of the most tasty selections. Combining two legumes with fresh green beans turns this salad into a good source of protein. At the same time, a single serving provides over 7 grams of dietary fiber (about 25% of the recommended daily intake). Additionally, the water soluble fiber found in beans has been shown to help reduce serum cholesterol levels.

Although Three Bean Salad can be served as soon as 30 minutes after preparation, the longer it marinates the more penetrating the taste. It will keep for 1 week in the refrigerator.

The texture of home cooked beans is best for this dish. If made with canned beans, be sure to rinse well to remove all salt and any of the starchy surrounding liquid.

Nutrition Information Per Serving	
Calories	178
Fat	1 gram
Percentage of Calories from Fat	5%
Cholesterol	0 milligram
Sodium	133 milligrams
Dietary Fiber	7.3 grams

three bean salad

prep time: 15 minutes

cooking time: 5 minutes

marinating time: 30 minutes

chilling time: 30 minutes

ingredients: ⅔ cup green beans, cut in ½-inch pieces

1 cup cooked garbanzo beans

1¼ cups cooked kidney or pinto beans

¼ cup sliced red onion

¼ cup apple cider vinegar

2 tablespoons honey

¼ cup water

2 tablespoons frozen apple juice concentrate

directions: 1. Steam green beans for 5 minutes, until barely tender. Remove from steamer immediately.

2. Combine all beans and onion in bowl or storage container.

3. Prepare dressing by beating the vinegar, honey, water and apple juice concentrate together with a fork until well blended.

4. Pour dressing over beans and mix well. Cover and let marinate at room temperature at least 30 minutes.

5. Chill for a minimum of 30 minutes. Toss again before serving. Use a slotted spoon to serve.

yield: 4 Servings

Cooking without Fat

YOU SAVE 116 CALORIES
This recipe contains 32 calories per serving
Typical recipe contains 148 calories per serving

italian vegetable marinade

The rousing flavor of marinated vegetables animates many mundane meals. They are a favorite component of an antipasto platter and a flavor booster in tossed salads. They even constitute a sound low calorie snack all by themselves.

What makes this recipe unique is the absence of salt. Those who avoid salt in their diets usually miss out on the pleasures of pickled and marinated foods, as most commercial choices are highly salted. (Just one medium dill pickle packs over 900 mg. of sodium.) Our Italian Vegetable Marinade gets its zesty flavor from garlic and herbs instead.

Don't feel constricted by our choice of vegetables in the ingredient listing. Other equally suitable selections include turnip rounds, radish halves, chunks of kohlrabi, quartered fresh baby artichokes, or other similarly firm vegetables. Although you can pick just one for a solitary vegetable marinade, we recommend an assortment balanced for color and taste.

Time is one of the key ingredients in a good marinade. A minimum of 2 hours marinating time is required. To maximize intensity, give the vegetables at least a day to season. Since Italian Vegetable Marinade keeps for a couple of weeks if refrigerated, and can do so much to liven up a meal, you might want to prepare enough at one time so you won't be caught short.

Nutrition Information Per Serving

Calories	32
Fat	Fat-Free*
Cholesterol	0 milligram
Sodium	15 milligrams
Dietary Fiber	.9 gram

*All foods contain some fat. Less than .5 gram of fat per serving is nutritionally insignificant and considered to be "Fat-Free."

italian vegetable marinade

prep time: 10 minutes

cooking time: 15 minutes

chilling time: 2-3 hours

ingredients: 1 ¼ cups water

2 tablespoons balsamic vinegar

⅓ cup apple cider vinegar

2 tablespoons lemon juice

2 teaspoons Italian seasoning blend

¼ teaspoon white pepper (optional)

2 cloves garlic, minced

¼ cup finely chopped parsley

2½ cups mixed cut vegetables (carrots cut in ¼-inch rounds, celery cut in ¼-inch pieces, red onion rings, green beans cut in 1-inch pieces, red or green pepper chunks cut in 1-inch pieces, small florets of broccoli or cauliflower)

directions: 1. Combine water, vinegars, lemon juice, seasonings, garlic and parsley in large saucepan.

2. Add vegetables. Bring to boil, cover and simmer 10-15 minutes until desired doneness.

3. Remove from heat. Cool to room temperature, cover and chill for at least 2-3 hours before serving. Use a slotted spoon to serve.

yield: 6 Servings

note: Keeps for several weeks if refrigerated.

YOU SAVE 116 CALORIES
This recipe contains 137 calories per serving
Typical recipe contains 253 calories per serving

rice salad

Leftover cooked grains provide the beginnings of a filling salad that can round out a fish or chicken dinner. In this model Rice Salad, the combination of colorful tomato, peas and corn adds visual appeal. The chewy rice and plump moist vegetables work together for texture. The simple lemon-vinaigrette dressing brings out the inherent flavors of the wholesome ingredients without overpowering them.

It is very easy to transform Rice Salad into a lunch or light dinner entree by introducing protein: tuna, cooked beans, tiny bite-size pieces of cooked turkey or chicken, or crumbled tofu. If you want to get fancy, spoon into hollowed out tomatoes or bell pepper halves.

Nutrition Information Per Serving	
Calories	137
Fat	.8 gram
Percentage of Calories from Fat	5%
Cholesterol	0 milligram
Sodium	27 milligrams
Dietary Fiber	5.7 grams

rice salad

prep time: 10 minutes

chilling time: 15 minutes

ingredients: 1 1/2 cups cooked brown rice*
1 cup chopped tomato
1/3 cup frozen peas, thawed
1/3 cup frozen corn kernels, thawed
1/3 cup chopped green onion
1 tablespoon lemon juice
1 tablespoon apple cider vinegar
2 teaspoons honey
1/8 teaspoon white pepper (optional)
1 clove garlic, chopped
1/2 teaspoon crushed dried oregano
1/2 teaspoon crushed dried basil

directions: 1. Combine rice, tomato, peas, corn, and green onions in serving bowl.
2. Beat together remaining ingredients for dressing and pour over rice. Mix well.
3. Cover and chill for a minimum of 15 minutes. Toss again before serving.

yield: 4 Servings

note: *If you have cooked wild rice on hand, mix it with the brown rice for an extra special dish. This salad can also be made with cooked millet or barley.

Cooking without Fat

lentil salad

Lentils are one of the oldest cultivated foods. Even people who shun beans generally like lentils, and of all the beans, they appear to be among the most digestible. Lentils are also quick cooking and don't require soaking beforehand. When preparing lentils for salad be sure to keep the heat down so they cook gently and hold their shape; too vigorous cooking will split the beans and their texture will become pulpy.

Lentils come in a range of colors including brown, green and a handsome red-orange. The directions here pertain to common brown or green lentils. Red lentils, or even yellow split peas, can be substituted but cooking time may be reduced slightly.

Nutrition Information Per Serving

Calories	102
Fat	Fat-Free*
Cholesterol	0 milligram
Sodium	61 milligrams
Dietary Fiber	3.7 grams

*All foods contain some fat. Less than .5 gram of fat per serving is nutritionally insignificant and considered to be "Fat-Free."

lentil salad

prep time: 10 minutes

cooking time: 30 minutes

chilling time: 1 hour

ingredients: ¾ cup dried lentils
2 cups + 2 tablespoons water
1 bay leaf
¼ cup chopped red pepper
¼ cup chopped green pepper
3 tablespoons balsamic vinegar
3 tablespoons lemon juice
1 clove garlic, chopped
¼ cup chopped green onion
½ teaspoon marjoram
½ teaspoon ground thyme
⅛-¼ teaspoon white pepper to taste (optional)
parsley sprigs

directions: 1. Wash lentils, remove any foreign matter, and drain.
2. Combine lentils, 2 cups water and bay leaf in medium saucepan. Bring to boil. Reduce heat, cover and cook just below simmering for 30 minutes, until lentils are cooked but still firm. Cook gently so lentils do not fall apart.
3. Combine red and green peppers in medium saucepan with 2 tablespoons water and cook over medium heat until vegetables soften. Set aside.
4. Drain cooked lentils, while still warm add peppers. Remove bay leaf.
5. Combine vinegar, lemon juice, garlic, green onion, marjoram, thyme and white pepper and pour over lentil mixture, stirring well to coat.
6. Put lentil mixture in a serving bowl and garnish with parsley.
7. Cover and chill 1 hour or longer before serving.

yield: 4 Servings

SALADS AS ENTREES

There's something exciting about eating a salad as an entree. Suddenly, you're free from actually cooking anything! Moreover, uncooked foods are full of vitamins, nutrients and fiber. Many of these recipes create one-dish meals, which will also save you time. Here are some tips on selecting canned fish, which is used in many entree salads.

SELECTING CANNED TUNA
Tuna varies in fat content depending on the species. The leanest is light tuna, followed by white albacore.

Be sure to select tuna canned in water, rather than oil, for a savings of 60 calories and 7 grams fat per 2-ounce portion and a bonus of 20% more protein. If an unsalted choice is not available, drain and rinse well.

SELECTING CANNED SALMON
When selecting canned salmon you may encounter several varieties: (1) chinook or king (the reddest and most costly); (2) sockeye, blueback, or simply "red"; (3) coho, which is lighter than sockeye, but still rich in color and flavor; (4) "pink," which has a paler flesh, less fat and correspondingly less flavor; and (5) chum, which is the least fatty and least tasty. The deeper colored salmons have the highest fat content and are richest in omega-3 fatty acids, but this makes them higher in calories. The red salmons are generally regarded as the most flavorful.

Another thing to look for when buying canned salmon is whether it has been canned with the bone-in (most of the bone softens and melts into the flesh although a few small pieces do remain) or is described as "skinless and boneless." Salmon that is canned with the bone still remaining is an excellent source of the mineral calcium, providing as much as 25% of the U.S. RDA in a 3½ ounce serving.

While it is easy to find solid packed salmon (without added oil or liquid) or salmon canned in water, finding an unsalted product is more difficult. Since sodium content can be quite high, if an unsalted choice is not available, it is best to drain and rinse the fish thoroughly before using.

Cooking without Fat

YOU SAVE 170 CALORIES
This recipe contains 193 calories per serving
Typical recipe contains 363 calories per serving

tuna nicoise

Nice, set in the heart of the famous French Riviera, is well known for its urbane visitors, trendy clubs, sun drenched beaches, and incredible cuisine. The famous Salade Nicoise that originated there is an artful melding of flavors and textures. Its success is built on the freshness and high quality of the ingredients found in the local markets: brilliant red tomatoes bursting with sun-ripened flavor, pencil thin green beans just off the vine, freshly dug potatoes, locally grown artichokes, and tuna of the highest caliber.

Those who have dined on Salade Nicoise in the past will note two key ingredients are missing—capers and olives. Both are extremely high in sodium. Olives, to many people's surprise, have too much fat to make them compatible with the healthiest eating strategy. If you can let go of preconceived expectations, we think you will find this a delightful dish.

Nutrition Information Per Serving	
Calories	193
Fat	.9 gram
Percentage of Calories from Fat	4%
Cholesterol	20 milligrams
Sodium	106 milligrams
Dietary Fiber	5.6 grams

tuna nicoise

prep time: 20 minutes

cooking time: 25 minutes

ingredients: 2 medium potatoes, cut in eighths
2 cups green beans, cut in 1-inch pieces
¼ cup lemon juice
2 tablespoons balsamic vinegar
2 tablespoons water
¾ teaspoon prepared mustard, spicy or dijon
1 tablespoon honey
2 teaspoons dried parsley flakes
⅛ teaspoon white pepper (optional)
6-8 canned artichoke hearts, rinsed and drained
   (14-ounce can)
small head of boston or red leaf lettuce, washed
1 can (6½ ounces) chunk light tuna, packed in water,
   drained
1 tomato, cut in wedges
4 thin red onion slices, cut in half

directions: 1. Place potatoes in vegetable steamer and steam 15 minutes. Add green beans and steam 10 minutes longer, until potatoes and beans are just tender. Remove from steamer immediately. If desired, place potatoes and beans in refrigerator or freezer for fast cooling.

2. Prepare dressing in blender or food processor by pureeing together lemon juice, balsamic vinegar, water, mustard, honey, parsley, white pepper and 2 of the artichokes.

3. Line large serving bowl with large lettuce leaves; tear remaining lettuce into smaller pieces and place in bowl. On top of lettuce add tuna separated into chunks, potatoes, green beans, tomato, onion and remaining artichoke hearts cut into quarters. Pour dressing over all and mix gently but thoroughly.

yield: 4 Servings

Cooking without Fat

YOU SAVE 309 CALORIES
This recipe contains 191 calories per serving
Typical recipe contains 500 calories per serving

tuna pasta salad

Pasta salads are a fitting lunch or light dinner entree. They are also a favorite for buffet service. As with many dishes, chilling has a tendency to dull the flavors. If you prepare this recipe well ahead of time, remove the bowl from the refrigerator and let the salad return to room temperature to restore its caliber.

By using water packed instead of oil packed tuna, nonfat yogurt in place of oil, and adding a variety of colorful crunchy vegetables in place of hard cooked eggs or capers and olives, this pasta salad adds up high in taste and low in calories, fat, cholesterol and sodium.

Nutrition Information Per Serving	
Calories	191
Fat	1.1 grams
Percentage of Calories from Fat	5%
Cholesterol	29 milligrams
Sodium	76 milligrams
Dietary Fiber	4.2 grams

tuna pasta salad

prep time: 20 minutes

cooking time: 15 minutes

ingredients: 1 cup uncooked whole wheat shells or spirals
(1½ cups cooked)

½ cup plain nonfat yogurt

1½ teaspoons honey

1 tablespoon lemon juice

1 teaspoon balsamic vinegar

½ teaspoon dried dill weed

¼ teaspoon celery seed

¼ teaspoon paprika

pinch white pepper (optional)

1 can (6½ ounces) light tuna, packed in water,
rinsed if salted, drained and flaked

⅓ cup frozen peas, unthawed

⅓ cup chopped celery

¼ cup chopped red pepper

2 tablespoons chopped green onion

directions: 1. Cook pasta in boiling water 10-12 minutes to taste.
Drain and rinse with cold water.

2. In large bowl combine yogurt, honey, lemon juice, vinegar, dill, celery seed, paprika and white pepper.

3. Stir in pasta, tuna, peas, celery and red pepper. Mix gently, but thoroughly until evenly coated with dressing. Sprinkle green onion on top.

4. Serve at room temperature. If salad needs to be held for more than 2 hours, cover and refrigerate. If chilled, let sit at room temperature a minimum of 15 minutes before serving.

yield: 4 Servings

Cooking without Fat

YOU SAVE 208 CALORIES
This recipe contains 232 calories per serving
Typical recipe contains 440 calories per serving

tuna bulgur salad

Bulgur is whole wheat that has been partially cooked, dried and cracked into small pieces for faster cooking. It has a nutty flavor and is sold in three grinds: coarse, medium and fine. Other terms for bulgur include cracked wheat, wheat pilaf, bulghur, burghul and parboiled wheat.

We developed this recipe using Health Valley Fat-Free Chicken Broth. It has a full, rich flavor and only 30 calories per serving.

Nutrition Information Per Serving	
Calories	232
Fat	1.1 grams
Percentage of Calories from Fat	4%
Cholesterol	28 milligrams
Sodium	211 milligrams
Dietary Fiber	6 grams

tuna bulgur salad

prep time: 10 minutes

cooking time: 20 minutes

chilling time: 30 minutes

ingredients: 1 ½ cups fat-free chicken broth
¾ cup uncooked bulgur
6 tablespoons apple cider vinegar
2 teaspoons prepared mustard, spicy or dijon
1 tablespoon honey
½ teaspoon crushed dried oregano
dash white pepper (optional)
½ cup chopped celery
½ cup frozen peas, thawed
¼ cup chopped red onion
¼ cup chopped red pepper
1 cup chopped tomato
1 can (6½ ounces) light tuna, packed in water,
rinsed if salted, drained and flaked

directions: 1. In medium saucepan, combine broth and bulgur. Bring to boil. Cover and cook over low heat for 20 minutes or until grain is tender and broth is absorbed.

2. In small bowl, beat together vinegar, mustard, honey, oregano and pepper.

3. When bulgur is cooked, transfer to a serving bowl and add vegetables and tuna. Mix well. Pour on dressing and stir to coat well. Chill for a minimum of 30 minutes before serving.

yield: 4 Servings

YOU SAVE 93 CALORIES
This recipe contains 218 calories per serving
Typical recipe contains 311 calories per serving

tuna salad

The sweetness of Delicious apples is an excellent contrast to the somewhat plain taste of tuna. If you favor tanginess, select a more tart apple instead. Peel or not, according to personal taste – the unpeeled apple contributes added fiber and makes this a more colorful dish. This salad is splendid served on a bed of lettuce garnished with orange slices, or in whole wheat pita pockets with lots of fresh alfalfa sprouts.

Nutrition Information Per Serving

Calories	218
Fat	1.4 grams
Percentage of Calories from Fat	6%
Cholesterol	42 milligrams
Sodium	149 milligrams
Dietary Fiber	3.5 grams

tuna salad

prep time: 15 minutes

ingredients: 1 can (6½ ounces) light tuna, packed in water,
        rinsed and drained if salted
    1 cup chopped red or golden delicious apple
    2 tablespoons orange juice
    ¼ cup chopped green pepper
    ¼ cup chopped celery
    ¼ cup chopped red onion
    dash white pepper (optional)
    ½ cup plain nonfat yogurt or ½ cup yogurt cheese*
    2 tablespoons unsweetened applesauce
    1 teaspoon prepared mustard, spicy or dijon
    lettuce leaves (optional)
    orange slices (optional)

directions: 1. Flake tuna with fork. Add apple, orange juice, green
       pepper, celery, onion, and pepper.
    2. Stir in yogurt, applesauce, and mustard; mix with fork
       until salad is well moistened.
    3. If desired, serve on a bed of lettuce and garnish with
       orange slices.

yield: 2 Servings

note: *Use a firm yogurt or yogurt cheese (see page 139) if a
    thicker dressing is desired.

Cooking without Fat

YOU SAVE 224 CALORIES
This recipe contains 159 calories per serving
Typical recipe contains 383 calories per serving

tuna sandwich spread

For those days when you are in a hurry or without fresh fish or poultry on hand, reach for a can of tuna and try this tasty spread. This easy recipe makes an excellent choice for a sandwich filling or cold salad plate. As a salad, it is particularly attractive presented on a red cabbage leaf.

This recipe can be prepared with tuna or salmon depending on your taste and nutritional preferences. By choosing tuna you save 4.6 grams of fat per serving; the trade-off is salmon is a richer source of beneficial omega-3 fatty acids.

A serving of this recipe prepared with salmon has 186 calories and 5.6 grams of fat with 29% of the calories coming from fat.

Nutrition Information Per Serving

Calories	159
Fat	1 gram
Percentage of Calories from Fat	6%
Cholesterol	58 milligrams
Sodium	199 milligrams
Dietary Fiber	.7 gram

tuna sandwich spread

prep time: 15 minutes

ingredients: 1 can (6½ ounces) light tuna or salmon,
packed in water, rinsed if salted and drained
¼ cup finely chopped celery
¼ cup finely chopped red onion
2 tablespoons finely chopped parsley
⅓ cup plain nonfat yogurt or ⅓ cup yogurt cheese*
½ tablespoon honey
1 teaspoon lemon juice
1 tablespoon prepared mustard, spicy or dijon

directions: 1. Flake fish with fork in medium bowl.
2. Add vegetables.
3. Combine yogurt, honey, lemon juice, and mustard. Mix
with fish and vegetables until evenly distributed and well
moistened.

yield: 2 Servings

note: *Use a firm yogurt or yogurt cheese (see page 139) if a
thicker dressing is desired.

Cooking without Fat

YOU SAVE 199 CALORIES
This recipe contains 276 calories per serving
Typical recipe contains 475 calories per serving

chicken salad oriental

Here is a salad I often prepare as a light lunch, especially during warm weather. It is as nutritious as it is refreshing and tasty. You'll get plenty of protein from the chicken and nonfat yogurt, calcium from the nonfat yogurt and greens, and vitamin C from the oranges, sweet pepper and greens. You also get potassium and vitamin B6 from the banana. The only thing you don't get is all the fat and calories in a typical Chinese chicken salad.

Nutrition Information Per Serving	
Calories	276
Fat	3.4 grams
Percentage of Calories from Fat	11%
Cholesterol	73 milligrams
Sodium	90 milligrams
Dietary Fiber	2.2 grams

chicken salad oriental

prep time: 15 minutes

ingredients: ¾ pound cooked boned, skinless chicken breast meat, diced

1 can (10½ ounces) mandarin oranges canned in juice, drained

½ cup sliced water chestnuts

2 tablespoons + 2 tablespoons chopped green onion

¼ cup chopped red pepper

½ cup plain nonfat yogurt or yogurt cheese*

½ cup mashed banana

3 tablespoons honey

1 tablespoon lemon juice

2 teaspoons apple cider vinegar

1 teaspoon finely chopped ginger

dash white pepper (optional)

3 cups chopped romaine lettuce or dark leafy greens of choice

directions: 1. In mixing bowl, combine chicken, ½ cup orange segments, water chestnuts, 2 tablespoons green onion and red pepper.

2. Combine yogurt, banana, honey, lemon juice, vinegar, ginger and white pepper in blender or food processor. Puree until smooth. Pour over chicken, mix well and chill.

3. To serve, arrange romaine lettuce on serving plate, spoon chicken salad on top, surround with remaining orange segments, and sprinkle remaining 2 tablespoons green onion over all.

yield: 4 Servings

note: *Use a firm yogurt or yogurt cheese (see page 139) if a thicker dressing is desired.

Cooking without Fat HOLIDAY MENU

We present for your holiday dining a festive menu of traditional favorites, including turkey, stuffing, yams and rich tasting desserts prepared the healthy low-fat way. We've kept all the flavor, while <u>eliminating over 95% of the fat and over 40% of the calories.</u>

Here is the complete holiday menu, with remarkable savings in fat and calories for you to compare. You'll enjoy every bite, as you start a new healthy holiday tradition.

	Cooking without Fat			**Traditional**		
	Calories	**Fat**	**% Cal Fat**	**Calories**	**Fat**	**% Cal Fat**
Carrot Orange Salad	65	0.2 gm	3%	161	11 gm	61%
Roast Turkey	153	0.8 gm	5%	210	7 gm	30%
Cranberry Sauce	35	0.0 gm	0	55	0 gm	0
Herb Cracker Stuffing	110	0.2 gm	1%	300	21 gm	63%
Peas with Water Chestnuts	187	0.8 gm	4%	247	9 gm	33%
Pineapple Yam Bake	176	0.2 gm	1%	298	11 gm	33%
Apple Raisin Cheesecake	228	0.3 gm	1%	480	28 gm	53%
Pumpkin Pie	216	0.4 gm	2%	326	12 gm	33%

This Holiday Menu, including ½ serving of each dessert totals:

	Calories	**Fat**	**% of Calories from Fat**
Cooking Without Fat	948	3 gm	3%
Traditional	1674	79 gm	47%

You save <u>726</u> calories by cooking without fat.

Cooking without Fat

holiday menu preparation

To make your holiday meal preparation go as smoothly as possible, we offer the following preparation suggestions.

The two desserts can be made the day ahead, but remember to start the yogurt cheese for the Apple Raisin Cheesecake two days ahead.

While the turkey is roasting, start with the Carrot Orange Salad and Holiday Cranberry Sauce. This will allow plenty of time for them to chill. If you have not stuffed the bird, prepare the stuffing and yams (except for the yam topping).

Top the yams just before baking. The last step is to make the Peas with Water Chestnuts.

Suggested Order of Preparation:
1. Apple Raisin Cheesecake
2. Pumpkin Pie
3. Roast Turkey
   (allow 4-5 hours to roast and ½ hour to cool before carving)
4. Carrot Orange Salad
5. Holiday Cranberry Sauce
6. Herb Cracker Stuffing
7. Pineapple Yam Bake
8. Peas with Water Chestnuts

carrot orange salad

prep time: 20 minutes

chilling time: 15 minutes

ingredients: 4 cups grated carrots (about 1 pound)

1 can (10½ ounces) unsweetened mandarin oranges, drained

⅓ cup finely chopped celery (optional)

1 tablespoon fruit juice sweetened orange marmalade

1 tablespoon honey

3 tablespoons orange juice

1 tablespoon lemon juice

1 teaspoon + 1 teaspoon dried dill

orange slices for garnish

directions: 1. In serving bowl, combine all ingredients except 1 teaspoon dill and orange slices for garnish. Mix well. Cover and refrigerate 15 minutes or longer.

2. Before serving, top with remaining dill and decorate with orange slices. Serve with slotted spoon.

yield: 6 Servings

note: If you have a food processor, I suggest you use the shredding blade to grate the carrots. This will dramatically reduce preparation time.

Nutrition Information Per Serving	
Calories	65
Fat	Fat-Free*
Cholesterol	0 milligram
Sodium	34 milligrams
Dietary Fiber	2.7 grams

*All foods contain some fat. Less than .5 gram of fat per serving is nutritionally insignificant and considered to be "Fat-Free."

roast turkey

prep time: 15 minutes

cooking time: 3½ to 4½ hours

ingredients: 1 12-15 pound fresh turkey hen

directions: 1. Preheat oven to 325°F.

2. Remove neck and organs from body cavity of turkey. Also remove any loose fat from body cavity. Rinse the bird on the outside as well as inside the cavity. Pat the bird dry with toweling.

3. Tie legs and wings close to body with string.

4. Place turkey breast side down on a rack in a shallow roasting pan. Insert meat thermometer in thickest part of thigh and roast in 325°F. oven, 15-18 minutes per pound or until thermometer registers 180°F. Remove the turkey from the oven; let stand 20 30 minutes before carving.

yield: 6-8 Servings

note: Times are for a 12-15 pound unstuffed bird. A stuffed bird will take 15 to 45 minutes longer depending on the size of the bird; insert thermometer in thigh or stuffing.

Roast Turkey can be stuffed with Herb Cracker Stuffing if you desire. The beauty of this recipe is its simplicity, allowing the turkey to cook slowly and baste in its own juices. Our nutritional information is based on 4 ounces of white meat without skin.

Nutrition Information Per Serving	
Calories	153
Fat	.8 gram
Percentage of Calories from Fat	5%
Cholesterol	95 milligrams
Sodium	59 milligrams
Dietary Fiber	0 gram

holiday cranberry sauce

prep time: 5 minutes

cooking time: 5 minutes

chilling time: 30 minutes

ingredients: 2 cups fresh cranberries
½ cup apple juice
⅔ cup honey
1 teaspoon finely chopped orange rind

directions:
1. Combine cranberries, apple juice and honey in a medium saucepan. Bring to a boil over medium heat, stirring constantly.
2. Reduce heat, simmer uncovered for 5 minutes or until berries pop.
3. Remove from heat and stir in orange rind.
4. Cool to room temperature, then chill thoroughly before serving.
5. This sauce will last for at least 2 weeks in the refrigerator.

yield: 1½ Cups

note: Cranberries generally appear on the market only during the Thanksgiving/Christmas season. If you would like to enjoy this fat-free relish at other times of the year, store a few extra bags of cranberries in the freezer. Frozen cranberries can be used exactly like fresh ones. Nutrition information is based on serving size of 1 tablespoon.

Nutrition Information Per Serving	
Calories	35
Fat	Fat-Free*
Cholesterol	0 milligram
Sodium	1 milligram
Dietary Fiber	.4 gram

*All foods contain some fat. Less than .5 gram of fat per serving is nutritionally insignificant and considered to be "Fat-Free."

herb cracker stuffing

prep time: 15 minutes

cooking time: 30 minutes

ingredients: 1 cup coarsely chopped celery

$\frac{1}{2}$ cup chopped onion

1 $\frac{1}{2}$ cups fat-free chicken broth

1 medium apple, cored and coarsely chopped

$\frac{1}{4}$ cup raisins

1 6$\frac{1}{2}$-ounce package fat-free crackers, coarsely crumbled

1 $\frac{1}{2}$ teaspoons Italian seasoning blend

directions: 1. Preheat oven to 350°F.

2. In medium skillet, simmer celery and onion in $\frac{1}{4}$ cup chicken broth until tender.

3. Add remaining ingredients and mix well. Place in covered casserole and bake at 350°F. for 30 minutes.

yield: 6 Servings

note: Herb Cracker Stuffing may be baked in the oven as a side dish, or used to stuff the turkey. If used to stuff the turkey adjust broth to one cup. The recipe is sufficient to stuff a 12-pound turkey. You can adjust the recipe proportionately according to the size of the bird.

We developed this recipe using Health Valley Fat-Free Chicken Broth. It has a full rich flavor and only 30 calories per serving. We also used Health Valley Fat-Free Herb Crackers. They have three times as much fiber as similar crackers.

Nutrition Information Per Serving

Calories	110
Fat	Fat-Free*
Cholesterol	0 milligram
Sodium	192 milligrams
Dietary Fiber	5.1 grams

*All foods contain some fat. Less than .5 gram of fat per serving is nutritionally insignificant and considered to be "Fat-Free."

peas with water chestnuts

prep time: 5 minutes

cooking time: 5 minutes

ingredients: ¼ cup fat-free chicken broth
⅓ cup chopped green onion
1 10-ounce package frozen peas
1 8-ounce can sliced water chestnuts, drained
1 teaspoon dried Italian seasoning blend

directions: 1. Add broth to skillet. Bring to a simmer and add green onions, peas, water chestnuts and seasoning.
2. Simmer uncovered about 5 minutes, until heated through. Drain, discarding liquid.

yield: 4 Servings

We developed this recipe using Health Valley Fat-Free Chicken Broth. It has a full, rich flavor and only 30 calories per serving.

Nutrition Information Per Serving	
Calories	187
Fat	.8 gram
Percentage of Calories from Fat	4%
Cholesterol	0 milligram
Sodium	84 milligrams
Dietary Fiber	7.1 grams

pineapple yam bake

prep time: 30 minutes

cooking time: 10 minutes

ingredients: 3 medium yams (about 1½ pounds total), peeled and sliced 1-inch thick

¾ cup crushed pineapple, packed in juice, drained

3 tablespoons + 1 tablespoon pure maple syrup

2 egg whites

directions: 1. Cook yams in boiling water for 25-35 minutes or until very soft and tender. Drain and mash thoroughly until consistency is smooth.

2. Preheat oven to 400°F.

3. Mix drained pineapple and 3 tablespoons syrup into mashed yams. Spoon into a 9-inch round or 8-inch square non-stick baking pan.

4. Beat egg whites to soft peaks; add remaining 1 tablespoon syrup and beat until stiff; spread with a spatula, using a swirling motion, on top of yam mixture.

5. Bake at 400°F. for 8-10 minutes, or until top is golden.

yield: 6 Servings

Nutrition Information Per Serving	
Calories	176
Fat	Fat-Free*
Cholesterol	0 milligram
Sodium	31 milligrams
Dietary Fiber	2.3 grams

*All foods contain some fat. Less than .5 gram of fat per serving is nutritionally insignificant and considered to be "Fat-Free."

pumpkin pie

prep time: 15 minutes

cooking time: 65 minutes

ingredients: 1 recipe Fat-Free Crust (see page 107) or
1½ cups fat-free cookies, ground into fine crumbs

3 egg whites, lightly beaten

1 can (16 ounces) solid pack pumpkin

½ cup pure maple syrup

1¼ teaspoons cinnamon

¼ teaspoon ground ginger

¼ teaspoon ground cloves

dash nutmeg

1 tablespoon arrowroot

1½ cups (12 fluid ounces) evaporated skimmed milk

directions:

1. Prepare crust for 10-inch nonstick springform pan, OR moisten fingers with water and press cookie crumbs over bottom and slightly up sides of 10-inch springform pan. Chill while preparing remaining ingredients.

2. Preheat oven to 425°F.

3. For filling, in large bowl, with electric mixer on high, combine egg whites, pumpkin, pure maple syrup, spices, arrowroot and evaporated milk until well blended. Pour mixture into prepared pie pan and smooth top with spatula.

4. Bake at 425°F. for 15 minutes, reduce temperature to 325°F. and bake an additional 40-50 minutes or until knife inserted near center comes out clean. Serve warm or at room temperature.

yield: 8 Servings

We developed this recipe using Health Valley Fat-Free Date Delight Cookies.

Nutrition Information Per Serving

Calories	216
Fat	Fat-Free*
Cholesterol	1.9 milligrams
Sodium	107 milligrams
Dietary Fiber	2 grams

*All foods contain some fat. Less than .5 gram of
fat per serving is nutritionally insignificant and
considered to be "Fat-Free."*

apple raisin cheesecake

prep time: 15 minutes

cooking time: 55 minutes

chilling time: 7 hours

ingredients: 2 cups yogurt cheese (see page 139. Drain yogurt 24 hours in advance.)

1 recipe Fat-Free Crust (see page 107.) or
1 1/2 cups fat-free cookies, ground into fine crumbs

2 large apples

1/4 cup + 1/2 cup honey

1 teaspoon vanilla

3 tablespoons arrowroot

3 egg whites

1/3 cup raisins

1/2 teaspoon + 1/2 teaspoon cinnamon

directions: 1. Prepare crust for 8-inch nonstick springform pan, OR moisten fingers with water and press cookie crumbs over bottom and slightly up sides of 8-inch springform pan. Chill while preparing remaining ingredients.

2. Preheat oven to 325°F.

3. Quarter, peel and thinly slice apples. Combine apples with 1/4 cup honey in small bowl and set aside.

4. Beat together yogurt cheese, 1/2 cup honey, vanilla, and arrowroot. In a separate bowl, beat egg whites to soft peak stage; fold egg whites into cheese mixture and mix until well blended. Pour half of the filling into prepared pan.

5. Drain excess liquid from apples. Cover filling with half apples. Sprinkle raisins and ½ teaspoon cinnamon over apples. Pour remaining filling on top and smooth with spatula. Arrange rest of apple slices on top and sprinkle with remaining ½ teaspoon cinnamon.

6. Bake at 325°F. for 55 minutes, or until center is set and surface is lightly browned. Remove from oven, cool to room temperature, then refrigerate until thoroughly chilled.

yield: 8 Servings

We developed this recipe using Health Valley Fat-Free Apple Spice Cookies.

Nutrition Information Per Serving

Calories	228
Fat	Fat-Free*
Cholesterol	1 milligram
Sodium	92 milligrams
Dietary Fiber	3.4 grams

*All foods contain some fat. Less than .5 gram of fat per serving is nutritionally insignificant and considered to be "Fat-Free."

chapter
seven

About Fat

What It Is

Fat is one of the six nutritional components of the food we eat. The other five are protein, carbohydrate, vitamins, minerals and water.

Fat is present in all living things and is the most concentrated source of food energy that there is, providing nine calories in every gram, compared to four calories per gram of protein and carbohydrate. The human body stores the vast majority of its energy reserves as fat.

The Three Different Types of Fat

The principal building blocks of fat are called fatty acids. In the most basic sense, fatty acids fall into three categories: "saturated," "monounsaturated" and "polyunsaturated". All fats are made up of a combination of these three different types of fatty acids, but there is usually one type that predominates. A fat is called either a saturated fat (butter), a monounsaturated fat (olive oil), or a polyunsaturated fat (soybean oil), depending on the type that is most prevalent.

A simple way to tell the difference is that saturated fats, like lard and butter, are usually solid at room temperature, while polyunsaturated and monounsaturated fats, such as safflower oil and olive oil are usually liquid at room temperature.

Food Sources of Fat

Foods that are rich in saturated fats

Chocolate
Coconut and coconut oil, palm oil
Meat, except for poultry, fish and pork
Whole milk, cream, ice cream, cheese and butter

Foods that are rich in monounsaturated fat

Avocados, canola oil, cashews,
Eggs, lard, peanuts, peanut butter, peanut oil, olive oil,
Margarine, pork, poultry, vegetable shortening

Foods that are rich in polyunsaturated fat

Corn, fish, mayonnaise
Safflower, soybean and sunflower oils
Walnuts

Cooking without Fat

The Answers to the Most Frequently Asked Questions About Fat

Q. Will it hurt me to dramatically reduce the amount of fat I eat?

A. Since there is fat present in virtually every whole food we eat, you can get all you need even from a very low-fat diet. Your body can make all the fat you need from the foods you eat, except for the "essential" fatty acids linoleic acid and linolenic acid, two polyunsaturated fatty acids that the human body cannot produce and therefore must get from food. The small amount of fat found in whole grains, vegetables and legumes can provide all the essential fatty acid you need every day, even in a very low-fat diet.

Q. How much fat do I need each day?

A. The National Academy of Sciences says that to stay healthy, you need three to six grams of fat per day in the form of linoleic acid. You can fulfill that amount with a fat level equal to just one or two percent of total calories. And other research[1] suggests that our need for dietary fat may be even less. The amount of linoleic acid you need can be easily obtained from a varied diet of whole grains, vegetables and legumes.

Q. What are the best sources of linoleic acid?

A. Take a look at the following chart for sources in grain. Each lists the amount of linoleic acid in 100 grams (3½ ounces) of each grain:

GRAIN SOURCES OF LINOLEIC ACID

Grain	Amount of Linoleic Acid in grams
Corn	1.15
Whole Wheat	0.83
Wheat Bran	2.68
Oatmeal	3.33
Amaranth	2.83
Millet	2.05
Brown Rice	1.00
Wheat Germ	5.82

1. American Journal of Clinical Nutrition, 1976; 29:559

Q. Are there really "good fats" and "bad fats?"

A. A diet that is too high in total fat can increase the risk of heart disease, obesity, diabetes and some forms of cancer. But eating too much of one kind of fat can also be a problem. Too much saturated fat can raise the level of cholesterol in your blood and raise the risk of heart attack and stroke. By cutting down on total fat and replacing some of the fat you eat with fats that are monounsaturated or polyunsaturated, you may be able to reduce your blood cholesterol and your risk of cardiovascular disease.

Q. What is the right balance of fats in my diet?

A. The leading health-promoting organizations all recommend that we should consume no more than 30 percent of our calories in the form of fat and that saturated fats, monounsaturated fats and polyunsaturated fats should make up no more than one-third each of our fat intake. There is now research showing that there can be significant health benefits to cutting your fat intake even lower – to no more than 15 percent of total calories.

Q. Does it really make that much of a difference if I get 30 percent of my calories from fat, rather than 40 percent?

A. Cutting fat from 40 percent of calories to 30 percent of calories can be critical.

There is now overwhelming evidence that too much fat in our diets increases our risk of heart disease, cancer, obesity and diabetes.

Societies throughout the world that consume diets high in fat have high rates of heart disease and cancer. Conversely, cultures that consume low-fat diets show significantly lower incidences of these diseases.

There are a number of examples to illustrate this, but in the interest of simplicity, we will cite only one. When Japanese immigrate from their homeland and give up their traditional low fat diets in favor of high-fat American diets, their incidence of heart disease and certain cancers rises dramatically. In Japan, heart disease and cancers of the breast, colon and prostate have all been rare. But once immigrants begin eating a high-fat, typical American diet, their incidences of these diseases soon reaches the same level as the rest of the American population.

The precise reason why excess fat seems to contribute to some forms of cancer isn't known, but researchers are looking into the possibility that high-fat diets may contribute to hormonal changes that may trigger the problem.

The National Cancer Institute estimates that a reduction in daily fat intake from 40 percent of calories to 25 percent of calories could reduce breast cancer mortality among women by 25 percent. Currently, some 36,000 American women die from breast cancer each year, so this dietary change alone could save as many as 9,000 lives a year!

Reducing fat intake from 40 percent of calories to 30 percent of calories or less is critical. To understand just how much more fat Americans consume than other societies, consider that the traditional Japanese diet contained only about 10 percent of calories from fat, although the introduction of Western "fast" food since the end of World War II has raised that figure to about 15 percent of calories.

That's why America's leading health-promoting organizations, including the National Academy of Sciences, the American Heart Association and the National Cancer Institute all recommend that you reduce your fat intake to no more than 30 percent of total calories. And some experts suggest that a cutback to 25 percent or 15 percent would be even better.

Q. Are saturated fat and cholesterol the same thing?

A. No. Although there appears to be a direct relationship between the intake of saturated fat and the level of serum cholesterol, they are different, and they perform different functions in the body.

Q. What is cholesterol?

A. Cholesterol is a waxy substance that is an important constituent of every cell in the human body. It is also a necessary component of many vital hormones. Cholesterol is only found in humans and animals, not in foods of plant origin.

Q. Where does the body get cholesterol?

A. The body gets cholesterol from one of two sources:
1. Cholesterol is supplied by the diet in foods from animal sources, such as meats and dairy products.
2. The body can also make all the cholesterol it needs from other raw materials provided in the diet, so it isn't necessary to consume any cholesterol for the body to be healthy.

Q. Should children follow a low-fat diet, too?

A. The American Heart Association has recommended that children over the age of two should follow the same dietary guidelines as adults and limit the amount of fat they eat to no more than 30 percent of calories. However, normal, healthy children under 2 years are growing rapidly and require fat for growth and energy, so their fat intake should not be restricted. Your personal pediatrician can give you the best advice about whether your child's diet is too high in fat.

Q. Shouldn't I be more concerned about saturated fat than about total fat in my diet?

A. It's true that saturated fat is the main factor in raising your blood cholesterol level, and that studies have linked a high cholesterol level to developing atherosclerosis. However, by concentrating your efforts on reducing the amount of total fat that you eat, you'll be increasing your scope, while simplifying your diet. First off, you'll save calories, since a gram of fat contains 9 calories, and both protein and carbohydrates contain only 4. This can help you to maintain your ideal weight level. Next, research has shown that a fat intake of over 30 percent is linked to a number of degenerative diseases. By keeping well under that figure you decrease your risk.

Cooking without Fat

Eating Too Much Fat and Health Problems

Eating too much fat can create conditions that may lead to a variety of health problems. Although no one person is likely to develop all these symptoms, and there can be other factors that contribute to all these conditions, here is a list of the disorders that may be related to eating too much fat:

Acne – Some dermatologists believe that excessive fat intake can result in increased production of sebum, an oily, waxy substance produced by the sebaceous glands in the skin. This, they believe, can contribute to acne.

Allergies – Many high-fat foods can be highly allergenic, including dairy products and eggs.

Bloating – Poor digestion of fatty foods can lead to an uncomfortable feeling of being bloated after eating.

Constipation – Foods that are high in fat usually contain little or no dietary fiber. And a diet that is low in fiber can result in constipation.

Dizziness – A decreased flow of blood in the arteries that supply the inner ear apparatus, which controls our balance, can result in dizziness. This decreased flow can result from a high-fat diet.

Fatigue – Poor digestion of fatty foods can result in feeling tired. But since high-fat foods tend to contain fewer essential vitamins and minerals than lower fat alternatives, fatigue may also result from an inadequate intake of these key nutrients.

Indigestion—Gas, indigestion and stomach pains can result from eating too much fat, which is hard to digest, or from allergies to fatty foods, such as milk, eggs and red meat.

Menstrual Cramps—A hormonal imbalance can sometimes be caused by excessive levels of estrogen that can in turn be the result of a diet high in fat.

Obesity—Eating fat can make you fat because fat contains more than twice as many calories as protein and carbohydrate. And while your body can speed up its metabolism to burn off excess protein and carbohydrate you consume, if you eat too much fat, your body simply puts it into fat cells to save it.

Premenstrual Syndrome (PMS)—This condition can also be related to excessive production of estrogen that in turn can be related to excessive intake of fat.

Skin Rashes—Skin rashes can often be the result of consuming food allergens. As mentioned before, many high-fat foods like dairy products and eggs are among those to which people are most commonly allergic.

Vertigo (loss of balance)—A condition similar to dizziness, this condition can be related to the reduction of blood flow to the inner ear structures that affect balance. Once again the culprit may be atherosclerotic plaques resulting from a high-fat diet.

Eating Too Much Fat
and Your Risk of Heart Disease

Heart attack, stroke and related diseases of the heart and blood vessels kill more than one million Americans every year. That's as many deaths as were caused by all other causes of death combined, including cancer!

The major cause of the high incidence of these diseases is **atherosclerosis,** the build up of fatty deposits in the arteries that restrict or totally block the flow of blood to the heart, brain and other vital organs. And there is no question that a major underlying cause of atherosclerosis is too much fat, especially saturated fat, in the American diet.

Too much fat can lead to an elevated cholesterol level, one of the principal risk factors associated with heart disease. This can happen in two ways. First, too much fat can rapidly lead to obesity, a condition that is associated with elevated cholesterol levels. When people who are obese lose weight, their cholesterol levels tend to go down. Second, saturated fat like the kind found in red meat and full-fat dairy products can directly increase the level of serum cholesterol, even if the person is not overweight. When people with elevated cholesterol levels reduce their intake of saturated fat, their serum cholesterol levels tend to go down.

While we have little control over the amount of fat used in preparing the foods we eat when dining out, we can exercise virtually total control over the amount of fat used in preparing our own foods at home. So one of the best ways to reduce your fat intake is to **prepare more of your own foods at home and cook without fat.** In fact, by following the nutrition guidelines of the American Heart Association, including eating less red meat and full-fat dairy products, and cooking without butter, cream, cooking oil, margarine, cheese and eggs, you can probably reduce your cholesterol level 5 percent or more, based on scientific studies. This translates into a reduction in risk of heart attack of 15 percent. That's because following the dietary guidelines and cooking without fat can easily reduce the percentage of calories you get from fat from the average of nearly 40 percent to a healthier level of 30 percent of calories or even less.

In scientific studies, those reducing the percentage of calories from fat from 40 percent to 30 percent have also reduced the level of cholesterol in their blood by five percent.[2] And other scientific studies have concluded that for every one percent that serum cholesterol is reduced, you reduce your risk of heart attack and stroke by three percent.[3]

So it's easy to see how cutting fat from your diet can substantially reduce your risk of heart attack and stroke.

Eating Too Much Fat and Your Risk of Diabetes

Eating too much fat can also raise your risk of developing a particular form of diabetes known as non-insulin dependent diabetes mellitus or, more commonly, adult or late onset diabetes. This form of diabetes represents about 90 percent of the cases of diabetes in America. And about 80 percent of the people who suffer from this ailment are obese. Adult onset diabetes usually develops subtly as a result of a gradual reduction in the body's insulin production. Additionally, many of the cells of the body become resistant to insulin, caused to a great extent by obesity. This reduction in the body's insulin production and in the cells' insulin sensitivity results in a decrease in the ability of body cells to use glucose. And ultimately it results in the elevated blood sugar levels associated with diabetes.

So a diet that is high in fat can certainly increase your risk of developing diabetes. And a low fat diet that is high in fiber and complex carbohydrates can certainly reduce your risk of developing this disease which ranks as the sixth most common cause of death in America.

Eating Too Much Fat and Your Risk of Cancer

Of all the different factors in our diet that have been found to have a relationship to cancer, fat has been the most studied and the one most frequently associated with the incidence of this most feared disease.

2. Journal of the American Dietetic Association, 1986; 759-764.
3. Lancet, 1990; 335:765-774.

Fat is thought to contribute to cancer in two ways.

First, a high intake of fat, particularly polyunsaturated fat, increases the possibility of the formation of unstable molecules known as "free radicals." It is believed that these molecules may actually be involved in initiating cancer by damaging the genes in our cells.

Second, once a cancer is initiated, research indicates that a high fat diet may help promote the growth of tumors. This is why certain cancers are much more common in societies that consume a high percentage of calories from fat.

While a high fat intake has not been associated with the incidence of all forms of cancer, it has been positively associated with breast cancer, prostate cancer, various cancers of the reproductive organs and cancers of the gastrointestinal tract.

Because of the strength of these associations, the National Cancer Institute, the American Cancer Society and the Surgeon General of the United States have all recommended a dramatic reduction in the consumption of fat.

It has been estimated that a 20 percent reduction in the incidence of cancer could be achieved from improving our diet. And the principal recommendation to accomplish this goal is *eat less fat!*

While the risk of heart disease and stroke is directly associated with both total fat and specifically the intake of saturated fats, the risk of cancer is directly associated with total fat and specifically with polyunsaturated fats. So again it's easy to see how important it is to select prepared foods that are low in fat or fat-free and to learn to cook nutritious, good tasting foods at home without fat.

The American Cancer Society has stated that up to 35 percent of all cancer deaths may be diet related and other health promoting organizations and nutrition professionals have suggested that improved diet, including a dramatic reduction in fat consumption, can reduce the occurrence of cancer by up to 50 percent.

3 kinds of fat

monounsaturated fats

avocados

eggs and pork

peanuts

poultry

canola, peanut and olive oils

margarine

OLIVE OIL

saturated fats

chocolate

ice cream, whole milk, cream and cheese

COCONUT OIL

coconut and palm oils

butter

red meat

polyunsaturated fats

corn

fish

Mayonnaise

walnuts

sunflower, safflower and soybean oils

chapter eight

Nutritional Information

nutritional analyses of recipes for "*Cooking without Fat*"

The Charts and How to Use Them

To provide you with the specific nutritional information you want about the recipes in "Cooking Without Fat" we have created the two sets of easy to use charts in this section.

In the first set of charts, we have looked at each nutrient individually, showing which recipes contain the most, or in some cases, the least amount of that nutrient per serving. We have also included a brief discussion of the nutritional role of each nutrient.

The second set of charts provides a complete nutritional profile for each recipe by section and in alphabetical order. Twenty-two values are given for each recipe.

All of the recipes in this book are a superior source of one or more nutrients. The nutrients for which each recipe is a superior source is highlighted in bold type. In designating a recipe a superior source of a nutrient, we compared the level of the nutrient to the level of calories. For comparison purposes, we chose 2000 calories as the standard level per day.

If a recipe provides a greater percentage of the U.S. RDA of a nutrient than it does of calories, then it is a superior source of that nutrient. For example, "Creamy New York Cheesecake" provides 31.3% of the U.S. RDA of calcium per serving. And since it provides only 10.7% of the 2000 calories daily standard it is a superior source of calcium.

We believe that these charts will make it easy for you to find the specific nutritional information you want and to select recipes based on your personal wants and needs.

calories

What is commonly referred to as a calorie is technically called a kilocalorie–the energy value of food expressed as a unit of heat. A kilocalorie is the amount of heat needed to raise the temperature of a kilogram (a little more than a quart) of water by 1 degree centigrade. By extension, 100 kilocalories would raise the temperature of water from 0 degrees centigrade (freezing) to 100 degrees centigrade (boiling).

Different amounts of dissimilar foods can provide the same amount of energy. For example, 4½ cups of cabbage, 1 tablespoon of vegetable oil and 2 tablespoons of sugar all provide 100 kilocalories.

Overconsumption of calories is a primary cause of obesity, which increases the risk of such serious degenerative diseases as cancer, heart disease and diabetes. The National Research Council has established recommended daily allowances for calories based on age, sex, weight and height. The RDA for a 138 pound woman between 25 and 50 years of age with moderate activity level is 2200 kilocalories per day. The RDA for a 174 pound man between 25 and 50 years of age with a moderate activity level is 2900 kilocalories.

Recipes with the Highest Number of Calories Per Serving

Peach Baked Chicken on Bulgur	317
Mushroom-Marinara Sauce on Pasta	314
Bombay Chicken	314
Black Bean Chili Bake	312
Tofu Mushroom Stuffed Baked Potatoes	294
Fish Stew	287
Pasta Primavera	285
Tex Mex Tortillas	281
Sweet and Sour Chicken	279
Chili Pie	279
Poached Fish Dinner with Mustard-Dill Sauce	278
Chicken Salad Oriental	276
Indian Style Turkey	274
Stuffed Peppers	272
Chicken Vegetable Stew	271
Poached Pears with Yogurt Sauce	264
Spanish Garden Chili	261
Banana Split	260
Curried Chicken	253
Orange Honey Baked Chicken	253

Recipes with the Lowest Number of Calories Per Serving *(Dressings and Sauces Excluded)*

Italian Vegetable Marinade	32
Gazpacho	42
Dijon Carrots and Zucchini	45
Honey Mustard Vegetables	56
Braised Red Cabbage	60
Healthy Coleslaw	61
Mediterranean Salad	64
Carrot Orange Salad	65
Red Cabbage and Apples	70
Orange Glazed Carrots	72
Honey Glazed Beets	73
Garden Vegetable Soup	75
Golden Squash Soup	77
Hot Borscht	78
Mexican Corn	80
Super Carrot Raisin Salad	93
Lentil Salad	102
Raspberry-Filled Melon	107
Honey Mustard Potato Salad	108
Creamy Skillet Cabbage	110

protein

Protein is a constituent of every living cell. In humans it accounts for half of the dry matter of an adult.

Protein is composed of 22 building blocks called amino acids. Our bodies manufacture 14 of these amino acids, but eight of these amino acids must be obtained from food. That is why they are called the "essential" amino acids. They are ISOLEUCINE, LEUCINE, METHIONINE, VALINE, PHENYLALANINE, THREONINE, LYSINE and TRYPTOPHAN.

Foods that contain all eight essential amino acids provide protein that is considered to be "high quality." Animal food sources contain high quality protein. Plant foods are frequently lacking in one or more of the eight essential amino acids. Combining complementary plant foods carefully improves the quality of the protein.

Protein is required for growth, and formation of essential body compounds including hormones, enzymes and coenzymes. It helps maintain both the water balance and acid-base balance, and is necessary for the production of antibodies.

The U.S. RDA for protein is 45 grams of high-quality protein, or 65 grams of lower quality protein. Good sources of high quality protein are poultry, fish and lean meat, egg whites, nonfat dairy products, and amaranth.

Recipes with the Greatest Amount of Protein Per Serving

Roast Turkey Breast	34 gm	Fish Cakes	28 gm
Indian Style Turkey	32 gm	Peach Baked Chicken on Bulgur	27 gm
Mexican Chicken	32 gm	Fish Stew	27 gm
Curried Chicken	31 gm	Bombay Chicken	27 gm
Chicken Salad Oriental	30 gm	Italian Meatballs	26 gm
Sweet and Sour Chicken	29 gm	Tuna Sandwich Spread	26 gm
Sloppy Joes	29 gm	Glazed Meatloaf	26 gm
Tuna Salad	28 gm	Orange Honey Baked Chicken	25 gm
Chicken Vegetable Stew	28 gm	with Mustard-Dill Sauce	
Chicken Cacciatore	28 gm	Poached Fish Dinner	24 gm
		Chicken Dijon	24 gm

carbohydrates

Carbohydrates are either starches or sugar. They are the body's primary and best source of energy, and the only source of energy for the nervous system. They are also essential for the proper oxidation of fats.

Carbohydrates are composed of carbon, hydrogen and oxygen, and are classified as "monosaccharides" (single sugars like fructose and glucose), "disaccharides" (double sugars like sucrose, lactose and maltose), or "polysaccharides" (complex carbohydrates like starch, dextrin and glycogen).

Carbohydrates make up about 46 percent of the typical American diet. Unfortunately most of these calories come from refined sugar, which provides only "empty calories." A healthy diet should contain 55 to 60 percent of its calories from carbohydrates, which include fruits, vegetables, legumes and whole grains.

Recipes with the Most Carbohydrates Per Serving

Mushroom-Marinara Sauce on Pasta	74 gm
Pasta Primavera	67 gm
Poached Pears with Yogurt Sauce	65 gm
Banana Split	62 gm
Tofu Mushroom Stuffed Baked Potatoes	59 gm
Black Bean Chili Bake	57 gm
Stuffed Peppers	56 gm
Tex Mex Tortillas	54 gm
Chili Pie	53 gm
Apple Raisin Cheesecake	53 gm
Spanish Garden Chili	53 gm
Pumpkin Pie	48 gm
Moroccan Eggplant and Garbanzo Beans	48 gm
Bombay Chicken	45 gm
Stuffed Baked Winter Squash	45 gm
Raspberry Cheesecake	44 gm
Old Fashioned Rice Pudding	44 gm
Frozen Fruit Creme	44 gm
Peach Baked Chicken on Bulgur	44 gm
Sweet and Sour Cabbage and Beans	43 gm

fat

Fats, like carbohydrates, are composed of carbon, hydrogen and oxygen. They are the most concentrated source of food energy supplying 9 calories per gram. Fats transport the fat soluble vitamins A, D, E, and K and are the source of the essential fatty acids necessary for normal growth. Fats are also necessary for the production of a variety of body compounds including hormone-like substances called prostaglandins which control a vast range of bodily functions.

The typical American diet contains 42% of calories from fat. The American Heart Association and the American Cancer Society recommend no more than 30% of calories be derived from fat, and saturated fat intake should be less than 10% of calories. Excessive fat consumption is a primary risk factor for heart disease and stroke, cancer and obesity. In *Cooking Without Fat* all the recipes are low in saturated fat and contain 15% or less of calories from fat.

Recipes with the Smallest Amount of Fat Per Serving *(Dressings and Sauces Excluded)*

Honey Glazed Beets	0.1 gm
Honey Mustard Vegetables	0.1 gm
Creamy Peach Cheesecake	0.1 gm
Herb Cracker Stuffing	0.2 gm
Dijon Carrots and Zucchini	0.2 gm
Pineapple Yam Bake	0.2 gm
Honey Mustard Potato Salad	0.2 gm
Super Carrot Raisin Salad	0.2 gm
Hot Borscht	0.2 gm
Italian Vegetable Marinade	0.2 gm
Baked Orange Beets	0.2 gm
Carrot Orange Salad	0.2 gm
Carrot "Cake"	0.2 gm
Raspberry Cheesecake	0.2 gm
Healthy Coleslaw	0.2 gm
Apple Raisin Cheesecake	0.3 gm
Orange Glazed Carrots	0.3 gm
Creamy New York Cheesecake	0.3 gm
Frozen Fruit Creme	0.3 gm

Recipes with the Greatest Amount of Fat Per Serving

Curried Chicken	3.5 gm
Bombay Chicken	3.5 gm
Sweet and Sour Chicken	3.5 gm
Chicken Cacciatore	3.4 gm
Chicken Salad Oriental	3.4 gm
Mexican Chicken	3.4 gm
Poached Fish Dinner with Mustard-Dill Sauce	3.3 gm
Stuffed Peppers	3.3 gm
Peach Baked Chicken on Bulgur	3.3 gm
Chicken Vegetable Stew	3.2 gm
Orange Honey Baked Chicken	3.0 gm
Tofu Mushroom Stuffed Baked Potatoes	2.9 gm
Easy Skillet Chicken	2.8 gm
Chicken Dijon	2.6 gm
Moroccan Eggplant and Garbanzo Beans	2.4 gm
Zesty Mexican Chicken Soup	2.4 gm
Southwest Garbanzo Beans	2.2 gm
Italian Frittata	2.1 gm
Fish Stew	2.0 gm

cholesterol

Cholesterol is a waxy substance found only in animal tissue. It is present in many of the foods we consume but can also be manufactured by the body as needed.

Cholesterol is necessary for the synthesis of important hormones including the sex hormones. It is necessary for the production of bile acids and therefore for the proper digestion of dietary fat. It is also necessary for the production of vitamin D in the body and helps protect the skin from a variety of chemical agents and helps prevent abnormal moisture loss through the skin. Cholesterol is part of the structure of every cell in the body and is found in the blood in combination with triglycerides and protein.

Excessive cholesterol in the blood is a primary risk factor for heart attack and stroke. To modify this risk it is recommended that a healthy diet contain no more than 300 milligrams per day. Only animal products, such as meat, poultry, fish, dairy and egg yolks contain cholesterol. Over half of the recipes in this book contain less than .5 milligram of cholesterol per serving. Thirty-nine contain no cholesterol at all. None of the recipes below have as much cholesterol per serving as is found in half an egg.

Recipes Highest in Cholesterol Per Serving

Roast Turkey Breast	95 mg
Indian Style Turkey	79 mg
Chicken Salad Oriental	73 mg
Sweet and Sour Chicken	72 mg
Curried Chicken	72 mg
Bombay Chicken	67 mg
Chicken Vegetable Stew	65 mg
Chicken Cacciatore	65 mg
Mexican Chicken	64 mg
Peach Baked Chicken on Bulgur	64 mg
Orange Honey Baked Chicken	64 mg
Chicken Dijon	64 mg
Glazed Meatloaf	63 mg
Italian Meatballs	63 mg
Tuna Sandwich Spread	58 mg
Easy Skillet Chicken	55 mg
Zesty Mexican Chicken Soup	48 mg
Turkey Vegetable Burgers	47 mg
Sloppy Joes	47 mg
Fish Stew	42 mg

dietary fiber

Dietary fiber is the portion of plant foods that cannot be digested by the human digestive system. There are two types of dietary fiber, water soluble and water insoluble.

Water soluble fiber binds with cholesterol-rich bile acids in the intestinal tract. Diets high in this type of fiber have been associated with lowered serum cholesterol levels and lowered risk of heart disease and stroke. Oat and rice bran as well as kidney and garbanzo beans are rich sources of soluble fiber.

Water insoluble fiber adds bulk to the diet and helps prevent constipation. Diets high in insoluble fiber are associated with reduced risk of some forms of cancer including cancer of the colon and rectum. Wheat bran is the most noted source of insoluble fiber. Figs and prunes are also good sources.

The National Cancer Institute recommends eating 25-35 grams of dietary fiber a day.

Recipes with the Greatest Amount of Dietary Fiber Per Serving

Black Bean Chili Bake	19.3 gm
Spanish Garden Chili	13.7 gm
Chili Pie	12.6 gm
Pasta Primavera	10.8 gm
Tex Mex Tortillas	10.6 gm
Moroccan Eggplant and Garbanzo Beans	10.4 gm
Mushroom-Marinara Sauce on Pasta	10.3 gm
Sloppy Joes	10.2 gm
Mexican Chicken	9.6 gm
Three Bean Salad	7.3 gm
Sweet and Sour Cabbage and Beans	7.2 gm
Peas with Water Chestnuts	7.1 gm
Southwest Garbanzo Beans	7.1 gm
Tofu Mushroom Stuffed Baked Potatoes	6.3 gm
Stuffed Baked Winter Squash	6.3 gm
Tuna Bulgur Salad	6.0 gm
Rice Salad	5.7 gm
Tuna Nicoise	5.6 gm
Stuffed Peppers	5.4 gm
Herb Cracker Stuffing	5.2 gm

vitamin a – beta carotene

Vitamin A is important for the health of the digestive tract, respiratory tract, eyes, skin and reproductive systems. It is necessary for proper night vision. Vitamin A aids in the detoxification of poisons, and is essential for resisting infections, allergies and the effects of air pollution. Diets high in vitamin A have been associated with a reduced risk in the incidence of cancers of the digestive and respiratory systems.

Vitamin A is present in foods of animal origin as pre-formed vitamin A, or in foods of plant origin as Beta Carotene, the non-toxic vitamin A precursor that the body converts to vitamin A as needed.

The U.S. RDA is 5,000 I.U. per day. Good sources of vitamin A include nonfat dairy products and certain fish. Good sources of Beta Carotene include carrots, dark green leafy vegetables, and both dark orange vegetables and fruits.

Recipes with the Greatest Amount of Vitamin A

Cream of Corn-Potato Soup	301 I.U.
Pumpkin Pie	188 I.U.
Poached Fish Dinner with Mustard-Dill Sauce	155 I.U.
Old Fashioned Rice Pudding	125 I.U.
Oven Fried Fish	95 I.U.
Frozen Fruit Creme	93 I.U.
Nonfat Whipped Topping	88 I.U.
Islander Fish Filets	81 I.U.
Orange Roughy in Citrus Sauce	79 I.U.
Tuna Salad	68 I.U.

Recipes with the Greatest Amount of Beta Carotene

Orange Glazed Carrots	31,970 I.U.
Glazed Curried Carrots	31,900 I.U.
Pineapple Yam Bake	24,760 I.U.
Carrot Orange Salad	21,330 I.U.
Pumpkin Pie	20,270 I.U.
Chicken Vegetable Stew	15,700 I.U.
Pasta Primavera	15,100 I.U.
Dijon Carrots and Zucchini	14,520 I.U.
Fish Stew	13,600 I.U.
Easy Skillet Chicken	10,770 I.U.

vitamin c

Vitamin C is necessary for the formation and maintenance of bones, teeth and gums, and connective tissue. It is required to maintain the strength of blood vessels and is an important antioxidant. It promotes good healing, aids in resisting infection, and enhances the absorption of iron. Vitamin C helps maintain a strong immune system and helps the body cope with stress. Diets high in vitamin C have been associated with a lower incidence of cancers of the esophagus and stomach.

The U.S. RDA for vitamin C is 60 milligrams per day. Due to its numerous functions in the body, many healthcare professionals feel that the body's need for vitamin C may be significantly greater. Vitamin C is found in citrus fruits, tomatoes, strawberries, melons, green peppers and dark green vegetables such as broccoli and spinach.

Recipes with the Greatest Amount of Vitamin C Per Serving

Stuffed Peppers	119 mg
Pasta Primavera	82 mg
Fish Stew	71 mg
Raspberry-Filled Melon	68 mg
Sweet and Sour Cabbage and Beans	67 mg
Mexican Chicken	65 mg
Sweet and Sour Chicken	56 mg
Chicken Cacciatore	55 mg
Orange Honey Baked Chicken	54 mg
Chicken Salad Oriental	53 mg
Tuna Salad	49 mg
Braised Red Cabbage	49 mg
Moroccan Eggplant and Garbanzo Beans	49 mg
Banana Split	42 mg
Tuna Nicoise	40 mg
Rice Salad	37 mg
Orange Roughy in Citrus Sauce	37 mg
Frozen Fruit Creme	36 mg
Easy Skillet Chicken	35 mg
Sloppy Joes	35 mg

calcium

Calcium is essential for the formation and maintenance of strong bones and teeth. It is involved in the regulation of heart beat, muscle action and transmission of nerve impulses. Calcium also aids in blood clotting.

The U.S. RDA is 1,000 milligrams per day. Good sources of calcium are nonfat dairy products, dark green leafy vegetables and canned salmon with the soft bones.

Recipes with the Greatest Amount of Calcium Per Serving

Creamy New York Cheesecake	313 mg
Raspberry Cheesecake	242 mg
Frozen Fruit Creme	207 mg
Pumpkin Pie	185 mg
Banana Split	181 mg
Cream of Corn-Potato Soup	177 mg
Tuna Salad	165 mg
Spinach Mushroom Lasagna	162 mg
Poached Fish Dinner with Mustard-Dill Sauce	156 mg
Carrot "Cake"	147 mg
Apple Raisin Cheesecake	137 mg
Creamy Peach Cheesecake	130 mg
Tofu Mushroom Stuffed Baked Potatoes	117 mg
Stuffed Peppers	114 mg
Poached Pears with Yogurt Sauce	112 mg
Chicken Salad Oriental	110 mg
Greek Rice	108 mg
Fish Stew	107 mg
Tuna Sandwich Spread	107 mg
Mexican Chicken	106 mg

sodium

Sodium regulates body fluid balance. It is involved in the maintenance of normal water balance as well as the body's acid-base balance. Sodium is also required for the absorption of glucose and the transport of other nutrients across cell membranes.

Although an essential mineral, sodium is abundant in our food supply. It is found in table salt and in all foods except fruits. An excessive intake of sodium is a risk factor for hypertension, which in turn is a primary risk factor for heart attack and stroke. The American Heart Association recommends an intake of no more than 1,000 milligrams per 1,000 calories consumed daily, and a maximum daily intake of no more than 3,000 milligrams. The recipes in *Cooking Without Fat* are all low in sodium with 64 containing less than 100 milligrams per serving.

Recipes with the Greatest Amount of Sodium Per Serving

Black Bean Chili Bake	460 mg
Chili Pie	366 mg
Tex Mex Tortillas	341 mg
Chicken Dijon	320 mg
Moroccan Eggplant and Garbanzo Beans	314 mg
Chicken Broth	309 mg
Poached Fish Dinner with Mustard-Dill Sauce	305 mg
Sloppy Joes	302 mg
Spinach Mushroom Lasagna	298 mg
Spanish Garden Chili	287 mg
Zesty Mexican Chicken Soup	263 mg
Southwest Garbanzo Beans	255 mg
Peach Baked Chicken on Bulgur	253 mg
Oven Fried Fish	248 mg
Curried Chicken	236 mg
Mexican Chicken	231 mg
Chicken Vegetable Stew	224 mg
Glazed Meatloaf	219 mg
Tuna Bulgur Salad	211 mg
Barley Pilaf	200 mg

potassium

Potassium is important in maintenance of both body fluid and acid-base balance, and transmission of nerve impulses. It is also necessary for the proper functioning of all muscles including the heart, and is involved in release of energy and production of glycogen and protein.

There is not an established U.S. RDA for potassium. An adequate intake is considered to be 2000 to 5000 milligrams. Most foods contain potassium. Rich sources include fruits–especially raisins, bananas and oranges, nonfat dairy products, whole grain bread and cereal products, legumes, potatoes and lean meat, poultry and fish.

Recipes with the Greatest Amount of Potassium Per Serving

Fish Stew	1477 mg
Poached Fish Dinner with Mustard-Dill Sauce	1341 mg
Sloppy Joes	1291 mg
Pasta Primavera	1120 mg
Tofu Mushroom Stuffed Baked Potatoes	1071 mg
Black Bean Chili Bake	1018 mg
Chicken Vegetable Stew	968 mg
Spanish Garden Chili	958 mg
Tuna Nicoise	943 mg
Stuffed Baked Winter Squash	914 mg
Indian Style Turkey	905 mg
Spinach Mushroom Lasagna	868 mg
Mexican Chicken	835 mg
Mushroom-Marinara Sauce on Pasta	834 mg
Stuffed Peppers	823 mg
Sweet and Sour Cabbage and Beans	806 mg
Moroccan Eggplant and Garbanzo Beans	798 mg
Tex Mex Tortillas	792 mg
Tuna Salad	757 mg
Chicken Cacciatore	718 mg

magnesium

Magnesium acts as a catalyst in hundreds of biological reactions. It is essential for cellular respiration and necessary for proper nerve and muscle function. Magnesium is also required for production of protein within the body.

The U.S. RDA is 400 milligrams per day. Magnesium is found in whole grain bread and cereal products, water chestnuts, legumes, spinach and nonfat dairy products.

Recipes with the Greatest Amount of Magnesium Per Serving

Mushroom-Marinara Sauce on Pasta	119 mg
Pasta Primavera	113 mg
Spinach Mushroom Lasagna	97 mg
Tuna Nicoise	82 mg
Oven Fried Fish	80 mg
Stuffed Baked Winter Squash	75 mg
Peas with Water Chestnuts	69 mg
Mexican Chicken	69 mg
Tofu Mushroom Stuffed Baked Potatoes	67 mg
Moroccan Eggplant and Garbanzo Beans	66 mg
Chicken Vegetable Stew	63 mg
Poached Fish Dinner with Mustard-Dill Sauce	63 mg
Sweet and Sour Cabbage and Beans	63 mg
Fish Stew	62 mg
Tuna Pasta Salad	61 mg
Chicken Cacciatore	59 mg
Sloppy Joes	57 mg
Indian Style Turkey	55 mg
Italian Meatballs	55 mg
Herb Cracker Stuffing	55 mg

iron

Iron is essential for the proper transportation of oxygen to the cells of the body. It is required for blood formation, and helps bolster the body's resistance to disease and stress.

The U.S. RDA is 18 milligrams per day. Foods rich in iron include legumes, dried fruit, green leafy vegetables, whole grain bread and cereal products, amaranth, lean meat, poultry and fish.

Recipes with the Greatest Amount of Iron Per Serving

Mushroom-Marinara Sauce on Pasta	8.0 mg
Pasta Primavera	7.2 mg
Spinach Mushroom Lasagna	4.8 mg
Tofu Mushroom Stuffed Baked Potatoes	4.7 mg
Fish Stew	4.0 mg
Moroccan Eggplant and Garbanzo Beans	3.9 mg
Southwest Garbanzo Beans	3.5 mg
Tuna Nicoise	3.3 mg
Tuna Pasta Salad	3.2 mg
Indian Style Turkey	3.1 mg
Tuna Bulgur Salad	3.1 mg
Chicken Cacciatore	3.1 mg
Sloppy Joes	3.1 mg
Sweet and Sour Cabbage and Beans	3.0 mg
Lentil Salad	2.9 mg
Italian Meatballs	2.7 mg
Peach Baked Chicken on Bulgur	2.7 mg
Sweet and Sour Chicken	2.6 mg
Southwestern Frittata	2.5 mg

zinc

Zinc is essential for normal immune function. It plays an important role in metabolism; it activates enzymes that are needed to break down protein and is required for the transport of carbon dioxide by red blood cells. It is necessary for the production of insulin which regulates blood sugar levels. Zinc is essential for normal growth and is necessary for normal wound healing. Low levels of zinc may impair the senses of smell and taste.

The U.S. RDA is 15 milligrams per day. Good sources of zinc are lean meat, poultry and fish, whole grain bread and cereal products, and legumes.

Recipes with the Greatest Amount of Zinc Per Serving

Mushroom-Marinara Sauce on Pasta	2.8 mg
Pasta Primavera	2.3 mg
Indian Style Turkey	2.2 mg
Roast Turkey Breast	2.0 mg
Spinach Mushroom Lasagna	1.9 mg
Italian Meatballs	1.8 mg
Tuna Pasta Salad	1.7 mg
Poached Fish Dinner with Mustard-Dill Sauce	1.7 mg
Sloppy Joes	1.6 mg
Glazed Meatloaf	1.6 mg
Tuna Salad	1.6 mg
Creamy New York Cheesecake	1.5 mg
Chicken Cacciatore	1.5 mg
Oven Fried Fish	1.4 mg
Chicken Vegetable Stew	1.4 mg
Chicken Salad Oriental	1.3 mg
Moroccan Eggplant and Garbanzo Beans	1.3 mg
Tuna Sandwich Spread	1.3 mg
Curried Chicken	1.2 mg
Fish Cakes	1.2 mg

phosphorus

Phosphorus is intimately involved in providing energy for bodily functions. It is essential for calcification of teeth and bones, and is part of many essential body compounds including DNA and RNA.

The U.S. RDA is 1,000 milligrams per day. Phosphorus is generally found in all lean meat, poultry and fish, nonfat dairy products, whole grain bread and cereal products, and legumes.

Recipes with the Greatest Amount of Phosphorus Per Serving

Poached Fish Dinner with Mustard-Dill Sauce	376 mg
Mushroom-Marinara Sauce on Pasta	371 mg
Fish Stew	364 mg
Oven Fried Fish	322 mg
Pasta Primavera	321 mg
Tuna Salad	300 mg
Indian Style Turkey	300 mg
Spinach Mushroom Lasagna	293 mg
Peach Baked Chicken on Bulgur	283 mg
Islander Fish Filets	282 mg
Chicken Vegetable Stew	281 mg
Chicken Salad Oriental	279 mg
Tuna Pasta Salad	264 mg
Bombay Chicken	263 mg
Fish Cakes	261 mg
Chicken Cacciatore	259 mg
Sweet and Sour Chicken	255 mg
Roast Turkey Breast	254 mg
Tuna Sandwich Spread	249 mg
Tuna Bulgur Salad	248 mg

thiamine – vitamin b1

Thiamine (B1) is necessary for the release of energy from carbohydrate foods. It helps maintain healthy nerves and muscles, including the heart. This vitamin is also necessary for normal growth and repair of body tissues, and promotes a healthy appetite.

The U.S. RDA is 1.5 milligrams per day. Good sources of thiamine include whole grain bread and cereal products, dark green leafy vegetables and legumes.

Recipes with the Greatest Amount of Thiamine Per Serving

Mushroom-Marinara Sauce on Pasta	0.80 mg
Pasta Primavera	0.67 mg
Fish Stew	0.46 mg
Spinach Mushroom Lasagna	0.38 mg
Stuffed Baked Winter Squash	0.37 mg
Stuffed Peppers	0.34 mg
Tuna Pasta Salad	0.33 mg
Tofu Mushroom Stuffed Baked Potatoes	0.31 mg
Poached Fish Dinner with Mustard-Dill Sauce	0.31 mg
Peas with Water Chestnuts	0.29 mg
Chicken Vegetable Stew	0.25 mg
Chicken Cacciatore	0.25 mg
Sweet and Sour Chicken	0.23 mg
Tuna Nicoise	0.22 mg
Bombay Chicken	0.21 mg
Tuna Bulgur Salad	0.21 mg
Rice Salad	0.21 mg
Chili Pie	0.20 mg
Chicken Salad Oriental	0.19 mg
Orange Roughy in Citrus Sauce	0.19 mg

riboflavin – vitamin b2

Riboflavin is necessary for the metabolism of protein, carbohydrate and fat. It is required for the formation of antibodies and red blood cells. In conjunction with vitamin A it helps maintain healthy mucous membranes lining the respiratory, digestive and excretory tracts, and the circulatory system.

The U.S. RDA is 1.7 milligrams per day. The best food sources are nonfat dairy products, green leafy vegetables, egg whites, whole grain bread and cereal products, lean meat, poultry and fish.

Recipes with the Greatest Amount of Riboflavin Per Serving

Spinach Mushroom Lasagna	0.49 mg
Creamy New York Cheesecake	0.42 mg
Pasta Primavera	0.40 mg
Mushroom-Marinara Sauce on Pasta	0.37 mg
Raspberry Cheesecake	0.33 mg
Banana Split	0.31 mg
Frozen Fruit Creme	0.29 mg
Chicken Salad Oriental	0.27 mg
Easy Skillet Chicken	0.27 mg
Pumpkin Pie	0.27 mg
Tuna Salad	0.27 mg
Islander Fish Filets	0.26 mg
Cream of Corn-Potato Soup	0.26 mg
Zesty Mexican Chicken Soup	0.24 mg
Carrot "Cake"	0.24 mg
Sweet and Sour Chicken	0.24 mg
Oven Fried Fish	0.23 mg
Mexican Chicken	0.23 mg
Poached Fish Dinner with Mustard-Dill Sauce	0.23 mg
Southwestern Frittata	0.22 mg

niacin – vitamin b3

Niacin (B3) helps to maintain healthy skin and a healthy nervous system. It is essential in the metabolism of protein, carbohydrate and fat. Additionally it helps promote good blood circulation.

The U.S. RDA is 20 milligrams per day. Good sources include lean meat, poultry and fish, nonfat dairy products, whole grain bread and cereal products, and mushrooms.

Recipes with the Greatest Amount of Niacin Per Serving

Chicken Vegetable Stew	13.3 mg
Sweet and Sour Chicken	13.2 mg
Peach Baked Chicken on Bulgur	12.6 mg
Chicken Cacciatore	12.5 mg
Chicken Salad Oriental	12.3 mg
Curried Chicken	12.3 mg
Bombay Chicken	12.0 mg
Mexican Chicken	11.5 mg
Fish Cakes	11.3 mg
Easy Skillet Chicken	10.9 mg
Orange Honey Baked Chicken	10.7 mg
Tuna Salad	10.7 mg
Chicken Dijon	10.6 mg
Zesty Mexican Chicken Soup	10.5 mg
Tuna Sandwich Spread	10.3 mg
Mushroom-Marinara Sauce on Pasta	10.0 mg
Poached Fish Dinner with Mustard-Dill Sauce	9.9 mg
Indian Style Turkey	8.8 mg
Roast Turkey Breast	8.5 mg
Pasta Primavera	8.2 mg

vitamin b6 – pyridoxine

Vitamin B6 is necessary for the metabolism of protein and for the conversion of glycogen to energy. It helps maintain a healthy nervous system. Vitamin B6 is essential for the production of antibodies and for the conversion of the amino acid tryptophan to niacin (vitamin B3).

The U.S. RDA is 2 milligrams per day. The best sources of B6 are lean meats, fish and poultry, whole grain bread and cereal products, potatoes and bananas.

Recipes with the Greatest Amount of Vitamin B6 Per Serving

Poached Fish Dinner with Mustard-Dill Sauce	0.92 mg
Chicken Vegetable Stew	0.88 mg
Tofu Mushroom Stuffed Baked Potatoes	0.82 mg
Indian Style Turkey	0.74 mg
Chicken Salad Oriental	0.73 mg
Chicken Cacciatore	0.72 mg
Mexican Chicken	0.70 mg
Sweet and Sour Chicken	0.66 mg
Roast Turkey Breast	0.63 mg
Sloppy Joes	0.62 mg
Easy Skillet Chicken	0.61 mg
Bombay Chicken	0.61 mg
Fish Stew	0.58 mg
Pasta Primavera	0.57 mg
Italian Meatballs	0.57 mg
Curried Chicken	0.57 mg
Peach Baked Chicken on Bulgur	0.53 mg
Orange Honey Baked Chicken	0.51 mg
Glazed Meatloaf	0.51 mg
Chicken Dijon	0.49 mg

vitamin b12 – cobalamin

Vitamin B12 aids in normal function of all cells. This vitamin is necessary for building genetic material, red blood cell formation, and maintaining a healthy nervous system.

The U.S. RDA is 6 micrograms per day. Good sources of this vitamin are nonfat dairy products and lean meat, poultry and fish.

Recipes with the Greatest Amount of Vitamin B12 Per Serving

Tuna Salad	4.22 mcg
Tuna Sandwich Spread	4.10 mcg
Fish Cakes	3.90 mcg
Islander Fish Filets	2.44 mcg
Oven Fried Fish	2.30 mcg
Orange Roughy in Citrus Sauce	2.27 mcg
Tuna Pasta Salad	2.11 mcg
Tuna Bulgur Salad	1.99 mcg
Tuna Nicoise	1.93 mcg
Poached Fish Dinner with Mustard-Dill Sauce	1.11 mcg
Creamy New York Cheesecake	0.94 mcg
Raspberry Cheesecake	0.70 mcg
Banana Split	0.66 mcg
Frozen Fruit Creme	0.61 mcg
Cream of Corn-Potato Soup	0.54 mcg
Spinach Mushroom Lasagna	0.49 mcg
Chicken Salad Oriental	0.46 mcg
Roast Turkey Breast	0.44 mcg
Indian Style Chicken	0.42 mcg
Carrot "Cake"	0.36 mcg

vitamin e

Vitamin E is a fat-soluble vitamin, best known as an antioxidant that protects the unsaturated fats in the body from damage by oxygen. It protects cell membranes from damage caused by pollutants, peroxides and unstable molecules called "free radicals." It also helps to keep other fat-soluble vitamins from being damaged by oxidation.

The U.S. RDA is 30 I.U. per day. Good sources of vitamin E include tuna, whole grain bread and cereal products, sweet potatoes and legumes.

Recipes with the Greatest Amount of Vitamin E Per Serving

Tuna Salad	7.9 I.U.
Pineapple Yam Bake	7.8 I.U.
Tuna Sandwich Spread	7.3 I.U.
Fish Cakes	7.0 I.U.
Mushroom-Marinara Sauce on Pasta	5.9 I.U.
Tuna Pasta Salad	5.6 I.U.
Pasta Primavera	5.2 I.U.
Southwest Garbanzo Beans	4.9 I.U.
Tuna Bulgur Salad	4.7 I.U.
Moroccan Eggplant and Garbanzo Beans	4.7 I.U.
Spinach Mushroom Lasagna	4.1 I.U.
Tuna Nicoise	4.0 I.U.
Rice Salad	3.2 I.U.
Sweet and Sour Cabbage and Beans	2.7 I.U.
Chicken Dijon	2.5 I.U.
Herb Cracker Stuffing	2.4 I.U.
Sweet and Sour Chicken	2.3 I.U.
Braised Red Cabbage	2.3 I.U.
Greek Rice	2.3 I.U.
Three Bean Salad	2.3 I.U.

Dessert Recipes

	Calories	Protein g	Carbohydrate g	Fat g	Cholesterol mg	Dietary Fiber g	Vitamin A I.U.	Beta Carotene I.U.	Vitamin C mg	Calcium mg	Sodium mg	Potassium mg	Magnesium mg	Iron mg	Zinc mg	Phosphorus mg	Thiamine mg	Riboflavin mg	Niacin mg	Vitamin B6 mg	Vitamin B12 mcg	Vitamin E I.U.
Apple Banana Bread Pudding	247	4.2	43	1.5	2.0	4.0	62.5	85	11.2	61	227	511	25.0	0.8	0.3	49	0.11	0.17	0.7	0.39	0.12	1.0
Apple Raisin Cheesecake	228	6.1	53	FF	1.0	3.4	2.8	21	4.3	137	92	392	16.5	1.0	0.6	100	0.10	0.22	0.6	0.07	0.36	0.3
Baked Apples	154	0.6	40	0.6	0.0	4.0	0.0	84	10.7	26	4	298	12.8	0.9	0.1	21	0.06	0.04	0.3	0.10	0.00	1.3
Banana Split	278	7.8	64	0.8	2.1	4.3	93.4	70	41.7	227	104	622	47.6	1.0	1.2	206	0.12	0.38	1.0	0.44	0.66	1.0
Carrot "Cake"	189	7.0	41	FF	1.0	3.1	2.8	7829	3.0	147	132	384	18.0	1.1	0.7	103	0.10	0.24	0.6	0.11	0.36	0.2
Creamy New York Cheesecake	214	11.0	43	FF	2.7	1.3	7.3	3	2.4	313	156	505	30.8	0.6	1.5	240	0.11	0.42	0.5	0.09	0.94	0.0
Creamy Peach Cheesecake	188	5.6	43	FF	1.0	2.2	2.8	303	3.7	130	85	349	15.2	0.9	0.6	97	0.09	0.20	0.8	0.05	0.35	0.0
Fat-Free Crust	79	15.0	145	FF	0.0	2.0	0.0	0	0.8	184	33	339	7.3	0.5	0.1	10	0.04	0.25	0.2	0.05	0.58	0.4
Fresh Berry Topping	39	0.9	9	FF	0.3	0.5	0.7	18	2.5	30	12	56	3.8	0.1	0.2	24	0.02	0.05	0.1	0.02	0.09	0.0
Frozen Fruit Creme	193	6.1	44	FF	2.0	2.4	93.1	22	36.2	207	91	348	25.2	0.6	1.0	167	0.07	0.29	0.5	0.08	0.61	0.5
Jumbo Lemon Delight	96	2.9	22	FF	0.3	3.0	25.6	0	15.9	48	40	237	7.6	0.7	0.1	29	0.08	0.08	0.4	0.01	0.09	0.0
Nonfat Dessert Topping	28	1.6	5	FF	0.5	0.0	1.4	1	0.2	57	22	74	5.5	0.0	0.3	45	0.01	0.07	0.1	0.02	0.17	0.0
Nonfat Whipped Topping	14	1.3	2	FF	0.7	0.0	87.9	0	0.3	47	21	65	4.5	0.0	0.2	38	0.02	0.06	0.0	0.01	0.15	0.0
Nonfat Yogurt Cheese	16	1.6	2	FF	0.5	0.0	1.4	1	0.2	57	22	72	5.4	0.0	0.3	44	0.01	0.07	0.0	0.05	0.17	0.0
Old Fashioned Rice Pudding	200	5.8	44	0.8	1.0	2.8	125.0	5	0.9	92	59	286	13.9	0.7	0.3	148	0.10	0.17	1.8	0.06	0.24	1.6
Poached Pears with Yogurt Sauce	264	3.2	65	0.9	0.8	4.9	2.1	35	9.0	112	38	448	21.3	0.9	0.7	93	0.07	0.20	0.5	0.09	0.26	1.2
Pumpkin Pie	216	7.3	48	FF	1.9	2.0	188.0	20267	6.2	185	107	511	36.4	2.2	0.6	128	0.11	0.27	0.8	0.08	0.12	0.1
Raspberry Cheesecake	213	9.1	44	FF	2.0	2.0	5.5	3	2.6	242	151	445	23.3	0.7	1.1	180	0.12	0.33	0.5	0.06	0.70	0.0
Raspberry-Filled Melon	107	1.6	26	0.7	0.0	4.1	0.0	3949	67.8	27	11	474	24.3	0.7	0.5	29	0.06	0.09	1.3	0.18	0.00	0.6

Poultry Recipes

	Calories	Protein g	Carbohydrate g	Fat g	Cholesterol mg	Dietary Fiber g	Vitamin A I.U.	Beta Carotene I.U.	Vitamin C mg	Calcium mg	Sodium mg	Potassium mg	Magnesium mg	Iron mg	Zinc mg	Phosphorus mg	Thiamine mg	Riboflavin mg	Niacin mg	Vitamin B6 mg	Vitamin B12 mcg	Vitamin E I.U.
Bombay Chicken	337	27.1	45	3.5	67	4.0	15.9	223	26.8	60	179	618	43.0	2.2	1.0	263	0.21	0.16	12.0	0.61	0.29	1.3
Chicken Cacciatore	226	28.0	21	3.4	65.0	2.7	16.0	2115	54.6	74	144	718	59.0	3.1	1.5	259	0.25	0.20	12.5	0.72	0.28	1.1
Chicken Dijon	188	24.2	11	2.8	63.9	0.8	15.8	586	9.8	52	320	401	38.3	1.5	0.9	206	0.10	0.13	10.6	0.49	0.25	2.5
Chicken Vegetable Stew	271	28.0	31	3.2	65.0	3.7	16.1	15700	21.5	72	224	968	63.3	2.3	1.4	281	0.25	0.19	13.3	0.88	0.31	1.9
Curried Chicken	253	30.6	26	3.5	72.2	3.7	17.8	216	3.6	35	236	540	41.8	2.1	1.2	240	0.17	0.15	12.3	0.57	0.29	1.0
Easy Skillet Chicken	162	22.3	12	2.8	55	3.4	13.5	10770	35.2	47	74	711	53.8	2.1	1.1	243	0.18	0.27	10.9	0.61	0.22	1.1
Glazed Meatloaf	224	26.0	26	1.2	63.0	2.3	0.0	1728	5.1	31	219	454	47.1	2.2	1.6	244	0.11	0.17	6.6	0.51	0.30	0.9
Indian Style Turkey	274	32.3	32	1.1	79	2.6	0.1	677	13.5	49	188	905	55.3	3.1	2.2	300	0.19	0.20	8.8	0.74	0.42	0.4
Italian Meatballs	227	26.4	28	1.3	63.0	2.3	0.0	1732	19.3	44	130	584	54.7	2.7	1.8	248	0.13	0.20	7.0	0.57	0.30	0.8
Mexican Chicken	246	32.1	22	3.4	64.2	9.6	15.8	1341	64.5	106	231	835	69.1	2.3	1.1	231	0.17	0.23	11.5	0.70	0.26	1.4
Orange Honey Baked Chicken	253	24.6	32	3.0	63.9	0.6	15.8	437	53.7	38	59	473	37.5	1.3	0.9	203	0.16	0.14	10.7	0.51	0.25	0.7
Peach Baked Chicken on Bulgur	317	27.4	44	3.3	64.0	4.8	15.9	504	10.8	36	253	534	36.2	2.7	1.0	283	0.17	0.16	12.6	0.53	0.30	1.2
Roast Turkey	153	34.1	0	0.8	94.5	0.0	0.0	0	0.0	14	59	331	33.0	1.7	2.0	254	0.05	0.15	8.5	0.63	0.44	0.0
Sloppy Joes	267	28.5	37	1.6	47.3	10.2	0.0	5317	35.1	44	302	1291	57.1	3.1	1.6	200	0.16	0.22	6.6	0.62	0.22	0.4
Sweet and Sour Chicken	279	28.9	34	3.5	72.0	3.7	17.8	592	56.0	50	105	600	52.5	2.6	1.1	255	0.23	0.24	13.2	0.66	0.30	2.3
Turkey Vegetable Burgers	116	19.3	7	0.8	47	1.1	0.0	125	3.9	32	58	297	33.5	1.9	1.2	172	0.07	0.14	4.6	0.37	0.22	0.3

Fish Recipes

	Calories	Protein g	Carbohydrate g	Fat g	Cholesterol mg	Dietary Fiber g	Vitamin A I.U.	Beta Carotene I.U.	Vitamin C mg	Calcium mg	Sodium mg	Potassium mg	Magnesium mg	Iron mg	Zinc mg	Phosphorus mg	Thiamine mg	Riboflavin mg	Niacin mg	Vitamin B6 mg	Vitamin B12 mcg	Vitamin E I.U.
Fish Cakes	171	27.9	12	1.4	41	1.8	65.0	37	0.2	20	158	362	48.3	1.6	1.2	261	0.04	0.14	11.3	0.33	3.90	7.0
Fish Stew	287	27.3	42	2.0	42.0	4.0	0.0	13600	70.8	107	158	1477	66.2	4.0	0.9	364	0.46	0.19	3.5	0.58	0.00	1.0
Islander Fish Filets	135	18.8	12	1.0	23.2	0.5	80.8	48	19.8	96	97	569	49.1	0.3	1.2	282	0.17	0.26	0.6	0.48	2.44	0.1
Orange Roughy in Citrus Sauce	163	17.4	21	1.0	22.7	0.2	79.4	437	36.6	50	99	532	45.1	0.7	0.9	244	0.19	0.20	0.6	0.38	2.27	0.0
Oven Fried Fish	166	19.8	19	1.7	22.8	3.5	95.0	0	0.1	49	248	515	79.7	1.1	1.4	322	0.14	0.23	0.6	0.41	2.30	1.8
Poached Fish Dinner with Mustard Dill Sauce	278	24.4	39	3.3	26.3	3.6	155.0	10350	32.4	156	305	1341	63.3	2.1	1.7	376	0.31	0.23	9.9	0.92	1.11	1.4

Pasta and Grain Recipes

	Calories	Protein g	Carbohydrate g	Fat g	Cholesterol mg	Dietary Fiber g	Vitamin A I.U.	Beta Carotene I.U.	Vitamin C mg	Calcium mg	Sodium mg	Potassium mg	Magnesium mg	Iron mg	Zinc mg	Phosphorus mg	Thiamine mg	Riboflavin mg	Niacin mg	Vitamin B6 mg	Vitamin B12 mcg	Vitamin E I.U.
Barley Pilaf	171	4.9	36	0.6	0.0	4.9	0.1	99	6.9	23	103	318	19.0	1.3	0.2	108	0.09	0.12	2.8	0.15	0.10	0.9
Basic Rice Recipe	123	3.4	24	0.6	0.0	2.2	0.1	0	0.0	12	106	109	0.7	0.6	0.1	85	0.11	0.03	2.2	0.01	0.05	0.0
Greek Rice	156	5.4	32	0.8	0.0	3.5	0.1	4235	13.7	108	171	345	42.3	2.2	0.5	118	0.16	0.14	2.6	0.11	0.05	2.3
Hawaiian Rice	180	2.7	23	1.0	0.0	2.7	0.0	199	8.0	15	152	129	3.9	0.7	0.1	68	0.10	0.04	1.7	0.01	0.04	0.1
Herb Cracker Stuffing	110	3.8	28	0.2	0.0	5.1	0.0	178	3.7	25	192	266	54.7	1.4	0.7	110	0.06	0.05	1.5	0.13	0.00	4.8
Mushroom-Marinara Sauce on Pasta	314	14.4	74	1.9	0.0	10.3	0.0	3398	20.8	71	53	834	119.0	8.0	2.8	371	0.80	0.37	10.0	0.47	0.01	6.0
Pasta Primavera	285	12.3	67	1.7	0.0	10.8	0.0	15100	82.2	103	75	1120	113.0	7.2	2.3	321	0.67	0.40	8.2	0.57	0.01	5.2
Risi e Bisi	127	4.7	25	0.7	0.0	3.0	0.1	608	10.8	36	128	245	15.3	1.3	0.4	103	0.19	0.07	2.5	0.07	0.05	0.3
Spanish Rice	159	4.6	32	1.0	0.0	3.3	0.1	771	22.4	48	120	361	15.8	1.5	0.3	113	0.17	0.07	2.9	0.12	0.05	0.2
Spinach Mushroom Lasagna	226	19.0	42	1.4	3	5.0	28.0	7026	26.4	162	298	868	96.9	4.8	1.9	293	0.38	0.49	4.9	0.43	0.49	4.1

Bean Recipes

	Calories	Protein g	Carbohydrate g	Fat g	Cholesterol mg	Dietary Fiber g	Vitamin A I.U.	Beta Carotene I.U.	Vitamin C mg	Calcium mg	Sodium mg	Potassium mg	Magnesium mg	Iron mg	Zinc mg	Phosphorus mg	Thiamine mg	Riboflavin mg	Niacin mg	Vitamin B6 mg	Vitamin B12 mcg	Vitamin E I.U.
Black Bean Chili Bake	312	20.4	57	0.8	0.5	19.3	1.4	106	1.4	67	460	1018	16.0	0.6	0.5	74	0.05	0.12	0.6	0.06	0.17	0.4
Chili Pie	279	15.2	53	1.1	1.1	12.6	10.1	97	1.6	52	366	679	42.7	1.6	0.9	120	0.20	0.15	1.2	0.12	0.07	1.2
Moroccan Eggplant and Garbanzo Beans	228	7.3	48	2.4	0.1	10.4	0.2	743	48.6	80	314	798	66.2	3.9	1.3	180	0.19	0.13	1.6	0.25	0.03	4.7
Southwestern Garbanzo Beans	170	5.8	35	2.2	0.0	7.1	0.0	568	18.8	67	255	455	50.0	3.5	1.1	135	0.08	0.09	0.9	0.12	0.00	4.9
Spanish Garden Chili	261	13.4	53	1.1	0.1	13.7	0.4	2760	30.5	40	287	958	32.2	2.5	0.5	137	0.18	0.14	2.6	0.23	0.03	1.0
Sweet and Sour Cabbage with Beans	192	6.6	43	0.7	0.0	7.2	0.0	1603	67.1	95	54	806	62.7	3.0	1.0	121	0.13	0.12	1.5	0.26	0.00	2.7
Tex Mex Tortillas	281	13.9	54	1.3	0.5	10.6	1.4	1037	18.4	75	341	792	35.5	1.1	1.0	109	0.13	0.13	1.0	0.20	0.17	1.5

Tofu Recipes

	Calories	Protein g	Carbohydrate g	Fat g	Cholesterol mg	Dietary Fiber g	Vitamin A I.U.	Beta Carotene I.U.	Vitamin C mg	Calcium mg	Sodium mg	Potassium mg	Magnesium mg	Iron mg	Zinc mg	Phosphorus mg	Thiamine mg	Riboflavin mg	Niacin mg	Vitamin B6 mg	Vitamin B12 mcg	Vitamin E I.U.
Italian Frittata	98	5.3	17	1.0	0.0	1.6	32	63	7.1	25	72	188	33.6	0.6	0.4	70	0.0	0.06	1.1	0.15	1.0	1.0
Southwestern Frittata	117	5.7	22	1.0	0.4	2.6	101	48	45.1	60	174	579	27.3	1.0	0.4	60	0.1	0.07	1.5	0.32	0.0	0.0
Stuffed Peppers	266	8.9	56	1.8	0.0	5.8	513	129	120.5	68	74	760	74.7	2.4	1.0	166	0.32	0.17	3.6	0.61	0.0	2.0
Tofu Mushroom Stuffed Baked Potatoes	254	8.6	52	1.1	0.0	3.0	22	0	49.1	62	215	656	55.2	3.8	0.9	213	0.3	0.36	2.6	0.69	0.2	0.2

Soup Recipes

	Calories	Protein g	Carbohydrate g	Fat g	Cholesterol mg	Dietary Fiber g	Vitamin A I.U.	Beta Carotene I.U.	Vitamin C mg	Calcium mg	Sodium mg	Potassium mg	Magnesium mg	Iron mg	Zinc mg	Phosphorus mg	Thiamine mg	Riboflavin mg	Niacin mg	Vitamin B6 mg	Vitamin B12 mcg	Vitamin E I.U.
Chicken Broth	36	3.3	1	FF	0.0	0.0	0.2	0	0.0	7	309	128	2.0	0.4	0.2	50	0.02	0.05	2.2	0.02	0.16	0.1
Cream of Corn-Potato Soup	192	7.0	25	0.5	2.6	2.9	301.0	256	5.1	177	211	409	32.6	0.4	0.9	179	0.12	0.26	1.2	0.18	0.54	0.8
Garden Vegetable Soup	75	2.3	17	FF	0.0	3.1	0.0	6982	29.6	54	186	442	27.2	1.7	0.3	57	0.10	0.07	1.1	0.25	0.00	1.0
Gazpacho	42	1.8	10	0.5	0.0	1.2	0.0	2860	34.9	24	24	415	24.6	1.5	0.4	42	0.09	0.09	1.3	0.16	0.00	0.4
Golden Squash Soup	77	3.9	14	0.7	1.2	2.5	10.4	697	13.9	84	156	391	33.3	0.9	0.7	102	0.09	0.14	1.6	0.13	0.16	0.6
Hot Borscht	78	2.1	18	FF	0.1	2.8	0.2	5424	29.8	41	177	437	29.8	0.8	0.4	51	0.10	0.06	1.0	0.21	0.03	1.4
Zesty Mexican Chicken Soup	164	22.0	12	2.4	48.1	2.1	12.0	2047	30.4	49	263	526	38.6	2.3	1.1	217	0.14	0.24	10.5	0.42	0.30	1.4

Vegetable Recipes

	Calories	Protein g	Carbohydrate g	Fat g	Cholesterol mg	Dietary Fiber g	Vitamin A I.U.	Beta Carotene I.U.	Vitamin C mg	Calcium mg	Sodium mg	Potassium mg	Magnesium mg	Iron mg	Zinc mg	Phosphorus mg	Thiamine mg	Riboflavin mg	Niacin mg	Vitamin B6 mg	Vitamin B12 mcg	Vitamin E I.U.
Baked Orange Beets	114	1.9	27	FF	0.0	3.2	0.0	82	34.7	28	66	506	49.9	0.9	0.4	51	0.09	0.04	0.5	0.10	0.00	0.2
Braised Red Cabbage	60	2.3	14	FF	0.2	2.3	0.6	266	48.8	74	75	352	21.5	0.8	0.4	51	0.07	0.07	0.5	0.15	0.07	2.3
Creamy Skillet Cabbage	110	3.2	17	1.8	0.4	2.3	0.9	1050	32.7	77	100	304	34.4	0.6	0.2	75	0.08	0.08	0.4	0.21	0.12	1.1
Dijon Carrots and Zucchini	45	1.2	10	FF	0.0	3.0	0.0	14520	4.5	29	75	313	22.6	0.7	0.3	48	0.05	0.06	0.7	0.20	0.01	0.5
Glazed Curried Carrots and Raisins	113	1.6	28	FF	0.0	4.3	0.0	31900	12.7	39	58	474	23.2	1.0	0.3	65	0.13	0.08	1.2	0.20	0.00	0.9
Honey Glazed Beets	73	1.5	18	FF	0.1	2.4	0.2	15	6.3	23	60	379	43.2	0.8	0.3	35	0.04	0.03	0.4	0.04	0.03	0.1
Honey Mustard Mixed Vegetables	56	1.0	12	FF	0.0	1.5	0.0	5380	27.3	26	111	186	12.6	0.6	0.1	32	0.04	0.04	0.4	0.09	0.00	0.7
Mexican Corn	80	3.0	20	FF	0.1	2.4	0.2	1228	28.5	22	18	247	22.2	0.9	0.4	56	0.09	0.10	1.3	0.11	0.03	1.0
Orange Glazed Carrots	72	1.4	17	FF	0.0	3.4	0.0	31970	23.6	34	44	433	21.0	0.7	0.2	56	0.14	0.07	1.1	0.18	0.00	1.0
Peas with Water Chestnuts	187	6.3	38	0.8	0.0	7.1	0.0	774	29.1	30	84	390	69.2	2.0	1.2	122	0.29	0.18	1.6	0.08	0.01	0.7
Pineapple Yam Bake	176	3.2	41	FF	0.0	2.3	0.0	24760	30.9	64	31	467	28.4	0.9	0.4	67	0.11	0.18	0.8	0.27	0.01	7.8
Stuffed Baked Winter Squash	177	3.4	45	FF	0.0	6.3	0.0	699	25.6	96	37	914	75.2	2.2	0.4	82	0.37	0.06	1.8	0.35	0.00	0.5

Salad Dressing Recipes

	Calories	Protein g	Carbohydrate g	Fat g	Cholesterol mg	Dietary Fiber g	Vitamin A I.U.	Beta Carotene I.U.	Vitamin C mg	Calcium mg	Sodium mg	Potassium mg	Magnesium mg	Iron mg	Zinc mg	Phosphorus mg	Thiamine mg	Riboflavin mg	Niacin mg	Vitamin B6 mg	Vitamin B12 mcg	Vitamin E I.U.
Buttermilk Yogurt Dressing	14	0.6	2	FF	0.4	0.4	2.1	96	1.7	20	14	34	2.6	0.1	0.1	15	0.01	0.02	0.0	0.01	0.04	0.0
Creamy French Dressing	14	0.7	3	FF	.17	.13	0.5	215	3.2	22	29	67	3.7	0.1	0.1	20	0.02	0.03	0.1	0.01	0.06	0.1
Creamy Tomato Curry Dressing	9	0.9	1	FF	.28	1.2	2.3	82	2.5	6	50	32	2.0	0.1	0.0	11	0.01	0.02	0.1	0.01	0.04	0.1
Holiday Cranberry Sauce	35	0.0	9	FF	0.0	0.4	0.0	4	1.2	1	1	17	1.0	0.1	0.0	1	0.00	0.01	0.1	0.01	0.00	0.0
Honey Mustard Dressing	17	0.8	3	FF	.25	0.0	0.7	0	0.1	29	19	38	3.0	0.0	0.1	23	0.01	0.03	0.1	0.01	0.09	0.0
Italian Dressing	13	0.2	3	FF	0.0	0.3	0.0	18	0.7	6	6	42	3.9	0.2	0.0	6	0.01	0.01	0.1	0.01	0.00	0.0
Mock Russian Dressing	10	0.6	2	FF	.17	0.1	0.5	150	1.8	21	24	47	2.7	0.1	0.1	18	0.01	0.03	0.1	0.01	0.06	0.1
Mustard-Dill Sauce	12	0.7	1	FF	.19	0.0	0.5	0	0.1	28	57	38	4.8	0.2	0.1	22	0.01	0.03	0.0	0.01	0.07	0.2
Salsa	5	0.2	1	FF	0.0	.32	0.0	223	8.3	3	2	46	2.8	0.2	0.0	5	0.01	0.01	0.1	0.02	0.00	0.1
Southwest Dressing	10	0.6	2	FF	.17	0.9	0.5	150	1.8	21	24	47	2.7	0.1	0.1	18	0.01	0.03	0.1	0.01	0.06	0.1

Salad Recipes

	Calories	Protein g	Carbohydrate g	Fat g	Cholesterol mg	Dietary Fiber g	Vitamin A I.U.	Beta Carotene I.U.	Vitamin C mg	Calcium mg	Sodium mg	Potassium mg	Magnesium mg	Iron mg	Zinc mg	Phosphorus mg	Thiamine mg	Riboflavin mg	Niacin mg	Vitamin B6 mg	Vitamin B12 mcg	Vitamin E I.U.
Carrot Orange Salad	65	1.2	16	FF	0.0	2.7	0.0	21330	24.4	38	34	333	17.2	0.6	0.2	42	0.10	0.06	0.8	0.14	0.00	0.7
Chicken Salad Oriental	276	29.8	32	3.4	72.7	2.2	19.2	1453	52.9	110	90	683	50.0	2.0	1.3	279	0.19	0.27	12.4	0.73	0.46	1.5
Healthy Coleslaw	61	1.8	15	FF	0.3	1.4	0.9	3949	28.7	68	28	228	14.4	0.6	0.3	49	0.05	0.07	0.4	0.08	0.12	1.2
Honey Mustard Potato Salad	108	3.4	23	FF	0.5	1.2	1.4	79	16.9	67	59	440	27.8	0.5	0.6	89	0.12	0.09	1.4	0.30	0.17	0.3
Italian Vegetable Marinade	32	0.6	9	FF	0.0	0.9	0.0	2673	9.0	22	15	126	7.7	0.6	0.1	16	0.03	0.02	0.2	0.06	0.00	0.2
Lentil Salad	102	7.4	18	FF	0.0	3.7	0.0	619	20.4	29	61	279	29.9	2.9	1.0	93	0.17	0.09	0.7	0.20	0.00	0.3
Mediterranean Salad	64	3.4	13	FF	0.8	1.9	2.1	835	16.1	100	40	334	21.9	0.6	0.6	94	0.08	0.15	0.6	0.09	0.26	0.8
Red Cabbage and Apples	70	1.6	17	FF	0.3	2.4	0.7	37	27.2	56	16	208	12.7	0.5	0.3	48	0.04	0.06	0.2	0.13	0.09	0.5
Rice Salad	137	4.2	30	0.8	0.0	5.7	0.0	2317	36.6	33	27	480	28.6	1.6	0.4	104	0.21	0.13	1.6	0.12	0.00	3.2
Super Carrot Raisin Salad	93	1.9	23	FF	0.3	2.6	0.9	10330	7.1	58	29	288	16.7	0.6	0.4	59	0.09	0.09	0.6	0.10	0.12	0.3
Three Bean Salad	178	7.4	38	1.0	0.0	7.3	0.0	218	6.7	41	133	298	28.1	1.9	0.6	70	0.04	0.06	0.4	0.06	0.00	2.3
Tuna Bulgur Salad	232	17.6	38	1.1	28.4	6.0	32.6	615	16.4	40	211	476	28.7	3.1	0.8	248	0.21	0.14	7.9	0.23	1.99	4.7
Tuna Nicoise	193	16.9	34	0.9	20.3	5.6	32.5	1685	39.7	88	106	943	82.4	3.3	1.2	209	0.22	0.20	7.2	0.46	1.93	4.0
Tuna Pasta Salad	191	18.4	27	1.1	28.9	4.2	33.9	209	9.2	83	76	396	60.5	3.2	1.7	264	0.33	0.21	7.9	0.30	2.11	5.6
Tuna Salad	218	28.4	25	1.4	41.6	3.5	67.8	915	49.0	165	149	757	52.7	1.8	1.6	300	0.15	0.27	10.7	0.45	4.22	7.9
Tuna Sandwich Spread	159	26.3	10	1.0	57.5	0.7	66.8	228	7.8	107	199	472	41.8	1.5	1.3	249	0.06	0.17	10.3	0.37	4.10	7.3
Waldorf Salad	118	1.8	30	FF	0.3	2.9	0.9	58	9.2	55	30	294	14.8	0.5	0.3	51	0.05	0.08	0.4	0.08	0.12	0.6

chapter nine

Testimonials

Cooking without Fat

From Our Fat-Free Success Story Contest

I was feeling badly and had to push myself to keep working. My husband was on the Health Valley fat-free diet and looked and felt great, so I decided to try it.

This is four months later and my cholesterol has gone from 279 to 167 and I have lost 25 pounds, and really feel great. If I had thought it could make you feel this much better, I would have tried it months ago.

       –Diana Delk, Buena Park, California

My husband's weight is 200 pounds, he's 56 years old and has had a serious cardiovascular problem for five years. When this illness began, I changed all my regular methods of cooking…my husband was still as chubby as ever. He never lost any weight until one of his work companions told me that he used to keep in his drawer all kinds of snacks and cookies, etc.

So I started switching these fatty products for all kinds of Health Valley products like those delicious apple cookies, or those raisin fruit bars. I discovered that there are many variations of these goodies.

Well, believe it or not, this first week (of eating Health Valley products) he has lost 5 pounds.

I'm so happy to have found these products, because now my husband has a better chance of living.

Thank you again,

       –Maria E. Quinones, Glendale, California

I've read all about it, convinced am I now
That I can lose weight eating your sav'ry chow.
I've lost every battle, but none of my weight
On foods that were bland–but now yours tastes just great.
So Health Valley Foods will enable me to win
To fight ugly fat and become nice and thin.
Praise God for you people who have made it fat free,
Delicious and healthy for people like me.

       –Fred "Cully" Wachtman, Pomona, California

In 1987, at age 64, my husband, Ed, was diagnosed as having a cholesterol count of 354. He was feeling dizzy in the mornings, and upon seeing his physician was told that he needed an angiography.

When the angiography was performed, a blockage was seen in the heart arteries. The solution was cardiac bypass surgery.

In June, 1987, surgery was performed with four grafts added to his heart. He was out of the hospital in 11 days and returned to work in two months. However, he was told he had to change eating habits or the cholesterol plaque would return in the arteries.

With this in mind, I started to change our eating habits and reduced fat to 10 percent in our meals. Everything we enjoyed was changed to fit his no-fat diet. I prepared recipes over and over to fit his taste, until it became a natural resource. Meats were dropped as well as butter and salt. Oils were changed and poultry was used without skin. I even made homemade bread and use flax seed oil for sauteing. I also included Health Valley foods in the schedule for him.

Ed's cholesterol count has remained at 181-to-186 since his surgery. He feels half the age he is and is active and conducts a part-time business.
–Virginia Defendorf, San Juan Capistrano, California

In 1964, I had two heart attacks. I went on a low-fat diet since then, but I still ate some red meat.

Then again in 1975, I had another heart attack because I was negligent and went off my low-fat, low-salt and sugar-free diet. I then realized how important it was to me to be on a strict diet if I wanted to live.

To date, I am very strict with my diet, because I have arteriosclerosis with one artery blocked and two that are 60 percent blocked. A vascular surgeon said that I was getting enough blood supply to my heart and said that I didn't need a bypass at that time even though I was getting slight angina pains.

Being on a cholesterol-free fat-free diet along with your Health Valley products has made it possible for me to maintain my cholesterol level at 150 and my angina pains have disappeared. I am 79 years of age, and can now dance for hours without angina pains.

Thought that you might be interested in my story and enter me in your fat-free success story contest.
–A.M. Glazer, Mt. Washington, Massachusetts

I am 61 years of age and run three to four miles every morning. I started using your products many years ago, and go out of my way to find stores that sell your product. If you check your records, you'll see all the boxtops I've sent to you over the years!

I also have your cookbook. What's amazing, your products taste so good; your products keep me slim and trim. I feel good knowing I'm eating the right food. I have a slim strong body. If you want my picture, I'll send it.

Health Valley, you deserve the award for developing such a fine product line and I think your product information sheets are great. I'm proud to be a family member, and a dedicated customer.

Thanks,

—Johnny Nixon, Rowland Heights, California

I'm writing this letter solely because I feel you should know about my own personal satisfaction with your products.

Six months ago, I was introduced to Health Valley Foods by a personal friend who owns a store and sells your product.

I am a 37-year-old male who at the time weighed 229 lbs. with a 42 inch waist.

With no exercise and your products, primarily cookies, muffins and chili consisting of about 80 percent of my diet, I have gone down to 164 lbs. and a 36 inch waist.

I eat healthier now and like I said, mostly supplement with your foods. No red meats, only chicken, fish, vegetables, fruits and the rest Health Valley foods. I could not have done this without the supplement of your foods. This has been the key and a God send that you are in the business you are in.

Since you have done so much for me with my health and feeling better, if there is anything I can do for you, please let me know.

I believe in your products, they taste great and I enjoy reading the boxes, with the informative information you provide.

Thank you again for providing me with this fresh alternative for eating healthy again.

—Jan Morris, Clearwater, Florida

My success story really is a success because it has to do with maintenance.

For several years, I needed to lose about 40 pounds, but all I was ever able to do was drop between five and 10. Then, no matter how much I didn't eat, I'd gain the weight back. In college doing a lot of walking I was able to lose the 40, but a new medication from my doctor helped me gain weight again. Then, no matter what I did, my weight kept going higher and higher. Most days all I had was diet soda and I was still gaining. Finally, my weight tapered off at a ghastly amount.

It was then I learned the dangers of not getting the right nutrients in one's system. So my main concern became getting my RDA (recommended daily allowance) of everything. This I did with Slim-Fast. This I did because I couldn't drop any weight without intaking less than 1,000 calories.

Health Valley played such an important part in this. I'm a vegetarian — a total vegetarian now. But I am able to maintain my weight. Thanks to Health Valley, I can keep my fat intake at 5 percent or less, and still enjoy muffins, cookies, bars, etc. The best part is that I now eat more than I did when I was heavier. I now eat full meals, regular meals, something I never, ever thought I'd ever do. There was a time when I thought I'd either have to fast completely or use something like Slim-Fast for the rest of my life. That is no way to live.

Thanks to Health Valley, I have a more normal eating life. I can be fat free and still enjoy certain things. These products have helped me have my only successful maintenance in my life.

—Michelle Gussow, Indianapolis, Indiana

After retiring I realized that, slowly but surely, I was gaining weight. Then I discovered Health Valley FAT-FREE foods. After six months, I am back to my normal weight.

The best part of eating Health Valley Foods is — euphoria, knowing that it is healthful — and convenient, saving precious time.

—Elvira Packer, Springdale, Pennsylvania

Cooking without Fat

I recently underwent open heart surgery and as an admonition from my physician, have been advised to limit consumption of fats and cholesterol. With this goal in mind, I became very conscious of ingredients found in the food I consume.

While shopping in one of the local food markets, I ran across a display of Health Valley FAT-FREE fruit cookies. I read the nutritional information on the side of the carton, and discovered a very healthful and appealing formula. I bought one carton of apple raisin jumbo fruit cookies and ate one when I returned home. The cookie was so moist, flavorful and delicious, I returned to the store and bought four more cartons.

I recently had a lipid profile run and discovered my cholesterol had gone down from 250 to 204, and my triglycerides had dropped to 156 from 369. I am certain that reduction of fat and cholesterol consumption coupled with an exercise program, resulted in such a dramatic improvement.

If Health Valley Foods ever goes public, I want to be one of the first investors to include Health Valley Foods in my investment portfolio.

—Bernard J. Stackhouse, Eau Claire, Wisconsin

On Aug. 23, 1990—at age 76—I had a stroke. My doctor said nothing could be done for me, that I would not live through the surgery.

In recent years, I'd followed what I thought was a reasonable diet, but I know it contained hidden fats.

My daughter had been reading for years about fat-free diets, encouraging me to follow one, because I'd had a severe weight problem for years. I felt it was too drastic for me.

She asked my doctor if he felt a fat-free diet could unclog my arteries, since my cholesterol level was around 200. I also had high blood pressure and diabetes. He said, "Yes, research does suggest it would. However, it isn't practical, for no one would stick to that diet."

My daughter replied, "It all depends on how scared they are, or if they wanted to live a normal life without fear of becoming a vegetable."

On Aug. 25, 1990 I began a fat-free diet, vegetarian and mostly sugar free. I began using Health Valley's FAT-FREE products regularly. My favorite is the FAT-FREE Apricot Delight Cookie. In six weeks, I was off all medication, and I added a regular exercise program.

In September, 1991, my cholesterol was 137, my weight dropped from 214 to 144, and all effects of the stroke have disappeared.

The renewed energy and great feeling of health and no hunger pangs are well worth doing without high-fat "goodies" I used to enjoy.

–Delilah Gile, Fresno, California

About our FAT-FREE products

POSITIVE CHANGES, INC. is a weight control program for sensible eating. Needless to say, we incorporate the FAT-FREE items from Health Valley in our program. I have recommended the FAT-FREE cookies to each class we have. They are wonderful.

–Carol Anti, Lincolnshire, Illinois

…Six months ago, weighing 255 pounds and having a cholesterol level of 239, I set out to go on a "Fat-Free" diet. …I quickly realized that besides most fruits and vegetables, finding "Fat-Free" foods was next to impossible. That was until I discovered your Health Valley products. My diet has consisted primarily of all your Health Valley foods for the past six months and I'm excited to tell you that I now weigh 195 pounds, losing 60 pounds and lowering my cholesterol level down to a now acceptable level of 170. All thanks to Health Valley!

Even though I have reached my goal weight, I still make all your Health Valley products a major part of my daily diet.

I work for a very large corporation and have shared my "Health Valley secret of quick weight loss" with all my fellow workers and they have all since become committed to using Health Valley products. I lost so much weight so quickly and easily they all wanted to be part of the Health Valley success story.

…I just want to say "thank you" from a very satisfied customer in Connecticut, for making a product that in my eyes is second to none! Keep up the good, no great, work!!!!

–Jerry Mattes, Clinton, Connecticut

...I have been eating an average of three cans a week of your FAT-FREE Soups, Chilis, etc. I want to tell you how delicious they are....

Your chilis are excellent. And a smash hit is definitely Amaranth Fast Menu...Keep up the good work.

— Philip Hull, New Paltz, New York

...I am writing to compliment you on developing FAT-FREE Muffins that are superior to any others I have tried. Not only are they deliciously moist and flavorful, but they are packed with nutritious ingredients and loaded with fiber!

...The American diet is slowly changing and thanks to you we have a wide range of items to choose from along with the knowledge that we are purchasing the finest products available on the market.

I am grateful to you for your efforts in ensuring the quality of everything you produce. You should be very proud!

I thank you from the bottom of my (healthy!) heart!

— Laurie Howe, Indianapolis, Indiana

I'm so excited!! I just purchased some of your Fat-Free cookies and fruit bars. They are absolutely delicious. I usually don't purchase "health foods" as displayed in many health food stores, as they usually are high in fat. But when I saw the bold FAT-FREE on your products, I immediately read the panel. And much to my surprise, I liked what I read. And after tasting how great these things taste I told myself, "I've got to let these people know how much their products are appreciated."

— Cathy Cooper, Centereach, New York

Today, I was in a crucial hearing in a highly publicized case. Because of this case I have barely enough time to sleep, much less eat. But what I do have time to do is drive several miles so that I can keep my briefcase stocked with at least a couple of boxes of your delicious FAT-FREE Cookies and Fruit Bars!! They are superb!!

— Kimberly M. Briggs, Oakland, California

I just purchased your FAT-FREE Raisin Oatmeal Cookies. They are delicious. These cookies taste like I made them. Now I don't have to spend as much time in the kitchen to prepare treats for my family. You have really helped me out. You didn't even add salt. How nice!!
— Claire Kauffmann, Willow Grove, Pennsylvania

The cholesterol-free, Fat-Free cookies you produce are a delight. I picked up some a while back just for the boxtop description. I bought more just for the taste. But then I found out that using these cookies as a snack-appetite appeaser has helped me reduce weight and increase pep. And they're still delicious!!
— Virginia Leipzig, Santa Fe, New Mexico

I was 275 pounds three years ago. My goal was to lose 3-5 pounds every month for two years. My idea was that if I took it slow and over a long period of time I would learn new eating habits. It worked, and now I am 198 pounds and have been using Health Valley's Fat-Free fruit bars as part of my diet. Even if I was not eating healthy I would like the fruit bars because they taste great. Thank you for a great product that both tastes great and is fat-free.
— Rodgers Allison, San Antonio, Texas

I am writing to you as both a consumer and a Registered Dietitian. For several years, my husband and I have enjoyed your products. Not only do you produce a very tasty line of foods (we have them all!), but you make it so very easy to follow a low-fat, high-fiber diet without any guilt. As a Registered and Licensed Dietitian in private practice, I appreciate your products even more.... When a client asks me to recommend a healthful soup, cereal, cookie, cracker, etc., my response is always Health Valley. It makes my job easier when I can simply refer him or her to one brand name that I can trust.
— Anne Dubner, RD, LD, Houston, Texas

Thank you for creating such wholesome, nutritious and delicious products... The diversity of products shows your progressiveness; yet you have never compromised on quality. The brand name Health Valley Foods is synonymous with excellence.
— J. Starr, San Juan Bautista, California

Cooking without Fat

I have been a fan of Health Valley products for a long time and plan on remaining so. Thank you and here's to a "FAT-FREE" future.

−Brooke Shields

I must tell you how much I love your products. Like most people, I am very careful as to what I eat, and am constantly watching my fat, cholesterol, and calorie intake. Your product has helped in my effort to maintain my 100 lbs. weight loss.

−Gloria A. Sanderson, Freeport, New York

What People Are Saying About Our Products in General

I want to thank you so much for making such healthy and delicious products! I have two children and it is wonderful to be able to offer a cookie, snack, etc. that is healthy! Working moms sure don't need any more guilt and this is one less to worry about. Sometimes my 1½ year old will only eat your Apple bars or your cookies for dinner, and I don't even mind!

−Thea Calhoun, RTR, CTRS, CCLS
Director of Recreational Therapy
Children's Hospital, Orange, California

Thank you for not only making delicious products that are not just empty calories, but including excellent labels for the products. After reading the label, I found your product was what the package said it was−not just misleading hype as many packages are. Your company means what it says.

−Sallie Shaw, R.N., Wheeling, West Virginia

In the 15 years I've been publishing this magazine I don't think I've ever met anyone with your level of consumer commitment and product quality.
–Jake Steinman, Publisher and Editor
City Sports Magazine
San Francisco, California

Without question, your Health Valley organic foods are the very finest in taste, quality and nutritional value available today. We are 100% users of your products.... We know of no other company on the market today that offers us such delicious products for breakfast, lunch and dinner, plus in between snacks.... We just want you folks at Health Valley to know what you have done for us.
–Mr. & Mrs. J.C. Nielson, Los Angeles, California

Thank you for your interest in providing a "healthy food" for consumers! It is obvious you take pride in your foods and want to help those who want to help themselves toward a healthier way of life.
–Margaret Frank, San Jose, California

I am writing to tell you how much I enjoy your products, and how happy I am that Health Valley exists. Your products provide me with a consistent supply of healthy, convenient and affordable meals. I appreciate your efforts to use organic ingredients and lead-free cans, and I always buy your new products, since they are all good.
–Michael D. Gurwitz, Monsey, New York

When I am eating your products, I feel as if I am doing my body a favor. You have enlightened me with your personal interest.
–C. Fitzgerald, La Canada, California

I can buy your products with my eyes closed, knowing that I can trust the quality.

— G. Moussalli, Denver, Colorado

I am impressed by the integrity and concern you show for the health and well-being of the people you serve.

— M. McElheny, Farmersville, New York

I think that your products are great. The depth of the company's concern for the client and product is excellent. My husband, a confirmed junk food fiend, has at last come to the realization that good-for-you food can taste great, thanks to you.

— L. Ratzmann, Madison, Wisconsin

I love and adore your products primarily because they are low in calories, high in nutrition and fiber, and low in salt and sugar. You make a superior product, and I always feel that I am doing myself a favor by purchasing them.

— K. Flowers, Albuquerque, New Mexico

What People Are Saying About Our Company in General

I just felt compelled to tell you that your company is truly the best. Your dedication to genuinely healthy products puts other food processors to shame (particularly one sugar-and-junk-laden company that has its world headquarters sitting in my home town). Every one of your employees should feel proud of their work at Health Valley. Your company is one of the precious few that are boldly paving the way for healthier, happier lifestyles, not just attempting to cash in on fads with as little effort as possible.

— Jeff Kimble, Battle Creek, Michigan

index

S